"The spiritual journeys of those living with mental health challenges, wrapped in webs of clinical complexity, offer profound insight if we learn to listen deeply to their stories, rather than stigmatize and label them. In this remarkable book, John Swinton helps us unravel the tangled threads of psychological definitions, biological explanations, psychotropic medications, and the authentic faith experiences of Christian disciples, sharing the gifts and courageous journeys of these souls. With well-researched psychological insight and theological wisdom, this book should be in the library of every pastor, and at the bedside of anyone seeking to understand how God's grace can weave through the disturbing pathways of those living with mental health challenges."

—Wesley Granberg-Michaelson
author of *Without Oars: Casting Off into a Life of Pilgrimage*

"Moving beyond the tired old language of 'illness' and 'battles,' Swinton invites us into the mental health journeys of a rich variety of people who speak in their own words, medically, theologically, and honestly. Focusing more on dignity than diagnosis, he shows that God works in all things, and healing comes in many forms. Sweeping aside the false dichotomy between science and faith, Swinton's readers are invited into a more nuanced theological world in which they may find themselves unexpectedly and lovingly represented. This is also a rich resource for pastors, teachers, parents and anyone else who has a stake in brain health, because, in the end, who doesn't?"

— Lillian Daniel
author of *Tired of Apologizing for a Church I Don't Belong To*

"*Finding Jesus in the Storm* first of all listens deeply, or, as John Swinton says, 'thickly,' to people with mental health challenges and helps a reader see, broaden, and reconstruct both the ways that people of faith might walk with people with mental challenges as well as help people with mental health challenges explore the spiritual dimensions of their own journey. As someone who has both worked with others and my own mental health challenges, this felt very real. Using insights from psychology, sociology, theology, and other disciplines, Swinton once again breaks past multiple forms of stigma and unexamined assumptions to help readers enter a space where we can once again see each other as children of God— pilgrims—doing the best we can to live into the embrace of God's love."

— Bill Gaventa
author of *Disability and Spirituality: Recovering Wholeness*

"With the nuanced perspective of a theologian and ordained minister who is also a psychiatric nurse, John Swinton offers here a rich 'theology that drops down into the heart' for people who live with mental health challenges. Refusing to reduce people to their neurons or to the labels that are assigned to them, he introduces us to the complex, lived experiences of real people as they live, wonder, worship, and love amid mental health challenges. In their close-to-the-ground stories, we find not only lament and loss but also joy, kindness, and grace. *Finding Jesus in the Storm* will challenge and bless all who care about the relationship between mental health and the life of Christian faith."

— Warren Kinghorn
Duke University Medical Center and Duke Divinity School

"In this remarkable book, John Swinton not only takes the spiritual lives of those living with mental health challenges seriously, he weaves together a beautiful, reflective theology of the cross and resurrection in the light of these experiences. This important and timely book is a must read for all of us who seek to live faithfully in the world today."

— Paula Gooder
author of *Body: A Biblical Spirituality for the Whole Person*

"*Finding Jesus in the Storm* is a masterful, wise, clear, and compassionate look at the experience of those struggling with mental health challenges such as depression, bipolar disorder, and schizophrenia, and the thin ways these are often described by mental health professionals, Western culture, and the church. Helped by refreshing philosophical insights, we are invited to listen to thicker descriptions of who these people are in relation to a theological, as well as a clinical horizon, and to better understand biblical healing—finding joy in Jesus while suffering. This book should be widely read."

— John R. Peteet, MD
Harvard Medical School

"John Swinton has listened well to Christians who have struggled with the unrelenting storms of severe mental health challenges. He has heard them tell of their experiences of the presence of God, and of the seeming absence of God, and of faith that grapples with the tensions between the two. *Finding Jesus in the Storm* provides a 'thick' description of Christian experiences of depression, schizophrenia, and bipolar disorder. Drawing on the author's experiences as mental health nurse, minister, and practical theologian, these accounts are engaged in conversation with both professional and Christian perspectives, scanning the horizons of mental health care, Christian Scripture, tradition, and church life. This book provides a unique, and hard won, account of journeys through deeply troubled waters. It is essential reading for all who are dissatisfied with superficial and second-hand Christian accounts of mental illness."

— Chris C. H. Cook
Durham University

FINDING JESUS IN THE STORM

The Spiritual Lives of Christians with Mental Health Challenges

John Swinton

WILLIAM B. EERDMANS PUBLISHING COMPANY

GRAND RAPIDS, MICHIGAN

Wm. B. Eerdmans Publishing Co.
4035 Park East Court SE, Grand Rapids, Michigan 49546
www.eerdmans.com

26 25 24 23 22 21 20   1 2 3 4 5 6 7

ISBN 978-0-8028-7372-9

Library of Congress Cataloging-in-Publication Data

Names: Swinton, John, 1957– author.
Title: Finding Jesus in the storm : the spiritual lives of Christians with mental
    health challenges / John Swinton.
Description: Grand Rapids, Michigan : William. B. Eerdmans Publishing
    Company, 2020. | Includes bibliographical references and index. | Summary:
    "Practical theology for Christians affected by mental health challenges"—
    Provided by publisher.
Identifiers: LCCN 2020012147 | ISBN 9780802873729
Subjects: LCSH: Mental health—Religious aspects—Christianity. | People with
    mental disabilities—Religious life.
Classification: LCC BT732.4 .S955 2020 | DDC 248.8/62—dc23
LC record available at https://lccn.loc.gov/2020012147

*To my good friend Allen Walker, for whom the storms
became just a little too powerful*

Contents

Part V: Redescribing Bipolar Disorder

Acknowledgments

There are many people I should thank in relation to this book. It has been a long time in the making, and it's been a difficult journey. My family have as always been remarkably supportive and forgiving as I have complained, moaned, and wrestled with this book. They always saw the end point even when I could not. I'd like to thank my friend and colleague Warren Kinghorn for his wisdom and insight, Katie Cross for her thoughtfulness in commenting on a later draft of the book, Joy Allen for her comments on depression, and Hannah Waite for her deep and personal insights into the important issues that this book wrestles with. I am grateful to Uli Guthrie for her guidance and insight, and I am thankful for the skills that Steph Brock brought to the project, and for her husband, Brian, whose constant encouragement has been a blessing on me for many years. Thank you also to the folks at Eerdmans, who have been extremely supportive and have encouraged me in times when I felt like finding something else to do! They have become friends, and I am grateful for all that they do. Thanks must also go to Michael Thomson for taking this project on before he moved on to Wipf and Stock. Thank you to Ronald Otto and the folks at Thresholds in Chicago (https://www.thresholds .org) for their help early on in the project. Most importantly, I want to thank the people who gifted me their life stories. This book is about you and for you, and I am thankful and humbled that you have trusted your stories with me. I only hope I have done your gifts justice. Finally, thank you to God for being gracious and kind and for teaching us that there is nothing in the realm of mental health and ill health or anywhere else that can separate us from God's love. That is the blessing that keeps us all on track.

Introduction: Life in All Its Fullness

Living Well with Jesus

> I have come that they may have life, and have it to the full.
> —John 10:10[1]

A FEW YEARS AGO, I ATTENDED A LECTURE ON THE POSITIVE RELATION-ships between religion and mental health given by an eminent professor of psychiatry. He opened his lecture with an intriguing, if somewhat disconcerting, statement: "I only have fifteen minutes to see a patient, and I spend the whole of that time looking at the computer screen trying to work out the patient's blood levels and checking the efficiency of the patient's meds." The rest of the lecture was excellent, but I couldn't get past that opening statement. As a former mental health nurse, I understand the pressures of a busy, understaffed, and often underfunded health-care system. Nevertheless, that the psychiatrist decided to spend *all* of the paltry fifteen minutes of each patient's visit looking at a computer screen is telling.

A person's biological functioning is certainly important. If one assumes that mental health experiences can be primarily or even fully understood and explained in biological terms, then scrutinizing a person's blood levels for chemical imbalances and checking the impact of medication on blood cell count make sense. However, human beings are not simply a conglomerate of chemical interactions. Humans are persons, living beings who have histories, feelings, experiences, and hopes, and who desire to live well. Living well is not determined by the functioning of our biological processes apart from our individual social, interpersonal, and spiritual experiences. Similarly, understanding the biological dimensions of mental health experiences may turn out to be helpful, but it is unlikely to solve problems that emerge from poverty, loneliness, war trauma, and abuse. It is also unlikely to tell us much about

---

1. Unless otherwise indicated, all biblical quotations come from the New International Version (2011).

1

what it means to live with and to experience these things scientists describe as "symptoms." If you don't know what these symptoms actually *mean* for an individual, it is difficult to know what you are trying to control and what a "good outcome" might look like. If you have only fifteen minutes with a patient, you don't need rich, thick experiential descriptions. Thin ones will do just fine. Time is an issue, but the problem of time reflects deeper issues.

THICK DESCRIPTIONS

The purpose of this book is to provide readers with rich, deep, and thick descriptions of the spiritual experiences of Christians living with mental health challenges. It assumes that in order to understand people's mental health experiences, we need to find time to listen carefully and cannot be bound by assumptions, even those of powerful explanatory frameworks like the *Diagnostic and Statistical Manual (DSM)*. This book is about how Christians living with severe mental health challenges—depression, schizophrenia, and bipolar disorder— experience their faith lives and strive to live life in all its fullness in the presence of sometimes deeply troubling experiences. The book is *not* about "severe mental illness" understood as a clinical category. Rather, it is about the experiences of unique and valuable disciples of Jesus who seek to *live* well with unconventional mental health experiences—experiences that some choose to describe as "severe mental illness" but that can also be described in other important ways.

Life in All Its Fullness

In John 10:10, Jesus makes an intensely powerful statement: "I have come that they may have *life*, and have it to the full." Life in all its fullness is certainly not life without suffering, pain, or disappointment. That much is clear as we reflect on Jesus's own life. Nor is it a life without joy, hope, and resurrection life in the Spirit. The quest for life in all its fullness is not the basis for a theology of glory—one that minimizes pain and looks past suffering.[2] Rather, it is the foundation for a practical theology of the cross that takes seriously the freedom and release that we have gained through the death and resurrection of Jesus at the same time that it recognizes that cadences of the cross still guide the rhythm and the tempo of the day-to-day life of the world. Life in all

---

2. For a very helpful overview of Luther's theology of the cross, see Gerhard Forde, *On Being a Theologian of the Cross* (Grand Rapids: Eerdmans, 1997).

its fullness is life with God—a God who accompanies us on a complex journey within which we live in the startling light of the resurrection but remain intensely aware that Jesus's cry from the cross, "My God, my God, why have you forsaken me?" still resonates throughout creation. Life in all its fullness is not life without tears but life with the one who dries our tears and moves us onward to fresh pastures.[3] Such fullness of life is what I mean when I suggest that this book is about the ways in which Christians with severe mental health challenges can *live* well and live faithfully even in the most disconcerting storms. Mental health challenges are difficult experiences, but they needn't prevent us from living well, living faithfully, and loving Jesus.

Understanding Explanation, Cure, and Healing

This book does not attempt to *explain* mental health challenges. It does not address causes directly, although I do clarify the problem of naming causation from both a scientific and a theological point of view. Instead, it intends to help all of us *understand* the experience of severe mental health challenges in general, and the role of Christian spirituality in particular, in ways that can bring about insight, compassion, empathy, and enduring faithful relationships. Its focus is on listening carefully to the ways people describe their spiritual experiences and trying to make theological and practical sense of lives that have been touched by difficult, troubling, but sometimes also profoundly revelatory challenges. The book is therefore *not* about curing mental health challenges. It is about healing, understood as the facilitation of understandings and circumstances in which people can live well with Jesus even when the prospect of cure is beyond our current horizons.

"Mental Illness" as a Journey

At heart, the book urges us to change our language about and modify our descriptions of mental health challenges in ways that can help all of us live peaceably and faithfully without misrepresentation and stigma. For the ways in which we describe the world determine what we think we see. What we think we see determines how we respond to what we think we see. How we

---

3. Rev. 21:4: "'He will wipe every tear from their eyes. There will be no more death' or mourning or crying or pain, for the old order of things has passed away." Ps. 23:2: "He makes me lie down in green pastures, / he leads me beside quiet waters."

respond to what we think we see is a measure of our faithfulness. Language and description matter.

Richard Arrandale, in his paper "Madness, Language and Theology," urges us to reconsider the ways in which we talk about the experiences some describe as "mental illness." He urges us to move beyond the language of illness, the limits of suffering, and the kinds of military metaphors that turn mental health experiences into battles that need to be fought and won. If "mental illness" is a war, then "those who professionally care for us are the allied forces deployed to win this war, and who often seem to do so with no consideration for the casualties. It is often the case that much of the treatment which is given has worse (and sometimes very long lasting) side-effects than the original problem itself."[4]

Military metaphors—*battling* with schizophrenia, *wrestling* with bipolar disorder, *fighting* depression—narrow the person's choice of description and "treatment" and easily preclude the development of "nonviolent" understandings and approaches. Instead, Arrandale urges the adoption of a kinder, gentler, and more generous hermeneutic that allows for forms of language that open up new worlds and new possibilities:

> If we dwell in the language of the negative and the military there is a serious danger that this will set the agenda for the people the language is used for/against. If we can learn to dwell in a language which is positive and liberating this may help in shaping that movement beyond enslavement and existential death. Language used in this way can be part of an exorcism of the linguistic demons which "possess" those with mental health problems—language (and thus a world-view) which, in its negative usage, is content to leave people to live in "the tombs" (Mark 5.2) of labelled madness. A more positive and theological language might enable people to break free from the chains and fetters with which they have been bound. Such a language exorcized of negativity and value judgements may allow people with mental health problems to be brought back into the kingdom from which they can feel alienated.[5]

If the church is possessed by linguistic demons that prevent it from talking faithfully about mental health issues, then exorcism is vital in order to ensure its present and future faithfulness. A primary intention of this book is

---

4. Richard Arrandale, "Madness, Language and Theology," *Theology* 102 (May 1, 1999): 195–202.

5. Arrandale, "Madness, Language and Theology," 197.

to facilitate faithful speech that moves us to faithful action. By developing a phenomenological approach that takes seriously the lived experience of unconventional mental health experiences, the book offers different ways of articulating the issues; different ways of understanding those who bear the weight of diagnoses; and different forms of description that I have seen bring about liberation and healing.

Arrandale asks us to consider framing mental health in terms of a journey. A journey is something we embark upon, willingly or otherwise, as we travel from one place to another. Sometimes we choose our journeys; at other times we are forced to go to places we do not want to. Along the way, we meet people and encounter situations—some helpful, some not—each of which changes the direction of our journey. Some change the meaning of the entire journey. Some journeys are easy and the burden light, like a summer hike; others feel like the winter journey of a refugee. Along the way, we may encounter enemies and become lost and confused. Some of these enemies are in our own heads, while others emerge as our perceived strangeness unsettles people and causes them to react with physical or psychological violence. Above all, the journey is surprising for us and for others. We will need maps, guides, friends, communities, equipment, and, for Christians, ultimately the guidance of God's Spirit if we are to negotiate our mental health journeys faithfully. But properly equipped, guided, supported, and faithfully accompanied, we can survive even the most powerful and disturbing storms.

The key thing about a journey is that we are always heading toward somewhere and something, not nowhere and nothing. Destination matters. The destination, like the winter road before us, can be cold and unclear. If it is uncertain or disappears from sight, we find ourselves in a very difficult, lonely, and deeply hopeless situation. But if we know our destination even in the midst of our sense of lostness, then we have hope. And if we can find hope (or if others can hold it for us), then the journey might actually be going somewhere rather than nowhere. Thinking of mental health challenges as a journey reminds us to hold on to the kind of destination we might want to reach. What that journey looks like in the context of severe mental health challenges is what this book is about.

ABOUT THE BOOK AND ITS LANGUAGE

The core of the book emerges from a series of qualitative research interviews that I carried out over a two-year period with Christians living with major depression, schizophrenia, and bipolar disorder. I chose to focus on these diagnoses not because they are representative of all mental health challenges but because they are generally acknowledged as particularly problematic and also because they raise important theological and practical issues for individuals, church, and society.

Through these interviews, I intended the following:

1   to capture some of the complexities of how people actually experience their mental health instead of how they or others interpret it, given their assumptions of what their diagnosis represents. This is the *phenomenological dimension*.

2   to gain insight into the ways in which people's unconventional mental health experiences affect their faith lives and relationships with God. This is the experience of lived *theology*.

3   to try to make sense of this in terms of the theology and practice of the church. This is *theological reflection and revised practice*.

Though these three foci formed the basis of our conversations, the richness of our conversations drew us to other interesting and surprising places. As people granted me entry into the intricacies of their mental health experiences, they helped me to recognize and accept profound insights into the ways in which God is present (or sometimes apparently absent) in their mental health experiences. This entry into their interior worlds quickly taught me that their assumed strangeness is not quite as strange as it first appears. People are just people, even in the midst of difficulties.

Much has been written on the relationship between spirituality and mental health.[6] Much of it assumes that spirituality is a broad and universal concept comprising a personal search for meaning, purpose, hope, value, and, for some people, God.[7] Yet my interviews for this book yielded a quite different understanding of spirituality—that it is not a general search for meaning but something quite specific. The interviewees perceived themselves as disciples of Jesus who were desperately trying to cling to him in the midst of complex

6. H. G. Koenig, M. E. McCullough, and D. B. Larson, eds., *Handbook of Religion and Health* (New York: Oxford University Press, 2001).

7. For a critique of this approach to spirituality, see John Swinton and Stephen Pattison, "Moving beyond Clarity: Towards a Thin, Vague, and Useful Understanding of Spirituality in Nursing Care," *Nursing Philosophy* 11 (2010): 226-37.

and difficult circumstances. Their question was not simply: "Where can I find meaning in the midst of my brokenness?" but much more specifically, "Where and how can I find Jesus and hold on to God in the midst of this experience?" The question is simple; the answer is much more complex.

Some of the people who share their experiences in the following pages find the language of mental illness beneficial and therapeutic and helpful for understanding and future development. Others do not. I believe people should be allowed to name their experiences in the way that is most helpful and pertinent for them. Readers will note that I don't use the term "mental illness" in this book. This is not because I am in any sense antipsychiatry or don't believe that people's suffering is real.[8] I know people's experiences are *very* real. Yet describing mental health experiences in terms of illness is only one way of naming and responding to such experience, and not necessarily the best way.

I use the term "mental health challenges" for two reasons. First, it focuses our attention on what enables us to remain healthy in the midst of psychological distress. While mental health challenges can cause great suffering and distress, it is possible to find hope and faith in the midst of the wildest storms. Second, the shift from illness to challenge offers a positive and forward-facing orientation. Whereas illness reminds us of what is wrong with us and narrows our range of options, challenge sees the situation as potentially constructive and leaves the door open for a variety of perspectives, interpretations, and descriptions. How to enable people to take up those challenges and learn to live life fully is a primary task of what is to come.

8. The term "antipsychiatry" refers to a movement that adopts the view that psychiatry and psychiatric treatments are more damaging than they are helpful. This movement considers psychiatry to be a coercive instrument of oppression based on unequal power relationships that lead to patients being treated for things the antipsychiatrists assume are problems of living rather than illnesses or diseases. Although I will critique psychiatry and also be quite critical of the idea of mental illness, I value psychiatry and consider it to have a legitimate and significant role in caring for people living with mental health challenges. Readers wishing to read more about antipsychiatry should see T. Szasz, "The Myth of Mental Illness," *American Psychologist* 15 (1960): 113–18; D. G. Cooper, *Psychiatry and Antipsychiatry* (London: Tavistock, 1967); P. Rabinow, ed., "Psychiatric Power," in *Ethics, Subjectivity, and Truth*, by M. Foucault (New York: New Press, 1997); and Peter Breggin, *Toxic Psychiatry* (New York: St. Martin's, 1991).

PART I

The Art of Description

1

REDESCRIBING THE WORLD OF "MENTAL ILLNESS"

Description, Explanation, and the Problem with the DSM

> I deliberately use the phrase "living under the description of
> manic depression (or bipolar disorder)" to refer to people who
> have received this medical diagnosis. The phrase is meant to
> reflect the social fact that they have been given a diagnosis. At the
> same time, it calls attention to another social fact: the diagnosis
> is only one description of a person among many.
>
> —Emily Martin[1]

THE FIELD OF MENTAL HEALTH IS HIGHLY CONTESTED. PEOPLE HAVE DE-
scribed, categorized, and responded to unconventional mental health experiences in a multitude of ways and have elicited a wide range of responses. At
any given historical or cultural moment, particular descriptions of the experience and explanations for its occurrence—that it is caused by demons, the
subconscious, chemical imbalances, genetics, neurology—become elevated
to the status of the "standard account." This account is assumed to provide
the interpretative framework used by a majority of people to explain unconventional thoughts, experiences, and actions. Each generation thinks that its
descriptions should be the "standard accounts," and each generation assumes
that its descriptions are more accurate than previous descriptions. The current
emphasis within Western cultures on describing mental health challenges in
biological terms is relatively new but nonetheless powerful. Genes, neurology,
and chemical imbalances all can easily serve as conversation-closing explanations for mental health challenges. Yet, while biology is an important factor, it
is not the only one. Running alongside this account are other important ways

1. Emily Martin, *Bipolar Expeditions: Mania and Depression in American Culture*
(Princeton: Princeton University Press, 2007), 10.

of describing such challenges, even if people do not necessarily give them the same social or scientific weight as the standard account. People still believe in demons, psychoanalysis, behaviorism, and many other descriptions. This book gives voice to some of these other forms of describing and understanding what is going on in people's lives.

But first, we must ask: What does it mean to describe something?

THE PRACTICE OF DESCRIPTION

In the epigraph to this chapter, the anthropologist Emily Martin refers to people living with bipolar disorder as *living under a description*, meaning that the diagnostic description "bipolar disorder" is only one way to describe an individual. "Bipolar disorder" is a powerful *clinical* description, one with a profound impact on a person's life not only in how the person's experiences are described and explained but also in how the person is perceived in the light of the professional and social interpretations of that particular diagnosis. Martin, however, reminds us that the clinical description "bipolar disorder," important as it may be, is *only* one description among many that apply to the life of any given person. Human beings do not live according to a single description. We live under multiple descriptions, some of them accurate, some of them not, but all of them significant in their potential to affect our identity (who we are, who we think we are, who others think we are), our perception (how we and others perceive ourselves), and our actions in relation to others and toward ourselves.

The conflict over terms occurs because culture, medicine, religion, personality, and the zeitgeist all shape and form particular descriptions and explanations of mental health phenomena and then offer ways of naming, controlling, and responding to people's experiences. Of course, more than one description can apply to any given experience. It is quite possible, for example, to argue that factors in mental health challenges are biological *and* cultural *and* spiritual—all at the same time. Nevertheless, we give certain descriptions more social and clinical power than others. At least part of the theological task of this book is to peel away those descriptions that are false, distracting, unfaithful, and damaging and replace them with ones that more accurately capture the nuances of people's experience.

Descriptions are thus identity forming, action oriented, and action determining. To repeat, the ways in which we describe the world determine what we think we see. What we think we see determines how we respond to what we see. How we respond determines the faithfulness of our actions. Descriptions matter because descriptions change things.

In her work on the nature of intention, the philosopher Elizabeth Anscombe highlights the way in which description (the way we describe something) and intentionality (our ability to act deliberately toward something in the light of that description) are deeply interwoven. In Anscombe's view, intentional actions, that is, actions that are *about* something as opposed to, for example, unintentional reflexes, are inevitably and irreducibly "actions under a description."[2] Descriptions define and confine the possible options open to us for comprehending and responding to any given situation. As Ian Hacking has put it: "All our acts are under descriptions, and the acts that are open to us depend, in a purely formal way, on the descriptions available to us."[3] Without a description there can be no intentional action. There is thus a dynamic interaction between describing something and the impact the description has on our responses to the things described. To suggest that descriptions shape our practices is not to suggest that the structure of the world is physically determined by our descriptions of it. Our descriptions do not have ontological power—meaning that things in the world do not actually come into existence because we describe them in particular ways. The universe will remain the universe regardless of my description of it. Nevertheless, my perception of and response to the universe are, to a greater or lesser extent, determined by how I choose to describe it.

Descriptions may not have ontological impact, but they do have *epistemological* power—meaning they shape and form the ways in which we come to know and respond to things in the world. This epistemological power of description is inseparably bound to practice: "Descriptions are embedded in our practices and lives. But if a description is not there, then intentional actions under that description cannot be there either. . . . What is curious about human action is that by and large what I am deliberately doing depends on the possibilities of description. . . . Hence if new modes of description come into being, new possibilities for action come into being as a consequence."[4] Much of the world around us exists for most of the time as nothing other than unnoticed background noise. Like the invisibility of water to the swimming fish, a good deal of our life in the world is lived unintentionally; it just hums

2. G. E. M. Anscombe, *Intention*, 2nd ed. (Oxford: Basil Blackwell, 1957).

3. Ian Hacking, *The Social Construction of What?* (Cambridge, MA: Harvard University Press, 1999), 31.

4. Thomas C. Heller, Morton Sosna, and David E. Welbery, eds., *Reconstructing Individualism* (Stanford, CA: Stanford University Press, 1986), 230.

along under the hood. When we bring certain things to the fore and choose to describe them, we bring them to attention. The nature of our descriptions determines the kind of attention we pay to those things. Once these things are described, we can act intentionally toward them. The same phenomenon can be described in many ways, and each description brings with it new sets of possibilities for intentional action. Different descriptions provide different modes of awareness, levels of intentionality, and possibilities for different forms of meaningful action.

The Problem of Thin Descriptions

There are different *kinds* of descriptions, depending on the angle from which one looks at a phenomenon, but there are also different *types* of descriptions. In his book *The Interpretation of Cultures*, the anthropologist Clifford Geertz presents us with the idea of *thick* and *thin* descriptions.[5] A thin description provides us with the minimum amount of information necessary to describe a situation or context. A survey, for example, provides a thin account of a phenomenon insofar as it captures only certain statistical aspects and provides no contextual, relational, experiential, or cultural information. Statistics also provide thin descriptions. So, for example, we might note that one in four people will experience mental health challenges over a lifetime. This emphasizes at a general level the fact that mental health challenges are a significant issue in the population. However, this statistic tells us very little about the particularities of either the one or the four. Thin descriptions provide us with high-level insights but no low-level details. Another example might be Google Translate, a web-based program that translates typed words into a different language. Through this process, you do get a rough understanding of what words mean in other languages, but that understanding is extremely limited and can even be quite badly skewed. It is an understanding of language stripped of culture, experience, history, or linguistic subtleties and idioms. It is too thin to provide more than a very basic level of insight into the language.

As we enter the world of mental health, it will quickly become clear that thin descriptions abound, both within public conceptions of people's experiences and within the mental health professions. In what follows, I examine four key areas where thin descriptions have become particularly problematic:

---

5. Clifford Geertz, *The Interpretation of Cultures* (New York: Basic Books, 1973), 33–55.

1   Stigma

2   The *DSM* diagnostic system

3   The turn to biology

4   The field of spirituality in mental health care

STIGMA AS THIN DESCRIPTION

We find a particularly powerful and devastating example of a thin description and its dangers in the phenomenon of stigma. Stigma is one of the most destructive aspects of living with unconventional mental health experiences and one of the most painful experiences that people have to endure. Stigma occurs when a person is reduced from being a whole to being a mere part; from being a full human being to being the sum of a single part. The sociologist Erving Goffman informs us that the concept of stigma originated in the Greek slave trade. After a slave was purchased, the slave was branded and, in branding, was reduced (or thinned down) to the size of the brand. The slave was no longer described as a person, a citizen, a friend, or a family member but was now simply property. Stigma functions in the area of mental health in a very similar way. Stigma reduces people living with unconventional mental health problems to the shape and form of their diagnosis, or more accurately, to people's perceptions and caricatures of the implications of their diagnosis. In this way, stigma thins down or reduces people's descriptions to impersonal caricatures based on the connotations of their diagnoses. People cease to be perceived as persons and become "schizophrenics," "depressives," "neurotics," or any other thin diagnostic facade that people choose to project when they don't want to engage with real individuals.

A Spoiled Identity

Goffman describes stigma as a phenomenon that occurs when an individual with an attribute deeply discredited by his or her society is rejected as a result of that attribute: "While a stranger is present before us, evidence can arise of his possessing an attribute that makes him different from others in the category of persons available for him to be, and of a less desirable kind—in the extreme, a person who is quite thoroughly bad, or dangerous, or weak. He is thus reduced in our minds from a whole and usual person to a tainted, discounted one. Such an attribute is a stigma, especially when its discrediting effect is very extensive."[6] Stigma is most powerful when it urges us to "reclassify an individual from one socially anticipated category to a different but equally well-anticipated one, and the kind that causes us to alter our estimation of the individual downward."[7] Such a powerful stigma redescribes individuals in negative ways that move them from one socially anticipated category to a different and lesser social category.[8] Stigma is thus a malignant mode of social description that is very often aimed at some of the most vulnerable people within society.

One of the problems with mental health diagnoses is that they are highly stigmatized categories that take their meaning not only from their clinical descriptions but also and sometimes primarily from the negative cultural accretions that accompany such descriptions. This is particularly true in the Western world, which has a preoccupation with intellect, reason, and clarity of thinking. In such a cultural milieu, mental health challenges can easily be perceived as challenging each of these socially valued attributes and, in so doing, challenging our conceptions of what it means to be fully human.

Tanya Luhrmann notices this particularly in the diagnosis of schizophrenia in America: "One of the challenges of living with schizophrenia in the United States is the clear identity conferred by the diagnostic label itself. To receive care in a society so acutely aware of individual rights is to receive an explicit diagnosis. A patient has the right to know. But the label 'schizophrenia' is often toxic for those who acquire it. It creates not only what Erving Goffman called a 'spoiled identity,' but an identity framed in opposition to the nonlabelled social world."[9] Describing someone as having schizophrenia or being a "schizophrenic" has significant social and relational consequences, at least in Western cultures. As Esmé Weijun Wang put it in relation to her personal experience of living with schizoaffective disorder: "Giving someone a diagnosis of schizophrenia will impact how they see themselves. It will change how they interact with friends and family. The diagnosis will affect how they are seen by the medical community, the legal system, the Transportation Security Administration, and so on."[10]

6. Erving Goffman, *Stigma: Notes on the Management of Spoiled Identity* (Englewood Cliffs, NJ: Prentice-Hall, 1963), 3.

7. Goffman, *Stigma*, 3.

8. Goffman, *Stigma*, 3.

9. T. M. Luhrmann and Jocelyn Marrow, eds., *Our Most Troubling Madness: Case Studies in Schizophrenia across Cultures* (Berkeley: University of California Press, 2016), 27.

10. Wang, *The Collected Schizophrenias*, Kindle locations 225–227.

Importantly, this "spoiled identity" stands in direct opposition to those claiming to bear witness to "normality." This is why schizophrenia can be so alienating. Built into the description is an assumption of distance and presumed Otherness. However, this is not true in all cultures, as we will see. Indeed, in certain cultures it is not possible to be "a schizophrenic"; constructing people in this way is just not what such cultures do. A question we will explore in various ways as we move on is this: What is it about Western culture that constructs schizophrenia (and other forms of mental health challenge) in such a way as to make it so dehumanizingly stigmatic?

Stigma Is Pathogenic

It is clear that thin stigmatized descriptions produce spoiled identities and force expectations downward. Stigma is thus *pathogenic* (it causes pathology) in that once it is named, the stigmatic description actively causes harm. Stigma dehumanizes people living with mental health challenges. But it also dehumanizes the stigmatizers, who are trained to see only parts of other people without caring for the whole of them (like the doctor in my opening vignette). Stigma thins our vision and hardens out hearts. It is destructive for all concerned.

The issue of stigma will come up throughout this book. For now, we just need to notice its devastating impact and the ways it thins people out and hurts them.

Making Up Thin People: The *Diagnostic and Statistical Manual of Mental Disorders (DSM)*

Psychiatry is a hermeneutical and descriptive discipline. It describes and interprets unconventional mental health experiences and responds in ways that bring hope, healing, and relief. We will focus on the issue of interpretation later. Here we concentrate on the descriptive dimensions of psychiatry. Historically via psychiatrists such as Karl Jaspers,[11] and in contemporary times through the detailed work of Andrew Sims,[12] an approach to description has emerged known as *descriptive psychopathology*. This phenomenological tradition provides rich and deep descriptions of psychopathology so that psychiatrists can gain insight and create rich and thick descriptions that help them

11. Karl Jaspers, *General Psychopathology*, trans. J. Hoenig and M. W. Hamilton, 7th ed. (Manchester: Manchester University Press, 1963).

12. A. Sims, *Symptoms in the Mind: An Introduction to Descriptive Psychopathology*, 3rd ed. (Edinburgh: Saunders, 2003).

develop deep and therapeutic understandings that lead to effective clinical intervention. Andrew Sims lays out this approach as follows:

> The study of individual personal experience is fundamental to psychiatry. Descriptive psychopathology is the precise description and categorization of abnormal experiences as recounted by the patient and observed in his behavior. There are two components to this: careful and informed observation of the patient, and phenomenology, which implies, according to Karl Jaspers, the study of subjective experience. The descriptive psychopathologist is trying to hear what the patient is saying without any theoretical, literary or artistic gloss of interpretation, and without the mechanistic explanations of science used inappropriately. In order to achieve understanding, phenomenology uses empathy as a precise clinical tool.[13]

The purpose of such a phenomenological approach is not to *explain* what is going on but to try to *understand* it: "In Jaspers' usage, understanding is contrasted with explanation. Understanding, in this sense, involves the use of empathy, subjective evaluation of experience by the 'understander' using his or her own qualities of observation as a human being: feeling inside. Explanation is the normal work of natural science involving the observation of phenomena from outside, and objective assessment. Both are required of the practicing doctor but whereas the method of observation in science is carefully and comprehensively taught, teaching the method of empathy to give subjective understanding is frequently neglected."[14] Sims draws attention to this phenomenological tradition but acknowledges that it does not get the recognition it deserves either in medical education or in practice.

One of the reasons this phenomenological tradition has been "lost" relates to the systems currently in place through which we make diagnoses and describe mental health challenges. These systems prefer thin descriptions to the richness and thickness of the phenomenological look. Part of the issue, as we have seen, relates to time. If you have only fifteen minutes with a patient, gathering rich phenomenological detail is not going to be high on your list of priorities. But lack of time is not the only reason for the thinness of psychiatric descriptions.

13. Andrew Sims, "Is Faith Delusion?," 2007, accessed October 28, 2019, https://www.rc psych.ac.uk/docs/default-source/members/sigs/spirituality-spsig/is-faith-delusion-andrew -sims-editedx.pdf?sfvrsn=59a019c0_2.

14. A. C. P. Sims, "Symptoms and Beliefs," *Journal of the Royal Society of Health* 112, no. 1 (1992): 42–46.

The Power of the DSM

The practice of psychiatric description (diagnosis) is organized according to the groupings and categorizations that compose diagnostic manuals such as the World Health Organization's International Classification of Diseases (ICD)[15] and the American Psychological Association's *Diagnostic and Statistical Manual of Mental Disorders (DSM)*.[16] These manuals contain the criterion used to redescribe persons' experiences in terms of commonly observed symptoms and to develop the formal names for mental health conditions. By "redescribing," I refer to the process whereby a person brings a set of experiences to the attention of the psychiatrist, who then redescribes them in terms of signs and symptoms of some kind of underlying pathological process.

The World Health Organization (WHO) claims that the "ICD is the foundation for the identification of health trends and statistics globally, and the international standard for reporting diseases and health conditions. It is the diagnostic classification standard for all clinical and research purposes. ICD defines the universe of diseases, disorders, injuries and other related health conditions, listed in a comprehensive, hierarchical fashion."[17] Defining the universe is a pretty impressive claim, even for an organization as esteemed as the World Health Organization! Nevertheless, the ICD criteria have been deeply influential in diagnosing mental and physical conditions and have been adopted in Europe, North America, China, Korea, Sweden, and Thailand.[18] The ICD and the *DSM* are closely connected:[19] "Although the [*DSM*] manual is American, it is much used elsewhere, despite the fact that the International Classification of Diseases, drawn up under the auspices of the World Health Organisation in Geneva, is usually seen as the official manual, if there is one. DSM-5 gives ICD codes when they match, and there is a project aimed at

15. World Health Organization, "The ICD-10 Classification of Mental and Behavioral Disorders: Clinical Descriptions and Diagnostic Guidelines," accessed October 28, 2019, https://www.who.int/classifications/icd/en/bluebook.pdf?ua=1.

16. American Psychiatric Association, *Diagnostic and Statistical Manual of Mental Disorders*, 5th ed. (*DSM-5*) (American Psychiatric Publishing, 2013).

17. World Health Organization, "International Classification of Diseases (ICD) Information Sheet," accessed October 28, 2019, https://www.who.int/classifications/icd/en/.

18. World Health Organization, "The ICD-10 Classification of Mental and Behavioural Disorders: Diagnostic Criteria for Research" (Geneva: World Health Organization, 1993), https://www.who.int/classifications/icd/en/GRNBOOK.pdf?ua=1.

19. M. First, "Harmonisation of ICD-11 and DSM-V: Opportunities and Challenges," *British Journal of Psychiatry* 195, no. 5 (1999): 382–90.

harmonising the two rulebooks."[20] While recognizing the importance of the ICD system, we will focus on the *DSM*, which is the main classification system used in the United States and is highly influential throughout the world.[21]

The most recent incarnation of the *DSM*, *DSM-5*, was published in May 2013 by the American Psychiatric Association and claims to offer standard criteria for the classification of mental disorders. The *DSM-5* provides a series of descriptions of mental health phenomena, which are clustered together to form various diagnostic categories. Each category is given a number: schizophrenia is 295.90, schizoaffective disorder is 295.70[F25.0], and so forth. In this way, a statistical system is merged with the self-narrated qualitative experiences of mental health, as numbers are assigned to people's experiences. The manual is statistical because "its classifications can be used for studying the prevalence of various types of illness. For that one requires a standardised classification. In a sense, the manual has its origins in 1844, when the American Psychiatric Association, in the year of its founding, produced a statistical classification of patients in asylums. It was soon incorporated into the decennial US census. During the First World War it was used for assessing army recruits, perhaps the first time it was put to diagnostic use."[22]

This manual is used by a wide variety of persons and groups: researchers, clinicians, drug regulation agencies, pharmaceutical companies, and health insurers. The presence of a *DSM* diagnosis is necessary, not only in terms of accurate diagnosis, but also (at least in the United States and parts of Canada) to access Medicare and insurance plans provided in Canadian provinces.[23] Its influence can be seen in the fact that the majority of English-language journals insist that the language of *DSM* be used to characterize any research published. The *DSM* is a purely descriptive document and offers no recommendations for treatment, although those who use it might argue that accurate diagnosis leads to the most appropriate treatment. In determining the kinds of areas that are fundable and not fundable for research, the descriptions contained in *DSM-5* are seen to serve bureaucratic as well as medical intentions. In short, *DSM-5* has a good deal of clinical, political, and financial power.

20. Ian Hacking, "Lost in the Forest," *London Review of Books* 35, no. 15 (August 8, 2013): 7–8, https://www.lrb.co.uk/v35/n15/ian-hacking/lost-in-the-forest.

21. For a fascinating insight into how this way of interpreting mental health issues is becoming globalized, see Ethan Watters, *Crazy like Us: The Globalization of the Western Mind* (New York: Little, Brown, 2011).

22. Hacking, "Lost in the Forest," 2.

23. Hacking, "Lost in the Forest," 1.

Categorizing Mental Health Experiences

The process for determining diagnostic categories begins when groups of psychiatrists meet in various hotels across America to discuss which mental health experiences should fit within the various diagnostic categories. After a lot of discussing, arguing, categorizing, and recategorizing, the psychiatrists judge which classifications, names, and criteria are appropriate descriptions to guide clinical practice. Thus is born the *DSM*.

Any given diagnostic category—schizophrenia, bipolar disorder, obsessive-compulsive disorder—comes into existence as it is constituted by the *DSM* criteria. The *DSM* has the power to establish, or at least to give formal, organized existence to, mental health experiences. As such, it is not only *descriptive* but also *formative*. Diagnoses are shorthand descriptions of complex human behavior. In descriptive mode, *DSM-5* provides clinicians with concepts and forms of language that can be used to make sense of clusters of unusual human experiences. However, such descriptions also *form* the ways psychiatrists (and others) see and describe the person before them. Once you accept the *DSM* as the basis for your diagnostic practices, that becomes the way you see people. Diagnoses will help you to see some things very clearly, but they will inevitably occlude other things. The *DSM* thus propagates a certain type of clinical gaze that is bounded by the parameters of the knowledge and expectations of the clinician. The expectations of the clinician are not free-floating. Clinicians are deeply aware of the expectations of the system and the limitations of time. Shorthand descriptions are very helpful within a system that is bounded and limited by the pressures of time.

There is thus a complicated dialectic between the consensus-based formation of diagnoses by clinicians and the pressures of the system clinicians have to use. A system like the *DSM* fits well into a pragmatic and instrumental system where therapeutic explanation and "getting things done" may be perceived as primary goals. There is little room here for thick descriptions that require more than fifteen minutes with a patient. This is why many people don't recognize themselves in the descriptions that emerge from the *DSM*. As Esmé Weijun Wang puts it: "To read the DSM-5 definition of my felt experience is to be cast far from the horror of psychosis and an unbridled mood; it shrink-wraps the bloody circumstance with objectivity until the words are colorless."[24] This is clearly a problem. However, there are other, perhaps greater problems with the thin descriptions that we encounter in the *DSM*. It is *descriptive* and

---

24. Wang, *The Collected Schizophrenias*, Kindle locations 183–184.

formative, but it is also a mode of *creation*: it brings mental health conditions into existence and takes some out of existence.

Making Up "Mentally Ill" People

The philosopher Ian Hacking opens his paper "Making Up People" with a quite startling assertion:

> Were there any perverts before the late nineteenth century? According to Arnold Davidson, "The answer is NO. . . . Perversion was not a disease that lurked about in nature, waiting for a psychiatrist with especially acute powers of observation to discover it hiding everywhere. It was a disease created by a new (functional) understanding of disease." Davidson is not denying that there have been odd people at all times. He is asserting that perversion, as a disease, and the pervert, as a diseased person, were created in the late nineteenth century. Davidson's claim, one of many now in circulation, illustrates what I call *making up people*.[25]

The description of someone as a "pervert" wasn't available before the late nineteenth century. It was only when law and medicine created a category and described those who fit that category as "perverts" that being a pervert became possible. Similarly, prior to formal categorization, again in the late nineteenth century, it was not possible to be either a homosexual or a heterosexual. There has been same-sex activity in all eras, but it was not until the legislative categories became available that one could be named "homosexual" or "heterosexual." Once these categories (kinds of people) came into existence, a variety of responses became possible: a position for or against homosexuality, heterosexuality, gay rights, homophobia, and so forth. Once these categories were created, it was possible to be these kinds of people.

However, the existence of such persons is fragile, determined by the shifting will of society and the transitive nature of the legislative system, which can in principle take them out of existence as well. For many people, it is not who they are as unique individuals that gives their existence substance and durability but the way society chooses to describe them at any moment in time. They remain

25. Ian Hacking, "Making Up People," in *Reconstructing Individualism: Autonomy, Individuality, and the Self in Western Thought*, ed. T. Heller (Stanford, CA: Stanford University Press, 1986), 99–114 (emphasis added). The interior quotation is from Arnold Davidson, "Closing Up the Corpses," in *Meaning and Method*, ed. G. Boolos (Cambridge: Cambridge University Press, 2001), 24.

in existence only as long as the category continues to be given social, political, and legal validation. It would be legislatively possible to eradicate homosexuality, heterosexuality, or perversion simply by changing the legal categories. We may find it difficult to imagine a society where people are forced to be homosexual. We may have less trouble imagining a society where people are forced to be heterosexual, as there are recent and even contemporary precedents to indicate that some would be quite comfortable with such a suggestion.[26] We would have no difficulty at all imagining a society where Jewish people were legislatively considered to be less than human. Europe has a dark history that makes this point tragically. Recognizing how and why we make up people is of the ultimate importance.[27]

What Hacking observes about the ways we make up people resonates with the people-making power of the *DSM*. It is possible for a particular form of mental health challenge to come into existence only if psychiatry continues to name the set of experiences that make up such a diagnosis in the same way it always has. The problem is that the *DSM* keeps changing its mind. Unlike the scientific process that goes into the development of the diagnosis of physical illnesses, a committee decides the presence or absence of particular forms of mental health challenges. One reason why the *DSM* has to be continually revised, updated, and rereleased is that the various committees vote to add, take out, or modify particular diagnoses or aspects of diagnoses. At the end of this process of discussing, arguing, and categorizing, these committees present the categories and criteria that, in their opinion, form the basis for classifying people's mental health experiences. The *DSM* has the power to create and establish, or at least to give formal, organized existence to, mental health experiences that are considered to be unconventional. These committees make up or invent mentally ill people, but they also reverse that process.

A good example of this de-creative process can be found in the response of psychiatry to homosexuality. In 1972, homosexuality was considered a treatable form of mental illness.[28] In 1973, the American Psychiatric Association

---

26. D. C. Haldeman, "Gay Rights, Patient Rights: The Implications of Sexual Orientation Conversion Therapy," *Professional Psychology: Research and Practice* 33, no. 3 (2002): 260–64.

27. I am aware and a little concerned that my usage of the term "homosexuality" may be problematic. The LGBTQ community tends to avoid the term "homosexuality," preferring to use the description "those attracted to the same sex." I acknowledge the importance of this linguistic change while also noting that this is a useful example of the way we create and re-create people in line with the politics and expectations of the moment.

28. Sarah Baughey-Gill, "When Gay Was Not Okay with the APA: A Historical Overview of Homosexuality and Its Status as Mental Disorder," *Occam's Razor* 1, no. 2 (2002): 5–16.

decided it was no longer to be described in this way. The change came about not because of any new scientific evidence but because of pressure from gay rights activists who felt the designation was unjust and unfair and that psychiatry was acting more in moral judgment than in the cause of clinical necessity. The description of homosexuality as a mental health issue was eliminated by the votes of the committee.

More recently, Asperger's syndrome has been taken out of existence. Prior to *DSM-5*, it was possible to have Asperger's syndrome. Now it's not. Asperger's has been subsumed into a broader category of autism. The National Autistic Society describes Asperger's syndrome in this way: "People with Asperger syndrome see, hear, and feel the world differently to other people. If you have Asperger syndrome, you have it for life—it is not an illness or disease and cannot be 'cured.' Often people feel that Asperger syndrome is a fundamental aspect of their identity."[29] Although some people choose to retain the term "Aspie," technically this way of being a person is no longer available. For many people, having Asperger's syndrome was important. It was not, and still is not, a problem to be solved but is more a way of life that provides an important source of identity:

> The news that the term "Asperger's syndrome" will soon cease to exist has some parents concerned—especially parents raising "Aspie" children. Starting May 2013, the American Psychiatric Association's new diagnostic manual, known as the DSM-5, will go into effect, stripping the well-known condition—a condition sometimes associated with loner geniuses like Albert Einstein and Andy Warhol—of its name. Instead, Asperger's syndrome will simply be known as ASD-Level 1 (mild), a top rung in the ladder of autism spectrum disorders. For those who viewed an Asperger's diagnosis as light-years away from clinical autism, this new classification may feel like a fall from grace.[30]

This change is problematic for some. Timothy Bumpus, who lives with autism, points out that "some of the most brilliant people had Asperger Syndrome, and you just can't put that under the title of Autism. . . . This disability, which is ironically not at all a disability, causes the recipient to be antisocial,

29. "Asperger Syndrome," National Autistic Society, accessed October 28, 2018, https://www.autism.org.uk/about/what-is/asperger.aspx.

30. Linda Federico-O'Murchu, "Farewell to Aspies: Some Families Reluctant to Let Go of Asperger's Diagnosis," *Today*, January 4, 2013, https://www.today.com/parents/farewell-aspies-some-families-reluctant-let-go-aspergers-diagnosis-1B7821891.

physically weak. . . . However, it is so much more. It allows a person to think in whole different ways, to see things in a different light than others."[31]

I met a young man at a conference in Atlanta a couple of years ago. At that time, he proudly proclaimed himself to be an Aspie! The next time I met him, something had changed. He said to me: "The last time I met you I had Asperger's syndrome. I was a wild, wild Aspie!! Now a committee has healed me of that, but they have given me autism . . . again!" We laughed. It was funny, but it was also telling. When something central to your identity can be changed by a committee without consulting you or others with similar experiences, you are forced to recognize that the fullness of your experience of mental health challenges is clearly not being incorporated into the diagnostic process.

Not all *DSM* diagnoses are as politically charged as same-sex relationships and Asperger's syndrome, but they all involve the same process of being created, modified, rejected, or incorporated according to committee votes. The potential difficulties and the inevitable thinness of the descriptions that emerge from this process need to be recognized. Diagnoses are more like social kinds than natural kinds;[32] they have a certain form of social existence in that at particular times society accepts them as useful explanatory concepts and acts accordingly. Diagnoses have an epistemology but no ontology. They are pencil sketches of human experiences that are frequently being erased and altered. On their own they tell us some potentially important things, but their descriptions are too thin to do all the work required for understanding mental health issues.

BIOLOGY AND THE THINNING OF MENTAL HEALTH CHALLENGES

The third area in which thin descriptions are given power is within the ongoing conversation around whether mental health challenges can be adequately explained by biology. On April 29, 2013 (just prior to publication of the fifth edition of the *DSM*), the director of the National Institute of Mental Health (NIMH), Thomas Insel, shook the world of psychiatry by stating that the diagnoses laid out in the *DSM* did not describe authentic disorders. They were constructs without any empirical basis. Because there are no biomarkers attached to the conditions the *DSM* describes as "mental disorders," they could

31. Federico-O'Murchu, "Farewell to Aspies."
32. Nick O. Haslam, "Natural Kinds, Human Kinds, and Essentialism," *Social Research* 65, no. 2 (Summer 1998): 291–314.

not be empirically verified and were therefore invalid as criteria for defining mental disorder. That being so, the *DSM* could not justifiably be considered clinically relevant. The NIMH is the leading federal agency for research on mental disorder in the United States. Insel said the NIMH would no longer fund research projects that rely exclusively on *DSM* criteria. The problem he highlights is that while the *DSM* criteria offer a measure of reliability, they are lacking in validity:

> The goal of this new manual [*DSM-5*], as with all previous editions, is to provide a common language for describing psychopathology. While DSM has been described as a "Bible" for the field, it is, at best, a dictionary, creating a set of labels and defining each. The strength of each of the editions of DSM has been "reliability"—each edition has ensured that clinicians use the same terms in the same ways. The weakness is its lack of validity. Unlike our definitions of ischemic heart disease, lymphoma, or AIDS, the DSM diagnoses are based on a consensus about clusters of clinical symptoms, not any objective laboratory measure. In the rest of medicine, this would be equivalent to creating diagnostic systems based on the nature of chest pain or the quality of fever. Indeed, symptom-based diagnosis, once common in other areas of medicine, has been largely replaced in the past half century as we have understood that symptoms alone rarely indicate the best choice of treatment. *Patients with mental disorders deserve better.*[33]

Insel urged the field to leave behind the descriptive approach of the *DSM* and to develop a new diagnostic scheme based on solid, verifiable scientific research that focused on finding the biological roots of mental disorders.

Insel is correct to suggest that there is a need for a more rigorous and thick process of diagnosis than the *DSM* can provide on its own. There is an obvious weakness in a system where decisions are made and diagnoses are constructed on the basis of consensus around flexible concepts and constructions, without evidence that stretches beyond the particularities of committee votes. But is his alternative really better or even possible? As Gary Greenberg noted recently in the *New Yorker*: "Doctors in most medical specialties have only gotten better at sorting our suffering according to its biochemical causes . . . [but] psychiatrists still cannot meet this demand. A detailed understanding of the brain, with its

---

33. Thomas Insel, "Transforming Diagnosis," National Institute of Mental Health, April 29, 2013, https://www.nimh.nih.gov/about/directors/thomas-insel/blog/2013/transforming-diagnosis.shtml.

hundred billion neurons and trillions of synapses, remains elusive, leaving psychiatry dependent on outward manifestations for its taxonomy of mental illnesses."[34] The evidence that Insel wants is, at least at the moment, simply not available. It may become available in the future, but for now, in general terms, the biological evidence for the root causes of *all* mental health disorders is at best speculative and at worst simply absent.[35] Insel may well be correct that patients deserve better, but will a shift from describing symptoms to describing biology really produce better descriptions?

At a personal level, making such a claim without evidence must be deeply troubling for people living with mental health challenges who have been treated under the "old regime." As Sarah Kamens has pointed out: "It's . . . akin to telling patients that we made a huge mistake."[36] If the *DSM* has interrater reliability—that is, all psychiatrists are using the same set of criteria—but no validity (no empirical evidence to indicate the truth of a given diagnosis), then people have been diagnosed by a set of criteria that is reliable across the sector but lacking empirical verification. This leaves people living with mental disorders in a difficult situation. It is possible that their current diagnosis could be redescribed in the future, and they would have to rebuild their lives and sense of identity accordingly.

It is true that the biological quest is intended to find better treatments and to eradicate symptoms. However, what if your symptoms are meaningful for you? If the only description of your situation is that you have a mental illness that is basically the same as a physical illness with symptoms that are meaningless, then your personal experience of your mental health challenges will be discounted as irrelevant. Critical as I have been of the *DSM*, at least it holds open the possibility that symptoms are more than mere biological malfunctioning. Such a suggestion—that symptoms are meaningful and should be responded to as such—is counterintuitive. For now, I urge the reader to remain open to the possibility. When we look more closely at the lived experience of mental health challenges, we will see the importance of recognizing the meaningfulness of symptoms and the dangers in trying to merge them into a single biological description. Insel is right: *patients deserve better*. The

34. Gary Greenberg, "Does Psychiatry Need Science?," *New Yorker*, April 23, 2013, https://www.newyorker.com/tech/annals-of-technology/does-psychiatry-need-science#.

35. My point here relates to biological explanations for *all* mental health challenges. It is not that there is no evidence for some. It is the assumption that all problems are based in biology that is problematic.

36. Sarah Kamens, "Dr. Insel, or: How Psychiatry Learned to Stop Worrying and Love the Biomarker; A Response to RDoC" (unpublished conference paper, May 2013).

problem is that within a universe of multiple descriptions, his solution may not be as helpful as he assumes.

The Danger of Reductive Explanation

It's not that biological descriptions are not relevant or important. The problem is that they can easily become *reductive*. In his work on the nature of explanation, the sociologist Alan Garfinkel points out the reductive tendencies of explanation. When people think they have explained something, they tend to exclude other explanations, thus reducing understanding of the situation to a single explanation. "The reductionist claims that one class of phenomena, more or less well explained by some body of theory, is really explainable by some other theory, which is thought of as deeper or more basic; this, we say, reduces the apparent complexity of the world."[37] Such explanations reduce the complexity of multifaceted situations and experiences to a single explanation. Explanations become hegemonic when they insist on explaining unconventional mental health experiences without reference to other possible explanations. Garfinkel suggests that we

> pay more attention to what exactly is being explained by a given explanation. Too often, theories *talk* as if they are addressing some problem, though they are really addressing different problems or different aspects, interpretations, or readings of the problem. For when a theory talks about a phenomenon, it inevitably does so in terms of its own representation of it. The phenomenon gets incorporated into the theory in a particular way, structured by a definite set of assumptions and presuppositions about its nature. This makes it very important that we recognize those presuppositions and discover how the theory has represented a particular object of explanation.[38]

For current purposes, it is important that we recognize the kinds of presuppositions that lie behind reductive biological explanations of mental health challenges and the dangers of uncritically accepting such explanations.

37. Alan Garfinkel, *Forms of Explanation: Rethinking the Questions in Social Theory* (New Haven: Yale University Press, 1981), 14.
38. Garfinkel, *Forms of Explanation*, 12.

"Mental Illness" Is Not like Measles

Take, for example, the common strategy of equating mental illness with physical illness. One reason people are keen on this way of thinking is that it destigmatizes mental disorder. It draws it out of the messiness of society, politics, and stigmatizing views and places it on par with forms of physical illness that tend not to attract stigma. In his book *Surviving Schizophrenia*, the psychiatrist E. Fuller Torey explains what he thinks mental illness is (in this case, schizophrenia): "Schizophrenia is a brain disease, now definitely known to be such. It is a real scientific and biological entity as clearly as diabetes, multiple sclerosis, and cancer are scientific and biological entities. It exhibits symptoms of a brain disease, symptoms which include impairment in thinking, delusions, hallucinations, changes in emotions, and changes in behavior. And, like cancer, [it] probably has more than one cause."[39]

Putting to one side the fact that the evidence for the biological roots of schizophrenia is not clear-cut,[40] let's think through how this explanation works. It claims to give us a plausible explanation of the various experiences that bring people under the description of schizophrenia. People experience symptoms because of an underlying biological condition. The primary task for mental health care is to adjust the person's biology in ways that will bring about relief from suffering. There may be other aspects to the patient and her care, but the central focus is on biology, because that is where the problems are fundamentally located. Schizophrenia is a malignant biological process similar to cancer, over which no one has total control. Within such an explanatory framework, people's mental health experiences are explained as the result of such things as chemical imbalances, genetic predispositions, neurological pathology, viruses, and so forth. The assertion "Mental illness is like any other medical illness" implies, as Insel suggested, that mental illness can be fully explained according to its biological basis.

Positively, as mentioned, one of the intentions of this kind of approach in general and Fuller Torrey's approach in particular is to destigmatize mental ill health. When Fuller Torrey wrote his book in 1982, there had been a strong tradition of blaming parents (often mothers) for the formation of schizophrenia. This blaming of family and mother had caused a lot of unnecessary grief

---

39. E. Fuller Torrey, *Surviving Schizophrenia: A Family Manual*, 6th ed. (San Francisco: Harper, 2013).

40. Richard P. Bentall, *Madness Explained: Psychosis and Human Nature* (London: Penguin Books, 2004).

for parents.[41] Recognizing this, Fuller Torrey had become a strong advocate for families. *Surviving Schizophrenia* was the first handbook designed specifically to help not patients but families "survive" schizophrenia. His strong emphasis on the importance of the biological had significant social and political as well as medical origins and intent.[42]

The ascription of biological explanations has also been used in an attempt to destigmatize the experiences of people living with mental health challenges. The suggestion that the causes of such challenges are similar to the causes of physical illnesses such as cancer, diabetes, and influenza is intended to reduce the stigma that surrounds mental disorders. The compassion behind this approach is clear, and the sentiment is laudable. The problem is, it doesn't seem to work.

Malla, Joober, and Garcia note that "Several well-conducted studies have concluded, almost uniformly, that this strategy—destigmatization by emphasizing the biological aspects of mental health challenges—has not only not worked, but also may have worsened public attitudes and behavior toward those with mental illnesses. Investigations of stigma have shown that those who consider mental disorders as primarily attributable to biological forces, just like other medical disorders, while absolving the mentally ill person of responsibility for their behavior and actions, tend to feel less optimistic about their ability to get better and function well, are less accepting of them and feel less positively toward them."[43] The problem seems to be that in using biology as an explanation for mental disorders, within the minds of the public *and* for the individual who lives with the experiences, the disorder becomes ontologized and totally defining of the person. People no longer *have* an illness; now they *are* an illness. The *DSM* offers descriptions that function epistemologi-

41. Denise Sommerfeld, "The Origins of Mother Blaming: Historical Perspectives on Childhood and Motherhood," *Infant Mental Health Journal* 10, no. 1 (Spring 1989): 14–24.

42. For a further development of this point and on the history of family blaming, see chap. 5 in Anne Harrington, *Mind Fixers: Psychiatry's Troubled Search for the Biology of Mental Illness* (New York: Norton, 2019).

43. A. Malla, R. Joober, and A. Garcia, "'Mental Illness Is like Any Other Medical Illness': A Critical Examination of the Statement and Its Impact on Patient Care and Society," *Journal of Psychiatry and Neuroscience* 40, no. 3 (2015): 147–50. See also S. Peerforck, G. Schomerus, and S. Pruess, "Different Biogenetic Causal Explanations and Attitudes towards Persons with Major Depression, Schizophrenia and Alcohol Dependence: Is the Concept of a Chemical Imbalance Beneficial?," *Journal of Affective Disorders* 168 (2014): 224–28; J. Read, N. Haslam, and N. L. Sayce, "Prejudice and Schizophrenia: A Review of the 'Mental Illness Is an Illness like Any Other' Approach," *Acta Psychiatrica Scandinavica* 114 (2006): 303–18; and N. Rüsch, A. R. Todd, and G. V. Bodenhausen, "Biogenetic Models of Psychopathology, Implicit Guilt, and Mental Illness Stigma," *Psychiatry Research* 179 (2010): 328–32.

cally rather than ontologically. Biological explanation does the exact opposite. A biological explanation is much deeper, much more personal, much more tied in with the "is-ness" of who and what a person is. Biological explanations are thus seen to have unfortunate side effects.

In his book *How to Become a Schizophrenic*, John Modrow, a psychiatrist who lives with schizophrenia, offers a powerful insider's critique of biological explanations and points out a hidden danger:

> I cannot think of anything more destructive of one's sense of worth as a human being than to believe that the inner core of one's being is sick— that one's thoughts, values, feelings, and beliefs are merely the meaningless symptoms of a sick mind. Undoubtedly the single most important causal factor behind my mental breakdown was a sense of worth so badly shaken that not even the most florid delusions of grandeur could save it. What the concept of "mental illness" offered me was "scientific proof" that I was utterly worthless, and would always be worthless. It was just the nature of my genes, chemistry and brain processes—something I could do nothing about.[44]

Schizophrenia is not like measles. One can *have* measles, but one *becomes* schizophrenia. Sally Clay addressed the First National Forum on Recovery from Mental Illness as follows: "Those of us who have had the experience called 'mental illness' know in our hearts that something profound is missing in these diagnoses. They do not take into account what we have actually endured. Even if the 'bad' chemical or the 'defective' gene is someday found, madness has its own reality that demands attention."[45] Stigma is a way of stealing someone's story and forcing the person to accept a false, negative identity. It needs to be fought against. Biological explanations may provide a helpful and nonstigmatizing version of disturbing experiences. However, such explanations can have a shadow side that we miss at our peril.

The point is not that biology may not be formative of mental challenges. We do not yet have the evidence to make such a case across the board, but in time it may emerge. The problem is that biological explanations on their own can be highly reductive, closing down aspects of our experiences and forcing us to

44. John Modrow, *How to Become a Schizophrenic: The Case against Biological Psychiatry* (Everett, WA: Apollyon, 1992), 147.

45. Sally Clay, "The Wounded Prophet" (unpublished paper presented at the First National Forum on Recovery from Mental Illness, National Institute of Mental Health and Ohio Department of Mental Health, April 1994).

interpret them in a very narrow and confined way. In the end, such attempts at destigmatizing "the mental" actually end up reinforcing the idea that there is a problem with that aspect of our humanness, rather than addressing the key issue—that there is no need to stigmatize issues of the mind dualistically. A psychological description is no different from a biological one; it simply addresses different aspects of our humanness—shifting the problem from the mind to the body is nothing more than another manifestation of Cartesian dualism. The unhealthy and inauthentic anthropology that underpins this way of thinking remains fully intact. Biological descriptions are simply too thin to do the work of realigning and clarifying that is necessary for the tasks of destigmatizing and healing.

The Thinning of Spirituality

The final area of thin description emerges from a rather surprising source: the ongoing conversation around the role of spirituality in mental health care. If systems of categorization such as the *DSM* tend to create diagnoses that can have thinning and objectifying effects, and if biological approaches risk turning people into bodies without persons, then conversations around spirituality reveal that even in the realm of the apparently holistic and spiritual dimensions of care, thin descriptions abound and hold hidden dangers. This may at first sound rather odd. We're tempted to say: "Surely, spirituality has to do with whole-person care and holistic ways of viewing people." Well, one might be forgiven for thinking that. However, closer scrutiny of what is actually going on in the realm of the spiritual as it is articulated within mental health care reveals something quite different.

Spirituality in Mental Health Care

I have been a part of the conversations around spirituality and mental health care for many years. In 2001, I wrote a book titled *Spirituality and Mental Health Care: Rediscovering a "Forgotten" Dimension*.[46] Among other things, that book pointed out the lack of research and practical attention being paid to spirituality within mental health care. It suggested that the "forgotten dimension" of spirituality was in fact crucial for good mental health care and

---

46. John Swinton, *Spirituality and Mental Health Care: Rediscovering a "Forgotten" Dimension* (London: Jessica Kingsley, 2001).

indicated ways in which mental health professionals could be encouraged to remember it and, in remembering, become people who care for the spirit as well as minds and bodies.

Since then, the situation has changed significantly. What appeared to have been "forgotten" in 2001 is well and truly remembered today! The literature emerging from the mental health-care professions reveals a burgeoning and vibrant interdisciplinary conversation that explores a variety of issues around spirituality, religion, and mental health. Religious spirituality has been positively associated with the alleviation of depression, anxiety, PTSD (post-traumatic stress disorder), schizophrenia, anorexia, and personality disorder.[47] The more generic forms of spirituality are not so closely tied to measurable outcomes, but they are assumed to be fundamental to genuinely person-centered care.[48] Some authors even suggest it is essential to our humanness.[49] This latter claim is probably not very wise, because highlighting any capacity or desire as fundamental to what it means to be human inevitably means that those who do not have that capacity or share that desire can be viewed as less than human. Nevertheless, the universality of spirituality is certainly a frequently made claim.[50] The presence of spirituality is recognized even at the level of policy, with governments insisting that all mental health professionals and indeed all health-care professionals take spirituality seriously.[51]

At first glance, this seems to be very good news! We may not be clear on what mental disorders are, but we do know what human beings are and what

47. On depression, S. Vasegh et al., "Religious and Spiritual Factors in Depression," *Depression Research and Treatment*, 2012; on anxiety, L. M. Steiner et al., "Spiritual Factors Predict State and Trait Anxiety," *Journal of Religion and Health* 56, no. 6 (2017): 1937–55; on PTSD, J. M. Currier, J. M. Holland, and K. D. Drescher, "Spirituality Factors in the Prediction of Outcomes of PTSD Treatment for US Military Veterans," *Journal of Traumatic Stress* 28, no. 1 (2015): 57–64; on schizophrenia, S. Grover, T. Davuluri, and S. Chakrabarti, "Religion, Spirituality, and Schizophrenia: A Review," *Indian Journal of Psychological Medicine* 36, no. 2 (2014): 119–24; on anorexia, Patricia Marsden, Efthalia Karagianni, and John F. Morgan, "Spirituality and Clinical Care in Eating Disorders: A Qualitative Study," *International Journal of Eating Disorders* 1, no. 1 (2006): 7–12; on personality disorder, K. Bennett, K. J. Shepherd, and A. Janca, "Personality Disorders and Spirituality," *Current Opinion in Psychiatry* 26, no. 1 (2013): 79–83.

48. Christina Puchalski, "Integrating Spirituality into Patient Care: An Essential Element of Person-Centered Care," *Polskie Archiwum Medycyny Wewnetrznej* 123 (2013): 491–97.

49. Pamela Reed, "An Emerging Paradigm for the Investigation of Spirituality in Nursing," *Research in Nursing and Health* 15 (1992): 349–57.

50. David Hay, with Rebecca Nye, *The Spirit of the Child* (London: HarperCollins, 1998).

51. NHS, Education for Scotland, *Spiritual Care Matters: An Introductory Resource for All NHS Scotland Staff* (Edinburgh: Scottish Government, 2009).

human beings need: they need *spiritual care*. Alongside the necessary care for mind and body, we also need to care for people's spirits. One might ask the question: "What could possibly be wrong with this?" Surely this puts things like religion and theology back on the map of professional credibility and offers important new possibilities for care. To an extent this is true, however, as useful as a focus on people's spiritual dimensions is, there are significant problems with this approach.

Spirituality as Self-Actualization

The basic understandings of spirituality in the relevant literature focus on the central features of what people assume spirituality to be: *meaning, purpose, hope, value, respect, love, dignity*, and (for some people) *God*.[52] Few of these definitions offer a strong philosophical or theological rationale for what spirituality actually is, and why it should be understood in such ways. Instead, many researchers simply create their own definitions of spirituality, which tend to focus on those things the researcher assumes to be most valuable in and, importantly, most absent from current caring practices. Their general assumption is that the content of spirituality emerges from the personal choice of the individual. Some people *choose* to express their essential spirituality in terms of religion, but others *choose* different ways of engaging with their spirituality (through nature, art, relationships, sport, and so forth).

Researchers think about spirituality in this way in order to ensure that it is *inclusive*. Put slightly differently, this is a spirituality designed to cater to people of "all faiths and none." It is nondenominational, open to the religious and the secular, and above all, *individualistic* and *personal*. Spirituality is thus perceived to relate to a series of personal *choices* that everyone should be given the *freedom* to develop on their own terms and in their own image. Spirituality relates to *my* meaning, *my* purpose, *my* value, and *my* choice about whether *I* believe in God. Viewed in this way, spirituality becomes a mode of self-actualization, a way of meeting personal needs and goals quite apart from others or God. This mode of spirituality fits neatly within the goals of modernity and the expectations of a culture that is deeply individualistic and fundamentally oriented toward personal choice as *the* moral arbiter.

52. For a useful review of this literature, see Deborah Cornah, *The Impact of Spirituality on Mental Health: A Review of the Literature* (London: Mental Health Foundation, 2006).

Thin Spirituality

What we end up with is a very thin mode of spirituality that is terrified of offending anyone. No longer do we have deep, thick descriptions of spirituality, richly narrated spiritual encounters with God, angels, or demons. We have prayer, worship, and sometimes a loose affiliation to religion, but involvement with what God is doing in the world is optional, if it is included at all. Instead, spirituality is thinned down and renarrated in terms of personal choices and practical psychological utility (does it make you feel better?). The efficacy and acceptance of spirituality are gauged by the effect of particular behaviors—prayer, meditation, church attendance—on a person's well-being, with "well-being," once again, being viewed primarily in relation to an individual's hopes and desires. One can *choose* the God who created the universe and who flung the stars into space, or one can *choose* a walk in the park. Both are assumed to be pretty much the same thing in terms of spiritual worth.

Practical utility is key. "Does it work?" "What benefits can it bring to people?" "How can it help us feel healthier?" This kind of spirituality is a spirituality from below—a spirituality that may include transcendence, but only as one option among many others. It makes little difference whether God is real. What matters is whether we *choose* God as a lifestyle option. Rather than introducing something that is radical and new, this mode of spirituality is designed to help certain culturally bound conceptions of spirituality fit in with current practices and assumptions. Instead of transforming mental health-care practices into something radically different from what is available currently, it is deeply shaped and formed by what is already going on in health-care institutions. It is a spirituality from below that takes its shape not from the urgings of the Spirit of God but from the nature and spirituality of health-care institutions.

The Spirituality of the Institution

An examination of the National Health Service (NHS) in the United Kingdom will illustrate this point. The NHS was launched in 1948. It is a system that assumes that good health care should be available to all people regardless of wealth. Health care is thus free at the point of use for all UK residents and is based on clinical need, not ability to pay.

The system is also designed to meet the needs of everyone; this is necessary for it to function effectively and fairly according to its expressed intentions. However, this universality inevitably problematizes and narrows the possible options for the kind of spirituality that might be acceptable within the system. In terms of spirituality, this ensures that the NHS is inevitably secular, because it cannot be connected directly with any one religion. It deals with a very broad range of people, and as such it must meet the needs of people of "all faiths and none." The particularity of religious traditions becomes problematic within a context that requires generalities in order to function. A general, generic definition of spirituality may be thin, but it is easy to implement.

Health and social care systems such as the NHS require generalities to function effectively. At a pragmatic level, it makes sense to deprioritize the particularities of religion and to develop a general mode of spirituality to which everyone can relate. Treatments—chemotherapy, medication, physiotherapy, pain control—must be universal and applicable across the whole system. You can't have an antibiotic that works only for one person! So, too, you can't have a spirituality that works for only one group of people. A system would not work well if each doctor had his or her own way of doing things that might conflict with how other doctors conducted their practice. So, while there is obviously diversity within the system, the principle of generalization is necessary and established.

Within this context, people may *think* they are acting counterculturally and taking spirituality *into* the system. However, a deeper reflection indicates that the system itself shapes and forms the spirituality that is acceptable; it silently places boundaries, parameters, and brakes on the activities of spiritual care and our articulations of spirituality and compels us to work with a thin model of spirituality that dovetails neatly with what is already there.

This model of spirituality seems to resonate with the idea of a universal spirituality that everyone shares, something that abounds in the literature. However, when one runs a critical eye across the ways in which people formulate spirituality, it becomes clear that, far from being universal, it is a very *Western* cultural model, which assumes the primacy of Western values such as individualism, freedom, autonomy, choice, and the right of people to create their own destiny. This is clearly a cultural model of spirituality rather than a universal one. It may raise our consciousness to certain important but overlooked aspects of health care, but by claiming that "everyone has a spirituality" and seeking to make a culturally bound model appear to be universal, we risk "baptizing people behind their backs," forcing them to accept thin, culturally bound models of spirituality and humanness that may satisfy certain desires and needs but in the end fail to meet those needs that can be discovered only as we engage with thicker descriptions. When this happens, we subliminally engage in precisely the kind of proselytizing behaviors that some consider a central danger of allowing religion to be a part of health care. There is clearly a need for a richer and thicker conversation around spirituality and mental health than is provided by current culturally bound models and approaches. The question is: *What might that look like? And how might we go about achieving such a goal?*

2

Resurrecting Phenomenology

Thick Descriptions and the Lived Experience of Mental Health Challenges

> The vital question is most often not if a particular kind of symptom is present, but what it means and why it is suffered. Causes for painful symptoms and deviant behaviors could be biological as well as psychological or cultural, but they always come together by way of the person who suffers from them.
>
> —Fredrik Svenaeus[1]

Useful in answering questions around what thicker conversations about spirituality might look like is Clifford Geertz's idea of *thick descriptions*. For Geertz, thick descriptions provide cultural context and help outsiders understand the meaning people place on actions, words, things, and situations. They are intended to provide enough context to enable those outside a particular situation to find meaning in the articulations of cultural experience.[2]

In the first chapter of his book *The Interpretation of Cultures*, Geertz focuses on the role of the ethnographer, a person who observes, records, analyzes, and interprets cultures. Interpretation of signs is the gateway into the meaning of a culture. To be authentic, such interpretation must be based in thick descriptions that help people see all the possible meanings. Geertz uses the example of the wink of an eye. At one level this is simply a muscular action that rapidly closes and opens a person's eyelid. However, at a thicker level, the one winking may be "practicing a burlesque of a friend faking a wink to deceive an innocent into thinking conspiracy is in motion." To understand the meaning of any particular wink, it is necessary to describe, interpret, and understand the

---

1. Fredrik Svenaeus, "Diagnosing Mental Disorders and Saving the Normal," *Medicine, Health Care and Philosophy* 17, no. 2 (2014): 241–44.

2. Clifford Geertz, "Thick Description: Toward an Interpretative Theory of Culture," in Geertz, *The Interpretation of Cultures* (New York: Basic Books, 1973).

culture in all its rich, thick fullness. Thick descriptions allow such description, interpretation, and understanding to occur.

The sociologist Norman Denzin notes that thick description "does more than record what a person is doing. It goes beyond mere fact and surface appearances. It presents detail, context, emotion, and the webs of social relationships that join persons to one another. Thick description evokes emotionality and self-feelings. It inserts history into experience. It establishes the significance of an experience, or the sequence of events, for the person or persons in question. In thick description, the voices, feelings, actions, and meanings of interacting individuals are heard."[3] Thick descriptions are necessary for deep understanding to occur. They provide a detailed account of a situation, phenomenon, or culture, an account that pays careful attention to the forms of behavior, language, interpretation, and relational dynamics. The thicker or richer the description, the broader the range of possibilities for interpretation, understanding, and action. Thick descriptions give the reader the opportunity to engage more deeply with the situation and, in so doing, begin to resonate with the issues in ways that thin descriptions simply cannot. Thick descriptions are multidimensional and rich in their *verisimilitude*; that is, they seem to be true or have the appearance of being real. Thick descriptions lead to thick and rich interpretations. Thick and rich descriptions and interpretations lead to thick and rich practices.

THE DEATH OF PHENOMENOLOGY

Nancy C. Andreasen is a prominent neuroscientist and psychiatrist whose book *The Broken Brain: The Biological Revolution in Psychiatry*[4] was a key text in psychiatry's movement from psychoanalytical to biological understandings of mental health challenges in the 1980s.[5] Although her strong biological position seems to stand at odds with some of the critique I offered in the previous chapter, she seems not to be completely bound by the hegemony of reductionist biological explanations. In her paper titled "DSM and the Death of Phenomenology in America: An Example of Unintended Consequences,"[6]

3. N. K. Denzin, *Interpretive Interactionism* (Newbury Park, CA: Sage, 1989), 8.

4. Nancy C. Andreasen, *The Broken Brain: The Biological Revolution in Psychiatry* (New York: Harper & Row, 1984).

5. Anne Harrington, *Mind Fixers: Psychiatry's Troubled Search for the Biology of Mental Illness* (New York: Norton, 2019), chap. 4.

6. Nancy C. Andreasen, "DSM and the Death of Phenomenology in America: An Example of Unintended Consequences," *Schizophrenia Bulletin* 33, no. 1 (2007): 108–12.

Andreasen contends that one of the unintended consequences of the introduction of the *DSM* criteria has been "the death of phenomenology."

In line with our previous comments on Jaspers's and Sims's perspective on the importance of thick descriptions for psychiatry, Andreasen notes that psychiatry has a long and rich history of descriptive psychopathology, a history at whose center have been phenomenological thinkers such as Martin Heidegger, Edmund Husserl, and Karl Jaspers. Psychiatrists such as Jaspers saw great benefit in constructing deep and thick descriptions of psychopathology that could provide in-depth understanding of the phenomenon of mental disorder. In so doing, they hoped to provide rich and thick possibilities for understanding, and thus more compassionate intervention. Andreasen points out that this kind of phenomenological approach to psychopathology has died with the implementation of the *DSM* criteria. The original creators of the *DSM*, she says, did not claim that it was definitive in containing the final, all-encompassing truth about mental disorder for psychiatry. They intended it to be seen as *a perspective* to guide clinical practice rather than an explanation that excluded other ways of describing and acting. Its authors recognized that it was a "best effort," a solid attempt to capture some aspects, but not every aspect, of people's mental health experiences.

What happened, though, at least in the United States, is that the *DSM* has been used more as a checklist than as part of a shared search for thick descriptions of people's mental health experiences. The *DSM* was originally intended to highlight only some characteristics of a given order. Andreasen notes that the DSM criteria

> were never intended to provide a comprehensive description. Rather, they were conceived of as "gatekeepers"—the minimum symptoms needed to make a diagnosis. Because DSM is often used as a primary textbook or the major diagnostic resource in many clinical and research settings, students typically do not know about other potentially important or interesting signs and symptoms that are not included in DSM. . . . DSM has had a dehumanizing impact on the practice of psychiatry. History taking—the central evaluation tool in psychiatry—has frequently been reduced to the use of DSM checklists. DSM discourages clinicians from getting to know the patient as an individual person because of its dryly empirical approach.[7]

7. Andreasen, "DSM and the Death of Phenomenology," 111.

The *DSM* certainly offers information about mental disorder. But if we assume that what it tells us is adequate for understanding, then we have a problem. From this perspective, we can see exactly why my psychiatrist friend didn't feel he needed to engage with his patients at any depth. Phenomenological engagement with thick descriptions was simply not a part of his worldview. The *DSM* may function more or less effectively as a general map of the terrain, but if we try to use it as a comprehensive guide to the territory, we will quickly become lost in the forest.[8]

To negotiate the territory effectively, we need a guide who is not functioning at a high level but is walking with us on the ground, noticing firsthand the details, the bumps, curves, turns, and hedges, that make the journey of mental health interesting, difficult, and complex. Andreasen suggests that we resurrect phenomenology; by returning to the rich and thick descriptions highlighted by people like Jaspers and Sims, we can more adequately capture the fullness of people's mental health experiences as they are lived out within the lives of real, meaning-seeking human beings. This does not mean rejecting other forms of description. It simply means starting in a different place and allowing that starting point to mark out, shape, and form the parameters of the journey and the ways we use, discern, and work with other descriptions.

Developing a Phenomenological Attitude

As I read Andreasen's paper, I began to see that the development of a phenomenological attitude might be a good way of founding a theological investigation that takes seriously the various descriptions of mental health challenges that are available, but in addition seeks to create new descriptions based on thick accounts of people's spiritual experiences. Such an approach would draw on the phenomenological tradition in order to create rich and thick description specifically focused on people's faith lives. Such thick descriptions have the potential to open up new avenues for understanding faithful practices.

Phenomenology seeks to move beyond standard assumptions about the way things appear to be and, as Edmund Husserl put it, get "back to the things themselves." The power of phenomenological description lies in its ability to describe the complexity of phenomena by getting behind the layers of theoret-

---

8. This metaphor comes from Ian Hacking's enlightening critique of the *DSM* criteria in his article "Lost in the Forest," *London Review of Books* 35, no. 15 (August 8, 2013): 7–8, https://www.lrb.co.uk/v35/n15/ian-hacking/lost-in-the-forest.

ical assumptions that are placed upon them. This makes it possible to capture something of the lived experience of a phenomenon, that is, the experience as it is lived out prior to the later attribution of theoretical interpretations to it. Phenomenology asks us to put aside our presuppositions, plausibility structures, standard explanatory frameworks, expectations, and assumptions and return to look at the thing itself, the experience as it is lived rather than as it is theorized. For example, rather than asking the question: "What is a hallucination?" (a medical question), we might ask a slightly different question: "What does it feel like to experience voices?" (a phenomenological question). We put to one side our technical language such as "symptom" or "hallucination," and its accompanying therapeutic or pharmaceuticals responses, and try to get back to the experience in and of itself—uninterpreted and lived. Using language such as "voice hearing" draws us into the phenomenological zone and opens up a different set of questions, a different type of description, and fresh possibilities for responding. Above all else, phenomenology urges us to remember that *before there was a theory, there was an experience; before there was a category, there was a person having a meaningful experience.*

Adopting a phenomenological attitude enables us to focus on understanding without forcing explanation. Explanation still has a place (although it may not be the role of theology to offer explanations), but our focus is on meaning and understanding, which takes us to quite different places and opens our journey up to new and fascinating possibilities.

Understanding Understanding

In the following chapters, I take up Andreasen's challenge and work toward resurrecting phenomenology as a significant dimension of theological reflection on the ways Christians experience mental health and ill health. This is not a formal exercise in phenomenological philosophy.[9] Rather, my intention is to develop a phenomenological attitude that questions and challenges the "natural attitude" toward mental health phenomena. My focus will not be on describing pathology per se, at least not in a clinical sense. I am a theologian,

9. I am not doing phenomenology in the way that a philosopher might. My intention is to use it as a perspective rather than as a strict method. Readers wishing to read some excellent phenomenology within this area written from the perspective of philosophy should explore the work of Mathew Ratcliffe and Eric Matthews: Mathew Ratcliffe, *Experiences of Depression* (Oxford: Oxford University Press, 2015); Ratcliffe, *Real Hallucinations* (Cambridge, MA: MIT Press, 2017); Eric H. Matthews, "Merleau-Ponty's Body-Subject and Psychiatry," *International Review of Psychiatry* 16, no. 3 (2004): 190–98.

not a psychiatrist, after all. My focus is not so much on eradicating or controlling pathology, but more on how people can live well with Jesus even in the midst of such experiences.

Everyday Naïveté

A good deal of the way we live our lives and engage the world assumes that the things we engage are simply there before us in an obvious and uninterpreted form, available to our understanding in their entirety "just as they are." Many of us do not question the validity of the ways we see the world; we just assume that what we see is what is actually there. The "lifeworld"—or what we experience prereflectively, prior to noticing and interpreting it—is invisible to us most of the time. Edmund Husserl calls this everyday naïveté the "natural attitude."[10] To get behind our everyday assumptions, it is necessary to reduce the phenomenological range of our focus of attention. We do this via what he describes as phenomenological reduction (*epoché*), otherwise known as bracketing.[11] *Epoché* is a Greek word meaning to suspend judgment or stay away from our normal commonsense ways of looking at things. Bracketing our assumptions does not mean that we pretend they do not exist. We cannot unknow the things we already know. To engage the process of phenomenological reduction, we begin by making our presuppositions and assumptions overt and clear. When we know what these things are, we can self-consciously put them to one side. We can then develop a consciousness of the ways our current knowledge impinges upon our ability to see things as they are. By reducing the lifeworld to a focus on specific phenomena, bracketing provides access to prereflective knowledge. We can then create rich, thick descriptions that help us see the thing in itself, untainted by our biases and prejudices.

Beyond Bracketing

Such bracketing is useful, for example, in getting behind the negative and stigmatic aspects of diagnoses and revealing cultural and religious accretions, caricatures, myths, and negative assumptions. As a basic technique, such an attitude is fine. However, in practice, it is impossible to bracket out our own experience. More than that, we actually need our experiences, biases, and

10. Edmund Husserl, *The Crisis of European Sciences and Transcendental Phenomenology*, trans. D. Carr (Evanston, IL: Northwestern University Press, 1970).

11. Edmund Husserl, *Cartesian Meditations* (The Hague: Martinus Nijhoff, 1973).

prejudices in order to make sense of the world. Human beings do not come to understand things in a vacuum. There is no such thing as an uninterpreted experience. Understanding requires something more than just bracketing.

That "something more" is ourselves! Central to the approach I am developing here is the recognition that our own interpretative horizon—our history, who we are, where we have been, what we know, what we believe about the world, what is ingrained in us by family, friends, culture, science, and religion—is fundamental to the ways we interpret the world and make sense of any new experience. Knowing and understanding come not simply from bracketing our biases and prejudices but also from recognizing the importance of our biases and prejudices for how we interpret the world, and utilizing those biases and prejudices as integral aspects of the way we make sense of any given experience or phenomenon. Positively construed, our history, our biases, and our prejudices are not obstacles to knowledge and understanding but the conditions for our knowledge. As the German philosopher Hans-Georg Gadamer has put it: "to interpret means to use one's own preconceptions to determine that the meaning of the text can really be made to speak for us."[12]

Understanding as Dialogical and Conversational

The process of understanding is thus seen to be *conversational and dialogical* rather than the product of isolated, bracketed personal reflection. Bracketing and the phenomenological attitude are useful for clearing the ground and enabling certain forms of description. However, the interpretative dimension of description is of fundamental importance. We come to know the world as we allow our horizon of understanding—the boundaries and parameters of our current knowledge, experience, and understanding—to enter into dialogue with other horizons of understanding. This process of dialogue forms the epicenter of how we come to know things.

Horizons both link and separate us. At one level, our horizons are distinct. As such, they divide and separate us from one another. The horizon of psychiatry, for example, is separate from the horizon of theology, as are the horizons of psychoanalytical theory and psychology. There is, however, a conversational flexibility within our horizons that allows such differences, if the conversation is properly and hospitably managed, to become the context for creative dialogue and deeper understanding. Charles Taylor observes

12. Hans-Georg Gadamer, *Truth and Method* (London: Continuum, 1981), 358.

that horizons are not fixed or immovable: "Horizons can be different, but at the same time they can travel, change, extend—as you climb a mountain, for instance."[13] Horizons can be shaped, extended, and changed: "Gadamer's concept 'horizon' has an inner complexity that is essential to it. On the one hand, horizons can be identified and distinguished; it is through such distinctions that we can come to grasp what is distorting understanding and impeding communication. But on the other hand, horizons evolve and change. There is no such thing as a fixed horizon. 'The horizon is, rather, something into which we move and which moves with us. Horizons change for a person who is moving.' A horizon with unchanging contours is an abstraction."[14] Knowledge and understanding come not through abstraction, distancing, and theorizing but through allowing the development of an openness to and awareness of other horizons that come from *listening* and *hearing*, not just talking. Such modes of listening and dialoguing help us to recognize and undo those aspects of our implicit assumptions that distort the horizon of the other. In this way we come to know the world not as an object to be mastered, fully fixed, conceptualized, and defined. Rather, we come to know things as we engage in dialogue with a variety of horizons of understanding. The delicate, patient, hospitable, and dialogical movement of interhorizontal conversation paves the way for understanding.

This is not an argument for relativism, that is, the suggestion that truth is always conditional and can be seen differently from a variety of viewpoints or perspectives: "Proposition p could be true from perspective A, false from perspective B, indeterminate from C, and so forth, but there would be no such thing as its being true or false unconditionally."[15] We simply want to point out that at different times and in different places, people ask different questions. Taylor illustrates this by reflecting on writing a history of the Roman Empire: such a history written in twenty-fifth-century China would be quite different from one written in twenty-first-century Europe. The difference is not because the basic propositions will have different truth claims and values. "The difference will be rather that different questions will be asked, different issues raised, different features will stand out as remarkable, and so forth."[16] In short, understanding is flexible and tentative, not because truth shifts and changes but

13. Charles Taylor, "Gadamer on the Human Sciences," in *The Cambridge Companion to Gadamer*, ed. Robert J. Dostal (Cambridge: Cambridge University Press, 2002), 126–43.

14. Taylor, "Gadamer on the Human Sciences," 136. The interior quotation is from Gadamer, *Truth and Method*, 304.

15. Taylor, "Gadamer on the Human Sciences," 134.

16. Taylor, "Gadamer on the Human Sciences," 135.

because our understanding and questioning of the world shift and change as we encounter new things and engage with different stories and fresh horizons. Understanding is a matter of hospitable, dialogical conversation that avoids relativism and refuses to be drawn into implicit or explicit reductionism.

It is precisely this kind of hospitable, dialogical, phenomenological conversation that the remainder of this book will try to generate. In so doing, I hope to create rich and thick descriptions of mental health phenomena that will allow us to work out the unique and vital contribution that theology and the practices of the church can make in facilitating life in all its fullness for Christians who live with severe mental health challenges.

Four Horizons: Creating a Thick Conversation around Severe Mental Health Challenges

What follows might best be described as a hermeneutical phenomenological conversation informed by the phenomenology and hermeneutics of Husserl and Gadamer and designed to create thick descriptions of the spiritual lives of people living with serious mental health challenges. The conversation partners that will work together to produce the narratives and perspectives presented in the remainder of this book represent four primary horizons:

1 The horizon of the author

2 The horizon of Christians living with mental health challenges

3 The horizon of the field of mental health care

4 The horizon of Scripture, Christian tradition, and reflection on the life of the church

The Horizon of the Author

My horizon emerges from my life history, which traverses three professions: psychiatric nurse, ordained minister, and practical theologian. These three professions combined with my personal life mean that my listening and interpreting are inevitably formed in quite particular ways. This horizon inevitably influences the way I write, interpret, organize, and present the various ideas and texts that make up this book. For many years I worked as a mental health nurse, and latterly as a community mental health chaplain, working alongside people living with a variety of mental health challenges. Many of my most formative years were thus spent with people who saw the world differently than others did. When you spend time with people who see the world differently, you begin to see the world differently yourself. As a community health chaplain, I was charged with the responsibility to be with people living with severe mental health challenges who were moving from formal psychiatric care into the community.[17] My job was to help them find a spiritual home. It was one of my most rewarding jobs. However, one of my biggest disappointments was that church communities could be just as stigmatizing and excluding as other communities. I realized very quickly how much work needed to be done in this area. I wish I could say that things are different thirty years on.

When I entered the world of academia in the early 1990s, I was given time and space to begin to think about these things in the light of who God is and who human beings are before God. I regard my nursing and chaplaincy experience as my place of *formation*, the place where I was shaped and formed to see the world in quite particular ways. My academic life has been my place of *vocation*—the place where I have, over time, discovered what God wants me to do with my formation.

This is the prehistory that I bring to this book. Throughout I have endeavored to remain aware of and reflexive about the ways my history has influenced my interpretation and presentation of the issues. I will leave it to you, the reader, to decide how successful I have been in that task.

The Horizon of Christians Living with Mental Health Challenges

The second horizon is of those living with serious mental health challenges. This is the phenomenological horizon that tries to get at people's experience as it is lived, without being overly influenced by theoretical overlay and presumptions. This horizon is *phenomenological* in that it seeks to get at an understanding of the thing-as-it-is. It is *interpretative* insofar as the stories upon which I reflect require careful consideration and thoughtful interpretation. My burden as the author has been to try to represent people's lived and interpreted

---

17. Readers interested in reading more about this mode of friendship ministry should see John Swinton, *Resurrecting the Person: Friendship and the Care of People with Mental Health Problems* (Nashville: Abingdon, 2000).

experience as authentically and faithfully as possible. The core conversations in this book emerged from research interviews I engaged in over a two-year period with Christians who lived with major mental health challenges, namely, schizophrenia, bipolar disorder, and major depression, which are generally agreed to be among the most serious mental health challenges. They also raise particularly sharp issues for theology, practice, and understandings of the nature of humanness. These conversations are not intended to be representative of the whole breadth of mental health challenges, but they do raise issues that have clear relevance to a broad range of mental health experiences.[18] If what follows is successful in developing rich, thick, and transformative descriptions of these forms of mental health challenges, it will, I hope, open the way for others to raise similar questions about other experiences of mental health challenges.

At a formal level, these conversations were qualitative research interviews—interpretive, phenomenologically oriented conversations intended to initiate open-ended inquiry into lived experience.[19] As a qualitative study, insights gleaned from them were not intended to be predictive, or generalizable to the population at large. Rather, I wanted to understand the uniqueness of what people were experiencing and to allow what emerged from their experience to inform understandings of mental health, theology, and faithful practice. The people I spoke with were kind enough to gift their stories without insisting that their experience was common to everyone. They made no claim to be representative of anything or anyone other than themselves. My hope was that if I could capture something of the depth of their experiences and engage these experiences with Scripture, tradition, and the practices of the church, others would be able to resonate and identify with the experience in ways that might bring about spiritual understanding and faith-full response.

At another level, these were clearly *spiritual conversations*—disciples talking to a disciple about the things of God. The content of these conversations was deeply spiritual, focusing on the things that were of the most profound importance to both the storyteller and the story receiver. Like all conversations, these were interactive and dialogical engagements, with each of us participating in the cocreation of the narrative.[20] Eileen R. Campbell-Reed and Christian

18. Over the period of the study, I spent time with thirty-five people living with the kinds of experiences highlighted in the book.

19. For a fuller understanding of the approach that I took in gathering and analyzing these interviews, see John Swinton and Harriet Mowat, *Practical Theology and Qualitative Research*, rev. 2nd ed. (London: SCM, 2017), especially chap. 4.

20. By this I mean that any narrative that is spoken and heard is created by two parties:

Scharen suggest that such spiritual conversations take place within "an *interhuman space*"—a space where relationality and empathy emerge, as we allow the Spirit to indwell our thoughts and our conversation in ways that are intimate, surprising, and sometimes revelatory.[21] These were spiritual people talking about the particularities of a living God within a context that was deeply spiritual. The social-scientific dimensions of the encounters gave structure and analytical space, which in turn opened up opportunities for shared spiritual experiences, fresh insights, and holy listening. Interviewing within practical theology is not simply information gathering; rather, it is gathering *testimony* and *bearing witness* to that testimony in ways that are authentic and faithful. My task as a practical theologian was to capture people's testimony and do all that I could do to bear faithful witness to that testimony.

Alongside these voices, I occasionally draw on the voices of writers elsewhere who offer perspectives about their experiences with mental health challenges that can help us understand the issues more clearly and intimately. Together, these various voices open up fresh space and offer shards of hope that can help us understand faithfully and practice well in the area of mutual mental health care.

The Horizon of the Field of Mental Health Care

This is a broad horizon that incorporates professional disciplines that offer a variety of descriptions of mental health and ill health. In addition to psychiatry, this horizon includes allied health professions such as psychology, nursing, neurology, genetics, and so forth. It also includes other associated disciplines, in particular, anthropology and cross-cultural studies.

It is important to be clear that this book is not intended to be seen as arguing against psychiatry. Likewise, it does not attempt to offer an alternative to psychiatry. My intention is to be a critical friend and not a psychiatry basher. Simon Wesley, president of the Royal College of Psychiatrists in the UK, observes that psychiatry bashing comes from inside as well as outside of

---

the narrator and the listener. In the context of qualitative research, the researcher chooses the area, constructs the questions, and shapes the answers by the responses to what is said. The interviewee creates the narrative as he or she responds to the questions and assumed perceptions of the interviewer. So, together, the two parties create a narrative that is cocreated and "truth-like," that is, it has verisimilitude.

21. Eileen R. Campbell-Reed and Christian Scharen, "Ethnography on Holy Ground: How Qualitative Interviewing Is Practical Theological Work," *International Journal of Practical Theology* 17, no. 2 (2013): 245.

the discipline of medicine: "There is no psychiatrist in the land who cannot remember the reactions they received from some colleagues—especially the senior ones—when they announced that they wanted to pursue a career in psychiatry. A bit of humour is all very well, but behind this is something unacceptable—an implication that the best and brightest doctors are somehow wasting their time in psychiatry. This has to stop. . . . People with mental disorders—just like those with physical disorders—deserve the best minds to find new treatments and provide the best care."[22]

Psychiatry bashing that comes from within medicine is just an extension of the stigmatization of mental health challenges that is rife in society. If psychiatrists are stigmatized, then so are those who receive treatment from them. Such stigma not only affects recruitment to the profession, it also further stigmatizes people with mental health challenges, who have more than enough stigma as it is. Doctors should know better! People deserve better. I see no reason why mental health professionals cannot be highly effective participants in God's work of redemption. One of this book's intentions is to tease out more specifically what that might look like. I will at points offer some critique of psychiatry, but always in the spirit of friendship and in the hope that together we can help people live out the fullness of life that Jesus promises.

The Horizon of Scripture, Christian Tradition, and Reflection on the Life of the Church

The final horizon is the theological horizon. This comes to us via Scripture, Christian tradition, and reflection on the life of the church. This horizon brings the knowledge, wisdom, and experience of the community of the saints into dialogical conversation with the other three horizons, with a view to allowing theology to *illuminate* and be illuminated by the issues under discussion.[23] Illumination refers to the work of the Holy Spirit as God strives to illuminate situations and experiences in the lives of believers in a way that allows us to grasp what we could not without such illumination and to respond in ways unavailable prior to our illumination. Saint Augustine describes illumination in this way: "When we lift up our eyes to the scriptures, because the scriptures have been provided by human beings, we are lifting up our eyes to the moun-

22. "Call for an End to 'Bashing' Psychiatrists," *Mental Health Today,* February 29, 2016, https://www.mentalhealthtoday.co.uk/call-for-an-end-to-bashing-psychiatrists.

23. I am grateful to my friend and colleague Tom Greggs for his insight into how illumination might be a useful concept for practical theology.

tains from where help will come to us. Even so, because those who wrote the scriptures were human beings, they were not shining on their own, but he was the true light who illumines everyone coming into this world (John 1:9)."[24]

Some things of God can be observed and grasped via human intellect. Other aspects have to be received via divine illumination. Illumination is a gift, not an achievement. The Trinity, for example, makes no logical sense, but through the illuminating light of the Spirit, human beings can at least partially grasp something of its truth and live into its implications. Humans are limited in their ability to know God, partly because of the limitations of their senses, and partly because of the barriers that sin puts up. Scripture shines "the ray of divine revelation," as Thomas Aquinas has put it,[25] which makes the knowledge of God available to human beings. Illumination breaks down barriers and opens up space for seeing things differently, or, as the apostle Paul has put it, for the transformation of our minds: "Do not conform to the pattern of this world, but be transformed by the renewing of your mind. Then you will be able to test and approve what God's will is—his good, pleasing and perfect will" (Rom. 12:2). Illumination reframes the world and throws fresh light on situations in ways that enable deep understanding, surprise, and enduring faithful action. When the horizon of Scripture and tradition is placed in dialogue with the other horizons, illumination transforms both theology and practice.

These are the four horizons that will shape and form the narratives and theological reflections that are to come: the horizon of the author; the horizon of Christians living with mental health challenges; the horizon of the field of mental health care; and the horizon of Scripture, Christian tradition, and reflection on the life of the church. If, as Charles Taylor suggests, understanding one another is the most important task of our age, engagement with these four horizons may be the beginning point for faithful understanding of mental health challenges and the development of descriptions that are rich, thick, godly, and truly illuminating.

---

24. Augustine, *Homilies on the Gospel of John (1–40)*, ed. Boniface Ramsey, trans. Edmund Hill, vol. III/12 of *The Works of Saint Augustine: A Translation for the 21st Century* (New York: New City Press, 2009).

25. Aquinas, *Summa theologiae* 1.9 ad 2.

PART II

REDESCRIBING DIAGNOSIS

3

Taking Our Meds Faithfully

The Ambiguity of Diagnosis and the Social Power of Medication

> The social power to define and categorize another person's experi-
> ence is not a power to be ignored. . . . In order to support persons
> who are trying to recover, we must attend to the fullness of their
> experiences, and not be distracted by their medical diagnoses.
> —Juli McGruder[1]

BEING DIAGNOSED IS OFTEN A PIVOTAL POINT IN A PERSON'S MENTAL
health journey. We have previously reflected on challenges that the *DSM* diagnostic system poses. It was suggested that its diagnostic descriptions are too
thin; they identify some aspects of people's experience but fail to recognize
other vital dimensions. The *DSM* cannot and does not capture the meaning
and impact of diagnosis, and indeed is not intended for such an interpretative
task. It is meant to offer a minimal amount of descriptive information that
can guide certain aspects of clinical practice. This can be helpful for clinicians
and for those living with unconventional mental health experiences. For the
former, it gives a basic descriptive structure that enables certain treatment
decisions. For the latter, it provides a name and an explanation for a series of
experiences that can be baffling to the individual and to others.

Jane lives with bipolar disorder and finds her diagnosis useful insofar as it
names her experience in a way that is helpful for her and for those around her.

> It's helpful when you are trying to tell your story to someone of what hap-
> pened. If I said I had a bipolar-depressive episode, they're like, Oh! OK,
> I understand that. Whereas if I say I had "this breakdown in my life," they're

---

1. Juli McGruder, "Life Experience Is Not a Disease or Why Medicalizing Madness Is
Counterproductive to Recovery," *Occupational Therapy in Mental Health* 17, nos. 3–4 (2002):
59–80, here 60.

a bit like, what? What does that mean? So, for people to kind of understand, or even just for me to be able to explain it to myself—what was going on during that time in my life—it is helpful. And for me it helps me to explain things like depersonalization, derealization, high anxiety, posttraumatic stress, and all that comes out of childhood stuff. Diagnosis has been helpful for understanding those things and having names for the symptoms, perhaps more so than having a label that fits the psychiatrist's diagnostic thing.

Diagnosis can name certain forms of experience in ways that make them understandable to self and others. The personal utility of diagnosis (how it relates to personal experience rather than its therapeutic utility) emerges not from the technical dimensions of the process of diagnosing but in its personal and social consequences.

Brian puts it like this:

> I've found it very helpful. It helps to sort of identify what medication can assist, but also provides me with an awareness around lifestyle and also around possible triggers for future relapse. This becomes much clearer with a diagnosis. I think . . . probably one of the things I struggled with early on was accepting the diagnosis as being helpful, but I think after many relapses that I've had since the first one, I've resigned myself and basically come to view it in a positive way as the best approach to take, not only for me but also for my family and loved ones and my friends who are supporting me. I think it's helpful . . . taking onboard all the years of research and how other people have experienced similar behavior for a similar diagnosis.

Brian's diagnosis of bipolar disorder helps him make sense of experiences that sometimes feel quite random. Randomness leads to anxiety and fear. Receiving a diagnosis can be a way of controlling the situation and driving out fear. Jane is a medical doctor. She is used to working with diagnoses and schemes of categorization. She says, "I need the diagnosis. I would be very uncomfortable just having experiences. It's very important to me to put something in a box and be, like, it has these characteristics and I can expect this, and these are the treatments. Of course, when I'm ill I don't feel like I have an illness at all because it's just what I'm doing. But when I am well it helps."

For Jane, diagnosis brings peace and a sense of control, at least when she is not experiencing those elements of her experience that she and others consider difficult. It also offers hope. If it is a recognizable condition, then she knows there are treatments available and that she is not destined to be "crazy forever"!

However, there is a more ambiguous side to receiving a diagnosis. Mary makes a poignant observation:

I think for some people diagnosis is a helpful way of being able to explain their story. But I think for me it is different. Yes, diagnoses can reduce anxiety, but at the same time they kind of lock the system. So, if you say to someone, Oh, you've got bipolar, they're like, OK, I've got bipolar. But what happens then is that it can stop them moving or changing, and they just kind of use it as an excuse and as a means to reduce their own anxiety. When I got the diagnosis (depression), we talked a lot about how actually it could be really unhelpful for me to label myself in a way that would stick, and a way that would stop me moving forward. Sure it makes you feel better and it reduces my anxiety because I can blame everything on this label. There are pluses, of course, but it does mean you are kind of stunted and you can't kind of grow. "Just take your meds for the rest of your life and you'll be fine." But who wants to be a patient forever!? (laughs) But then at the same time, I know that actually some diagnoses are helpful. Well, my friend, for example, was diagnosed with bipolar. It was just incredibly helpful for her, because she'd been, like, just all over the place, different diagnoses, different drugs and treatments, and it was just horrible. Awful for her, so when she was finally told actually you've got bipolar, she was, like, Oh, I don't really know what that means, but great, I can explain myself in some way.

There is an uncomfortable and awkward ambiguity that accompanies the ascription of a diagnosis. It can be helpful and unhelpful at precisely the same time.

DIAGNOSIS, ALIENATION, AND RESIGNATION

Allen was fifty-one years old. He studied divinity at the University of Aberdeen in Scotland before beginning a PhD in immunology at the University of Glasgow. That program didn't quite work out for him, but his desire for God and his longing to help people remained a primary mark of Allen's life. He was an interesting man—clever, thoughtful, but with a rather unusual way of expressing himself. His sharp, high voice was distinct and could be rather disconcerting. For his friends, however (and I include myself within this category), that was just how Allen was. Allen also lived under the description of schizophrenia.[2]

2. The study that underpins this book was approved by the ethics committee of the

His schizophrenia began to seriously impinge on his life in January 1976. It was small things at first. Paranoia—specifically the feeling that someone was following him around—"started big time in 1976," he said. "I kept feeling there was someone walking behind me. I just felt that if I walked around fast enough, I would see them, but I never did. They were always there but I just couldn't quite see them." Then came the feeling that people were against him, at first certain people, and then *everyone*: "There was this real fear. I was convinced everyone in the world was going to kill me if I left my room, but I'm not quite sure why. I talked to my classmates about it [Allen was a university student at the time], about what would hurt me, and that people were turning against me. They started to avoid me. That kind of made my point! People *were* against me, even my friends. So, it was kind of like a self-fulfilling prophecy."

Things went from bad to worse. Allen's feelings that people were against him became more intense. He also began to think that someone was stealing his thoughts:

> I was only sleeping like an hour a night. It was the beginning of June. I felt that I had to have a hat on all the time to protect my thoughts, because I believed that people were looking at my thoughts and were interfering with them. But if I had on this hat, it protected me from that. So, I kept the hat on at all times, even like, I was having a shower. I would leave it on until the last minute, go to the shower, take it off quick, have a quick wash of my head and then put back on my hat. That sort of thing.

Gradually Allen's life became quite disorganized and miserable. His paranoia increased, angry voices surrounded him, and his friends abandoned him (or at least that was how he felt). Even his own thoughts became his enemy. His experience resonates deeply with the experience of the psalmist:

> Even my close friend,
>   someone I trusted,
> one who shared my bread,
>   has turned against me. (Ps. 41:9)

University of Aberdeen, Scotland, UK. The people whose voices fill this book have all given permission for their words to be used. All of the participants' voices have been fully anonymized, apart from Allen's. Tragically, Allen died by suicide before this book was completed. His mother has granted permission to use his real name as a sign of respect and in the hope that his posthumous testimony can help others.

> How long must I wrestle with my thoughts
> and day after day have sorrow in my heart?
> How long will my enemy triumph over me? (Ps. 13:2)

Allen felt afraid, alone, and very lonely.

After several months of these deeply troublesome experiences, Allen finally received a formal diagnosis of schizophrenia. He knew there was something seriously wrong and that he needed ongoing help, but receiving this diagnosis did not bring relief. It made him sad: "I remember I was in the hospital when they asked if I wanted to know my diagnosis. And I said yes. They told me that I had schizophrenia. It made me a bit sad because it was sort of like, 'Oh! that's me forevermore now,' kind of thing. But it was also sort of like, I sort of felt useless a bit because I wasn't studying (I couldn't at that point), and I wasn't doing anything, so it's like I'm no use to anyone. And that just made it worse."

Some diagnoses may bring about a lessening of anxiety, but the diagnosis of schizophrenia had no such palliative effect. We will look at why this diagnosis is particularly destructive later in the book. Here we note that Allen equated this diagnosis with the end of a creative and productive life. "I just felt like giving up."

His initial visceral fear and disappointment at being diagnosed with schizophrenia were compounded by an encounter he had on a bus shortly after he was diagnosed.

> When I was a student I used to always see this woman on the bus, because she went home at the same time as me. We used to talk from time to time, but after she found out I had schizophrenia she stopped speaking to me and kept away from me. I think probably she misunderstood me, because I was no threat to her before and I'm no threat to her now. But I think she maybe thought of like a violent person with schizophrenia and thought, "Oh, I better watch myself and keep away." I think she was reacting to the name: schizophrenia. Because I remember she gave this shocked look at me when I said I had schizophrenia. That's why I tend not to tell people unless I know they're going to be OK, like I can tell you [John Swinton] because you won't turn against me for it, I know that.

Something in the diagnosis of schizophrenia seems to have deeply negative connotations. The shift in the woman's attitude from friendliness to fear is indicative of spoken and unspoken connotations that accompany the name "schizophrenia." Allen hadn't changed the way he was interacting with her. What had changed was the way he *described* himself to her. From the perspective of the woman, nothing had changed since she last willingly chatted with him. However, the introduction of the description "schizophrenia" instantly closed down her relational horizon. Allen's already-growing alienation was exacerbated by his self-stigmatizing view of schizophrenia, which was then confirmed by the bus lady's instant withdrawal. It may be that withdrawal and social isolation can be perceived as "symptoms" of schizophrenia, but the reasons for that may be more complex than the simple outworking of individual psychopathology.

Mental health diagnoses are not like physical health diagnoses. They are sticky labels that reduce people's vision to the shape and form of their assumptions about what people living with a diagnosis should be, how they should behave, and how best one should relate to "such people." It is true that some things in Allen's life had changed. His diagnosis captured some dimensions of the nature of these changes, but he hadn't suddenly become another person! The problem was that the diagnosis of schizophrenia made it difficult for people to see Allen as Allen. The presumed connotations of his diagnosis presented an unwanted persona that blinded people to the fullness of being with him. But not everyone stopped seeing Allen as Allen.

Recognition as a Lifeline

In his book *Alien Landscapes? Interpreting Disordered Minds*,[3] the philosopher Jonathan Glover draws attention to the alienating way in which mental health diagnoses can function in the lives of individuals with mental health challenges and those around them. He uses a rather unusual illustration to make his point. Drawing on the work of the Finnish children's author Tove Jansson, Glover narrates a story about an incident that occurred within the mythical (and somewhat mystical) family of creatures called the Moomins, fairy-tale characters that resemble hippopotamuses with long snouts. In Jansson's book *Finn Family Moomintroll*, the character named Moomintroll has a strange and difficult encounter. During a game of hide-and-seek, he crawls under a hobgoblin's hat and experiences a radical change, so much so that no one is able to recognize him: "All his fat parts had become thin, and everything that was small had grown big. And the strangest thing about it was that he himself didn't realize what was the matter."[4]

3. Jonathan Glover, *Alien Landscapes? Interpreting Disordered Minds* (Cambridge, MA: Harvard University Press, 2014), 373.

4. Tove Jansson, *Finn Family Moomintroll*, trans. Elizabeth Portch (London: Puffin Books, 1961), 23.

Moomintroll wandered back to his friends, who, of course, don't know who he is. They ask him who he is, and he, thinking it is still part of the game, claims to be the king of California! They believe him and instantly reject him. "'Go away!' said the Snork to Moomintroll. 'Otherwise we shall have to sit on your head.'"[5] Things go from bad to worse, and the encounter ends with Moomintroll and his friends exchanging insults and ending up in a fight. "Isn't there anyone who believes me?" laments Moomintroll. It is then that Moominmamma (Moomintroll's mother) intervenes: "Moominmamma looked carefully. She looked into his frightened eyes for a very long time, and then she said quietly: 'Yes, you are Moomintroll.' And at that same moment he began to change. His ears, eyes, and tail began to shrink, and his nose and tummy grew until at last he was his old self again. 'It's all right now, my dear,' said Moominmamma. 'You see, I shall always know you whatever happens.'"[6]

Glover concludes: "It would be wonderful if such recognition could dispel psychiatric changes in this way. It cannot, of course. But the recognition can still be a lifeline."[7] Such recognition may or may not be able to dispel psychiatric changes, but it can change the way we look at people and the ways we choose to describe their changes. There is a tremendous power in looking beyond diagnoses and simply recognizing someone for who he or she is.

Recognition and Love

Allen's mother powerfully gave him this gift of recognition. Her response to Allen's diagnosis was quite different from his own and from that of the woman on the bus. She didn't allow his new description to change the way she saw him. She continued to recognize him for who he was . . . Allen. He said, "One good thing I remember when I went home and told my mum because I really didn't feel good about it. I said, 'Oh no, they're telling me I'm schizophrenic!' And my mum said, *'No, you're not a schizophrenic, you have schizophrenia. That's different.'* Yes. Sometimes, if I ever feel down about it, I remind myself of what my mum said. Yes, it's just like any other illness. It doesn't define a person, it's just something you have."

The diagnosis of schizophrenia carried with it connotations of hopelessness, helplessness, and fearfulness and a sense of being at the mercy of unfixable broken biology. Allen reacted with sadness, withdrawal, and resignation. Allen's mum's counterdiagnosis or reframing told a very different story. Like

5. Jansson, *Finn Family Moomintroll*, 24.
6. Jansson, *Finn Family Moomintroll*, 26.
7. Glover, *Alien Landscapes?*, 374.

Moominmamma, she looked at him carefully. She looked into his eyes and saw Allen. And at that moment he began to change. His symptoms did not go away, but his sense of worth and value began to return. She recognized him and continued to recognize him even in the midst of the changes. Yes, he had very difficult and debilitating experiences, and yes, he would more than probably need the assistance of the mental health professions for the rest of his life. But his diagnosis was not who or all that he was. He was Allen, and she loved him. Allen's mother could see him for what he was: sometimes difficult but always lovable. All of us need someone like that. Not all of us find such people.

A Bipolar Story

The practice of diagnosis is essentially a hermeneutical enterprise. Someone encountering unconventional mental health challenges brings a set of experiences to the attention of a psychiatrist. The psychiatrist interprets these experiences according to the particular health-care traditions in which he or she has been trained and applies a diagnosis that is more or less in line with the interpretative guidance of one of the standard diagnostic assessment manuals. Once diagnoses are applied, certain potential options for treatment and intervention become available: psychotherapy, counseling, psychopharmacological intervention, and so forth. The problem, of course, is that as these forms of practice emerge in relation to diagnostic descriptions, other modes of practice that could emerge from other descriptions recede into the background.

Diagnoses are technical stories that occur in the midst of people's personal stories. This is an important recognition. A diagnosis contains a story; indeed, it *is* a story. It has a beginning, a middle, and an imagined end. It lays out the causes of people's mental health experiences and offers a narrative (sometimes a quite fixed narrative) to explain them and to indicate the likely trajectory of people's lives. This story then enters into the ongoing story of the recipient of the diagnoses. Such a story can bring about healing and relief. But, as we have seen, it can also prompt sadness and disruption. To receive a mental health diagnosis is to encounter a radical change in identity that can be helpful, but it can also thin out our life possibilities. No longer is life the way we had always assumed it to be. Now our narrative involves a new and alien description: *schizophrenia, depression, bipolar disorder, personality disorder,* or whatever. It is true that the diagnosis may be helpful in that it explains some aspects of our experience that may be disturbing or upsetting. But it also gives a person's life a certain meaning and direction that is rarely welcomed. Hearing the words

"You have schizophrenia, and you will have it for the rest of your life. You will have to take medication, and as long as you do, you may do well" may offer some understanding and control, but it can also strip one's life of control and purpose and can push a person into the thin and limited role of patient-with-a-mental-health-diagnosis, a role that may or may not be desirable and is liberating and deeply limiting at the same time. These kinds of tensions are well illustrated within the life of the theologian Monica Coleman and her encounter with bipolar disorder.

In her memoir *Bipolar Faith: A Black Woman's Journey with Depression and Faith*,[8] Coleman lays out in sometimes painfully raw detail her journey with bipolar disorder.[9] In a chapter titled "Diagnosis,"[10] she helps her reader understand both the problems and the blessings that diagnosis can bring. She describes two incidents—one medical and the other theological—that were formative in her experience and understanding of diagnosis. In this chapter, Monica is wrestling with severe depression and how best she should deal with it. At that stage in her journey she wasn't on medication, and she had been reluctant (partly on theological grounds: "I should depend on God . . .") to get involved with mental health professionals. Eventually she gives in and visits a mental health nurse:

> I told the nurse that I was sad, tired, and uninterested in eating. She told me that I was depressed and needed medication. In fact, she added, I would probably have to be on medication for the rest of my life. "Can't I just see a doctor? Isn't therapy included in my health plan?" The nurse refused to schedule an appointment with a doctor until I agreed. Until I told her I would take medication for the rest of my life. I was desperate, but there was no way I was letting these people give me another pill. Ever. I took my weak sad self home.[11]

This encounter illustrates well a clash of descriptions. "I'm sad, tired, and uninterested in eating." "You are depressed, and you can only get help if you describe your situation in the way that I tell you to!" There is no discussion

---

8. Monica Coleman, *Bipolar Faith: A Black Woman's Journey with Depression and Faith* (Minneapolis: Fortress, 2016).

9. This conversation around Coleman's experience of diagnosis originally appeared as a discussion piece in the online book discussion forum called Syndicate and is available at https://syndicate.network/symposia/theology/bipolar-faith/.

10. Coleman, *Bipolar Faith*, 271.

11. Coleman, *Bipolar Faith*, 273.

and no other descriptions are allowed, just a statement about how the world *really* is for you, even if your experience doesn't mesh with that declaration. What we find here is an uncomfortable mixture of medical paternalism and biological explanation: "You have an illness like any other illness. You will have to take your medication and continue to take it for the rest of your life." The nurse here describes depression as a fundamentally incurable illness that can be ameliorated only via medication.

But how accurate is this description? We have already seen that, on their own, biological explanations are too thin to help us understand the fullness of the experience of mental health challenges. In Monica's story, it is clear that while biology and biochemistry may be involved in her depression, trauma and sexual abuse are also fundamental to her experiences of depression. Does it really make sense to suggest that medication can eradicate the significance of her memories and the impact of her historical exploitation? The nurse seemed to view depression as similar to a viral infection. She considered it to be a "thing," like an elephant or a tree. Depression, however, is not like that. The Duke University psychiatrist Dan Blazer highlights the dangers of this kind of reification of depression and an overemphasis on biological roots: "The assumption seems to be that there is a 'real disease' called major depression and, by attaching the label, the psychiatrist pronounces that the patient has this disease. (This process of making an idea real has been labelled 'reification.') Reification numbs us to the possibility that depression can be more a signal of the emotionally toxic society in which we live than a thing in and of itself. And if the effects of this toxicity are initially expressed through depression, then depression should signal a need to better understand and improve society."[12]

There may be such a thing as purely biological depression. Biology certainly plays a part in all our experiences. But many people's depression is most likely deeply rooted in their history. If depression is reified and assumed to be nothing but a biological disorder, serious problems arise. Monica's lament, "Can't I just see a doctor? Isn't therapy included in my health plan?" is basically a cry for someone to listen to her story and her history without imposing deterministic biological frameworks. It is a cry for the nurse to let go of her thin account of Monica's situation and to hear and recognize that she has a story to tell that cannot be understood by thinking about her biology apart from her life as a person. Some things cannot be healed by medication alone.

12. D. B. Blazer, *The Age of Melancholy: "Major Depression" and Its Social Origins* (New York: Routledge, 2005), 6.

Medication and Faith

At that stage in her journey, Monica was avoiding taking medication, but not simply because of the unpleasant side effects. She looked upon it as being forced to make a major change in her identity. She had no desire to become a "chronic mental health patient." She saw the taking of medication as a transition point from one identity into another, less valued identity: *a spoiled identity*. She knew that there were other ways in which her situation could be described, different ways to respond to it.

Eventually she got to a stage where she could no longer cope with the darkness of her depression. She didn't want to become a "mental patient," but she also didn't want to live within the exhausting shadow of depression. Medication loomed large on her horizon, but still she hesitated: "I held the green-and-white rectangle of pills in my hands. It was a simple question that required a tectonic shift in my own understanding of myself."[13]

She stood on the precipice, gazing across at the possible new identity that she was about to take onboard. She hesitated, but her friend called her attention to something she hadn't considered: *faith*. There is a lot of evidence to suggest that faith helps people cope when they are depressed.[14] However, the form of faith into which Monica's friend invited her was not faith as a mode of coping. It was something quite different. Monica was a lover of Jesus. She had faith. But the faith toward which her friend urged her was different:

> "You have to have faith," he insisted. "I do," I immediately replied. "I don't think God hates me or anything. I believe in God." "No. Listen. You have to have faith in the medication. You have to believe it will help you. Or it won't. You're going to have to trust this too. . . . It's not idolatry. If you really believe God is in everything, if you really believe that, then you have to know that God is in the medicine too."[15]

This was a breakthrough moment for Monica. Nestling at the back of her theological concerns was the fear that taking medicine was an act of faithlessness. Her friend's reformulating the act, from a secular, medical perspective to a spiritual perspective, gave her the sense of safety that she needed. She took the medicine.

---

13. Coleman, *Bipolar Faith*, 285.

14. Artin Mahdanian, "Religion and Depression: A Review of the Literature," *Journal of Psychiatry and Behavioral Health Forecast* 1, no. 1 (February 23, 2018): 1–6.

15. Coleman, *Bipolar Faith*, 285.

Theologically, I am not convinced that "God is in the medicine," or that God is *in* everything in the way that Monica's friend articulated it. I am not certain that is the best way to conceptualize the relationship between God and creation. Nevertheless, there remains something powerful about recognizing that medication and faith do not belong to two different realms and that God can work *through* the medicine. Depression is a certain kind of pain. Pain prevents us from relating to ourselves, to one another. Having faith that medication can open up new spiritual connections—with God, self, and others—draws the mundane practice of taking medication onto a spiritual plane where this technical human practice can be transformed into a mode of divine relational healing. We will explore this suggestion in more detail later in the book.

Theological Diagnosis

Monica's encounter with her medical diagnosis was ambiguous. That ambiguity became even sharper when she encountered something strangely similar within the Christian community. The practice of administering a diagnosis to unconventional mental health experiences is not confined to the realm of medicine. One might have assumed that the perfect counterstory to the kind of thin medical reductionism that Monica had encountered would be the gospel. The gospel's wonderful and transformative story about God, who in Jesus and through the power of the Holy Spirit offers love, acceptance, salvation, and a place of belonging for all in the coming kingdom, seems like the perfect counterpoint to perspectives that place all hope in inducing biochemical changes within individuals. Jesus the healer promises to end our suffering and heal our brokenness.[16] What better way to redescribe experiences such as Monica's? Yet what Monica encountered was something quite different. She loves and trusts Jesus very much, but his followers . . . not so much.

Monica tells the story of her encounter with two Christian psychiatrists, one of whom happened to be the mother of her best friend:

> [The assessment of the Christian psychiatrist was that] I wasn't depressed. I was lonely. I just needed better social connections. She recommended a local church I might like. I had a church. I had God. I knew the difference between loneliness and illness. I tried another psychiatrist—the mother of a good friend. She knew I was a minister. She even knew my Nashville church. I began to feel comfortable. As we talked on the phone, I told her about the

16. Coleman, *Bipolar Faith*, 276.

terrible HMO people. I told her about the woman at the counseling center. I told her that I was looking for a referral for a psychiatrist in my part of town. She told me that I didn't need a doctor; I needed Jesus. I didn't hear a word she said after this. I made up an excuse to get off the phone. I tried to be polite because she was my friend's mother. But no, this was not about religion. The conversation added an hour to my daily crying session. Why was it so hard for people to understand? Aren't I telling people I am sad?[17]

The first psychiatrist, to her credit, did seem to push toward a perspective that recognized that Monica's depression may have had social and relational dimensions. However, she simply didn't listen to Monica's description of her story. Had she listened, she would have known that Monica loved Jesus and was deeply engaged with God's people even if, at times, that was a hard thing to hold on to. Instead she explained Monica's sadness via a social model, as if Monica were somehow incapable of seeing the difference between loneliness and the deep darkness she was going through. Had the psychiatrist listened to her story instead of trying to write her story for her, things might have been quite different.

Lazy Theodicy

The second psychiatrist was so deeply immersed in her spiritual projections that she was unable to hear any story other than her own. Worse, by implying that Monica was out of touch with Jesus, she engaged in what we might call *lazy theodicy*. Lazy theodicy is a form of thinking in which Christians ascribe sinful distance from God, sin, or the demonic to explain the presence of un-explainable (in their view) psychological distress. Lazy theodicy often ends up blaming the individual, locating the problem not in the social realities of a person's experiences but in the realm of individual spiritual alienation, sin, and ultimately evil. This is a trope we will see again and again as we move on. It is lazy because it takes no time and makes no effort to explore the processes and experiences involved in the development of mental health challenges and the complexity of what is required for people to move toward healing and under-standing. This way of thinking is not just lazy, it is also malignant, choosing to point the finger of "evil" at some of the most vulnerable people in our society rather than taking the time to work through the complexities of living with a mental health challenge. It would be rather unusual (but not unimaginable) for

17. Coleman, *Bipolar Faith*, 276.

a person stricken by cancer to be advised by a pastor that what is needed is not chemotherapy or radiotherapy but simply Jesus. Thin theological diagnoses can bring out the worst in Christian people.

The beauty, courage, and elegance of Monica's story of diagnosis are highlighted in the way she refuses to yield to reductionist descriptions and explanations, be they medical or spiritual. She keeps things thick. In the end, she accepts the necessity for diagnosis and medication. However, that acceptance is as much theological as it is medical. The reasons for her taking medication become clear only as we read them through the thickness of her story. Her thick story helps us see that depression, like all human experience, is multifaceted and multistoried. Depression, like all diagnoses, needs to be narrated in its fullness if it is to be understood and responded to with compassionate faithfulness.

PART III

REDESCRIBING DEPRESSION

4

LAMENT AND JOY

Depression, Antifeeling, and the (Sometimes Vague) Possibility of Joy

> Consider it pure joy, my brothers and sisters, whenever you face trials of many kinds.
>
> —James 1:2

FIVE YEARS AGO I RECEIVED A TELEPHONE CALL FROM A FRIEND. SHE told me that one of our mutual friends had taken his own life. No one knew why. Brian was a successful health-care professional, with a wife, a family, and an apparently very bright future. Many of us had not seen any indications that something was wrong, although those in close contact with him knew there were problems. He just got up one morning and was never seen alive again. Everyone was devastated. What do you do with such news? One of the most painful human experiences must be to say good-bye to a loved one in the morning and then never see that person alive again. I was asked to do the sermon at the celebration of Brian's life. I preached on the psalms of lament and the unending, unfailing love of God. I tried to help people see that the joy that God promises includes suffering and that the psalms of lament offer faithful language to express our hurt, brokenness, anger, and disappointment at what my friend had done and what God had clearly *not* done: save him.

Brian was a Christian; he was a lover of Jesus, as were his family and many of his friends. And yet, despite the profound consolation of the gospel, for some, the first response to his death by suicide was not comfort but fear. In spite of the apostle Paul's firm assurance that "neither death nor life, neither angels nor demons, neither the present nor the future, nor any powers, neither height nor depth, nor anything else in all creation, will be able to separate us from the love of God that is in Christ Jesus our Lord" (Rom. 8:38–39), they were afraid for Brian's eternal future. I guess that is the problem with hyper-cognitive theologies that assume that our eternal futures lie in our own hands rather than in the loving hands of God. If it is the case that neither death nor life can separate us from God's love, then we need not fear death, even death by suicide. We simply need to trust in God's grace.

There is a difficult tension between recognizing that God does not abandon those who end their own lives and the imperative that such actions are not God's desire for human beings. As my good friend and colleague Warren Kinghorn reminded me, two affirmations are indispensable for a Christian approach to suicide:

1   Suicide is a tragedy and a loss, and never to be encouraged or seen by Christians as a positive good.

2   *Nothing* will be able to separate us from the love of God in Christ Jesus our Lord.

If we Christians say either of these things without the other, we fall into error.[1] My sermon at Brian's funeral tried to capture the complex dynamics of these two statements. The lament psalms articulate the reality of tragedy and loss alongside the reality of God's unending love. Such an approach does not take away our pain, but it does provide us with a certain kind of consoling hope. I think people were helped by that sermon.

But then something changed.

The autopsy results came back, and it turned out that Brian had had a problem with his pituitary gland that may have contributed to his depression and ultimate demise. Some people seemed strangely relieved when they heard this. "Ah! It wasn't really his mind. It was his body that had gone wrong." Now, that may have been the case, but there are two things to consider as we reflect on this reaction. First, the spiritual dualism is quite startling. If his death has something to do with Brian's mind, then it is a spiritual problem, but if it has to do with his body, it is a medical issue. Second, and connected to the first point, it is interesting how medicine became, for some, a therapeutic theodicy, a way of explaining the presence of perceived evil and suffering.[2] If the problem lies within the human psyche, and if the human psyche is the place where we determine our salvation, then Brian has a real problem. But if the

---

1. Warren Kinghorn, personal correspondence.

2. For a deeper discussion of this and other issues relating to theodicy, see John Swinton, *Raging with Compassion: Pastoral Responses to the Problem of Evil* (Grand Rapids: Eerdmans, 2007).

issue is biological, then medicine can explain it without the need for awkward questions around the nature of God and the meaning of human suffering.

One of the problems for modern Western people is the tendency to equate the soul with the mind. Culturally we place inordinate social value on intellect, reason, quickness of thought, and academic ability. Certain strands of theological thinking can be sucked into this hypercognitive trap when defining emphasis is placed on intellect and verbal ability, with the verbal proclamation of the name of Jesus assumed as a central and vital aspect of our salvation.[3] When we think like this, any damage to the mind implicitly or explicitly morphs into damage to the soul. This can make it particularly difficult for Christians to live well with mental health challenges, brain damage, or something like dementia.[4] The implication that the *real* problem is soul damage prowls around like a roaring lion. The palpable sense of relief that some of my well-meaning Christian friends expressed as they encountered a medical theodicy is but one instance of a cultural phenomenon that is, to say the least, troublesome.

Fast-forward five years to a few weeks ago. I had just flown from Aberdeen to London and was walking toward the airport exit when a man I had never met before stopped me. "You're John Swinton?" he said. Now, I can never be certain whether to own up to a question like that! But on this occasion I did. He said, "You spoke at Brian's funeral five years ago. I just want to thank you. I had never thought of suffering and joy in that way, and I had certainly never thought that it was OK to be angry with God and to speak out that anger and frustration through the psalms. I just wanted to say thank you." With that he walked on.

I left the airport and got on a train to central London. As I thought about that brief encounter, I began to realize that the problem that many people encountered when Brian took his life was that they were *speechless*. His friends had no effective language to articulate the pain, lostness, and indeed anger that they felt toward the situation and in many ways toward God. They had become monolingual in their faith lives, sure and confident in the language of happiness and hope, but completely lost when it came to the language of suffering, brokenness, disappointment, and in particular, a biblical understanding of joy. They had heard Jesus say: "Very truly I tell you, you will weep and mourn while the world rejoices. You will grieve, but your grief will turn to

3. For a discussion of this in relation to profound intellectual disability, see John Swinton, *Becoming Friends of Time: Disability, Timefullness, and Gentle Discipleship* (Waco, TX: Baylor University Press, 2017).

4. For a discussion of this in relation to dementia, see John Swinton, *Dementia: Living in the Memories of God* (Grand Rapids: Eerdmans, 2012).

joy" (John 16:20), but they had not experienced the illumination of his words. This lack of language led them to turn to medicine and biology for intellectual and spiritual relief. They turned to them as theodicies not just because they alleviated their fears about Brian's eternal destiny but because they spoke in a language with which they were familiar. Medicine and biology represented a safe place. Within their theological tradition, they couldn't find the right kind of language to articulate their feelings and fears. The language of medicine and biology filled the gap. What the stranger in the airport taught me was that the words of my sermon had given him a language to express his sadness, his pain, and his anger, and that this language came from within his faith tradition in a way that he had not noticed previously. My articulation of the power of the psalms had moved him from silence into speech. I had helped him to reframe both lament and joy.

I have looked at lament in some detail elsewhere,[5] and it is not my purpose here to repeat those arguments. Instead, I will look at depression, with lamentation as a backdrop and joy as foreground. In the remainder of this chapter and in line with James's words in the chapter epigraph, I will explore the ways in which a focus on joy can help us understand the experience of Christians who wrestle with the darkness of depression. By understanding the nature and purpose of joy, we can understand depression in a different way, and that will give us a way to talk about depression (and to remain silent) that is both liberating and, I hope, healing. Understanding depression through the lens of Christian joy can help us understand depression more thickly and respond more faithfully.

Depression

Depression is the leading cause of disability around the world. The World Health Organization estimates that approximately 322 million people (4.4 percent of the world's population) live with depression.[6] I imagine that all the readers of this book have had some contact with depression, either in their own lives or in the lives of people they know and for whom they care. The experience of major depression is extremely deep, dark, dangerous, and serious. When your world tumbles into black and gray, when meaning is stripped from

5. Swinton, *Raging with Compassion*, 90–130.
6. M. Friedrich, "Depression Is the Leading Cause of Disability around the World," *Journal of the American Medical Association* 317, no. 15 (2017): 1517.

your existence and God seems to vanish, you find yourself cast into a realm the likes of which you really have to experience in order to understand.

Yet there is a problem with depression, beyond the obvious. Because we use the language of depression so frequently and in so many different contexts, it has become flattened, thinned, and reduced in such a way that it sometimes fails to convey the raw power of deep depression. There are at least three dimensions to this flattening and thinning, one biological, one linguistic, and the other spiritual. Each dimension can be deeply unhelpful in its own particular way.

Biological Thinning

For many people, medication is an important aspect of dealing with depression. But while medication has the potential to bring relief and release for people living with enduring depression, the growing domination of biological descriptions, assumptions, and explanations can be problematic. In his book *Lost Connections: Why You're Depressed and How to Find Hope*, the journalist Johann Hari offers a critique of the overmedicalization of depression.[7] He highlights the fact that there is an epidemic of depression and anxiety and suggests that scientists have discovered nine different causes. While some forms of depression may have a biological component, Harri argues that most are deeply tied in to the ways in which we live our lives and the sense of dissatisfaction that people experience in the day-to-dayness of our shared existence. Human beings need love, belonging, and meaningful and purposeful existence. If they don't get that (and many do not), then there are consequences. These consequences may be connected to our biology, but they are also deeply connected with our culture and social experiences. Interestingly, Harri says a major protector from depression is meaningful work: work that people feel they are genuinely participating in, have ownership of, and can feel productively engaged with. Harri describes such work as an *antidepressant*. This is a fascinating suggestion. By using the term "antidepressant" but recontextualizing it outside of pharmacology, he asks what other nonmedical antidepressants might be available in nonmedical settings.

The turn to biomedical descriptions and explanations of depression is partly caused by the influence of pharmaceutical companies, who, as Ben Goldacre has shown, tend to fund and publish research that supports the po-

7. Johann Hari, *Lost Connections: Why You're Depressed and How to Find Hope* (London: Bloomsbury, 2019).

tency of their particular brand of medication.[8] By funding drug trials and controlling which results are made public, they shape our assumptions about what an effective response to depression might actually look like. Goldacre argues that good science is necessary in order for doctors and patients to make informed decisions. However, often the kind of science we're given in relation to psychopharmacology is not good. He provides evidence that indicates that drug companies run bad trials on their own drugs, and so deliberately distort and exaggerate the benefits. If the results are not in favor of the company, the data is buried. Astonishingly, all this is perfectly legal.[9]

In short, there is a problem with the way we are informed about the efficacy of psychopharmacology. That does not mean that it should be rejected. I am *not* arguing against medication; it is, after all, helpful for some people. However, we must remain critically aware of the politics of medication and the ways an automatic turn to medication without proper consideration of other possible interventions places full responsibility for dealing with depression on medicine and the makers of pharmaceuticals and ignores any conversation about the need for cultural change. It gets society off the hook. It also tempts doctors and patients alike to narrow their options for intervention. David's experience helpfully illustrates this point:

> The doctor's account was that my serotonin levels were low, and that medication could raise that. So, I was told that I was literally chemically deficient and that this would help. I had suffered terribly with depression and anxiety for years, and I had always tried to deal with it through prayer and meditation. So, the very fact that I had decided to go to a doctor indicates just how bad things were. But I wasn't even offered counseling through it all. The doctor just went straight to medication. He was good though. Very compassionate. Compassion with a different shared framework of what compassion might look like.

The doctor had a genuine and compassionate desire to alleviate David's distress. However, the focus of his intervention was on the chemical dimensions of David's experience rather than the spiritual dimensions that had been David's usual way of dealing with depression. It was not that giving medication

8. Ben Goldacre, *Bad Pharma: How Medicine Is Broken, and How We Can Fix It* (San Francisco: HarperCollins, 2012)

9. For a further critique of questionable pharmacological practices, see Irving Kirsch, *The Emperor's New Drugs: Exploding the Antidepressant Myth* (London: Bodley Head, 2009).

was necessarily the wrong thing to do. The problem was that the doctor assumed it to be the *only* thing to do. David's natural spiritual resources and coping mechanism were not taken into consideration. The medication "worked" insofar as it lessened David's distress, but it had the side effect of flattening everything. "The medication took the edges off everything. So, I couldn't actually work through the issues that I needed to work through at a spiritual level." Medication has its place, and that may well be an important place. But it needs to be seen within a broader spiritual context that recognizes the importance of biology but is not defined or confined by it.

Linguistic Thinning

Depression has also been thinned and flattened by the mundane way many of us talk about it; we don't adequately recognize the true depth of the pain and suffering those who are depressed go through. We call it "the Monday morning blues"; we feel sad and state that we are "feeling a bit depressed." This is an unusual way to talk about a serious mental health condition. We would not normally say we have "a touch of cancer" or "a bit of a stroke," but many of us seem to think it is appropriate to downgrade depression to the language of mild sadness or "feduppedness":

> I hope that doesn't sound awful or like I am invalidating others' experiences. It's just that I keep finding myself battling with the issue when people mention having a "depressed day," and I'm like, mate, my depressed day is lying in bed, not eating, not moving, barely able to get out of bed to go to the bathroom, and if I am able to do anything, it exhausts me, so I may be able to read for a bit or watch TV, but those are on "good" days. . . . On a bad day I will cry or be a zombie or think/attempt suicide.

The tension between having major, enduring depression and having a season where one is depressed can even be missed by those who have received a diagnosis of depression. Amy puts it in this way:

> So, I am just in my own mind trying to figure out how I should deal with that tension [between a season of depression and a lifetime of being depressed] while saying both experiences are valid but there is a demarcation between a "bout" or season of depression in comparison to a diagnosis of major depression that will more than probably live with me as long as I live. Let me give you an example. One of my friends got a diagnosis of

depression, and I helped her through it. She was on antidepressants for six months and came off them and no longer has feelings of depression. So, her depression is "cured," and she has talked to me about giving up my medication because she was able to do it (which experience informs me is not a good idea for me!). But then how do I deal with the tension that, yes, she had some experience or a season of depression for six months (and is now apparently the oracle on all things depression), while I have had a diagnosis of major depressive disorder since I was thirteen, so for thirteen years. And I wouldn't say it's a depression that has been on and off, but one that has continuously been there every day. Sure, some days are better than others, and my medication has made a massive difference in my ability to control my emotions and not be governed or ticked off by my own mind. I think what I am struggling with is how do I value those experiences and say, yes, you had a season of depression, but explain (if I even need to explain to myself) that there is difference between a season of depression and years of depression. And I know some people may say it's a season of depression, but in my own mind thirteen years is more than just a season.

The language of depression has become so normalized and thinned down (even sometimes for those who have lived through it for a short period) that it has lost the power to describe the true, raw power of the experience of major depression.

Spiritual Thinning

The third dimension of thinning occurs when the complexities of depression are reduced to a single, often ill thought through spiritual explanation. This is the spiritual equivalent of biological reductionism. The general trope here runs along the lines of "Come on now! Pull yourself together. If you just prayed a little harder and opened yourself to the Spirit, you wouldn't be feeling the way you do. Didn't Jesus tell us to have faith and be joyful?" (subtext: "Be happy, just like I am, because my happiness proves how close I am to God"). As Stephanie put it: "Often what I hear is people saying things like 'Oh, I got through my period of depression by just praying more.' And I just wanted to say, 'OK, you weren't depressed! Maybe you had a bad day.' So, I think there's still misunderstanding about what constitutes a mental illness. It's not just a bad day, it's not just a series of bad days, it's bloody hell."

Prayer and the healing work of the Holy Spirit are of course vitally important for Christians. But attributing human suffering to a lack of human effort
feels more like works than grace. Depression is certainly a spiritual crisis but,
as will become clear, not in this way. Talking faithfully about depression requires more than glib and easy assumptions that low mood is equal to sinfulness or faithlessness. It is unlikely that we would invest our hard-earned cash
in a business venture without doing extensive amounts of homework and risk
assessment alongside our prayers for discernment. It is interesting and revealing to ask why some are unwilling to work as hard to understand and respond
to the spiritual dimensions of depression or any other mental health challenge
as they are manifested in the lives of their brothers and sisters in Christ.

Thickening Our Understanding of Depression

I want us to approach this issue in a slightly unusual way. One of the marks
of Western culture is the desire for happiness. It seems natural to assume that
in the midst of the many other things we might want, above all else, we want
to be happy. Happiness is a positive emotion that provides us with a sense of
well-being, hope, and enjoyment of the way our lives are and the way we want
them to be in the future. There is nothing wrong with desiring happiness.
However, the fact that the apostle Paul does not mention happiness as a gift
of the Spirit might make us a little wary of its spiritual validity as a primary
life goal.

Paul does name joy as a gift of the Spirit, however. The absence of happiness and the presence of joy in Paul's list of spiritual gifts affect how we might
describe and understand depression. Intuitively we may think that depression
is an absence of happiness. However, in Scripture *joy*, not happiness, is considered a gift of the Spirit. So, what might depression look like if we thought
of it as a disturbance of joy rather than a lack of happiness? The concept of joy
symbolizes for many people the exact opposite of depression. Depression is
assumed to be a set of experiences where one loses one's joy. So, when Scripture
urges us toward the experience of joy: "the joy of the Lord is our strength"
(Neh. 8:10), it can become quite oppressive for those who appear to live without joy. They are tempted to assume that their perceived lack of joy indicates
a spiritual deficit. However, when we begin to tease out what biblical joy is, we
discover that it is actually a potential source of liberation and hope for people
living with enduring depression.

Thinking about Joy

In teasing out this suggestion, let me begin with three propositions:

1   Theologically, joy is best not equated with happiness.

2   Sadness and suffering are not the opposite of joy. Indeed, they are aspects of joy.

3   The primary problem for those living with major depression is *not* sadness but an experience of a deep loss of joy.

As we reflect on these three propositions, it will become clear that depression is a deeply spiritual experience with profound theological implications.

What Exactly Is Joy?

The Yale systematic theologian Willie Jennings defines joy this way: "Joy is an act of resistance against all of the forces of despair. Joy is a work that can become a state which can become a way of life."[10] Jennings is speaking into the history of oppression and slavery that has been the experience of African Americans. Finding joy—being able to celebrate the goodness of Jesus even during horrendous struggles—is an act of resistance that stands firmly against those powers and principalities that desire nothing but despair for human beings. It is a collective work that involves spiritual formation. As we engage in worship, we become people who embody joy. As we embody joy, it becomes a way of life. Joy also requires political striving and a form of church that stands clearly against injustice based on the enduring presence of Jesus. The key thing for current purposes is the suggestion that joy is not the *outcome* of resistance. We do not struggle against despair so that we can find joy. Joy is not the product of human effort. Quite the opposite. Joy is the key point of resistance *within* the struggle.

Unlike happiness, joy is not an emotion or a feeling. Rather, it is an assured presence—the presence of Jesus. Karl Barth helps us draw out this perspective on joy a little further:

10. Willie James Jennings, "Joy That Gathers" (unpublished essay, presented as a work in progress to the Theology of Joy Project at the Yale Center for Faith & Culture consultation on "Religions of Joy?," August 21, 2014). Quoted here with the author's permission.

Jesus Christ enters human existence as the great joy which shall be to all people. He breaks down this resistance to grace by Himself appearing as grace triumphant, as the royal removal of our sin and guilt by the action of God Himself. Because our sin and guilt are now in the heart of God, they are no longer exclusively ours. Because He bears them, the suffering and punishment for them are lifted from us, and our own suffering can be only a reminiscence of His. As He takes to Himself our sin and guilt in His Son, we are freed from the necessity of seeing and suffering and lamenting except as His and by faith in Him, i.e., except as a burden of sin and guilt which is lifted from us by Him. It remains for us only to be the sinners whose place He has taken and who must therefore really have their life in Him.[11]

For Barth, *Jesus is joy*. In the incarnation, Jesus enters creation and initiates our redemption. That is our joy. When we think of joy, we should think not simply of happiness but of the presence of Jesus, which may include happiness but, in the light of the cross, also includes sadness and suffering. The power of the incarnation is God's empathic movement into the suffering of the world in order (a) to reveal a solidarity that we were not aware of before and (b) to share in human suffering in a way that gives hope to the pain of death and suffering and creates streams of possibility even within the most hopeless of situations. This is not a theodicy. It is not an explanation of evil and suffering. It is a statement about the nature of joy and the location of God within human suffering. Jesus our joy inhabits our suffering in hopeful ways.

Joy as Gift

In Galatians 5:22 the apostle Paul offers a description of the fruits of the Spirit, that is, the things that come to us in the presence of the Spirit of Jesus: "the fruit of the Spirit is love, joy, peace, forbearance, kindness, goodness, faithfulness." Joy is not a human work, an emotion or a feeling. *Joy is a gift*. It is something that God simply and lovingly chooses to give to us. Joy is not synonymous with happiness. It is not a coincidence that Paul does not name happiness as a gift of the Spirit. It's not that God does not desire us to be happy. It is simply that joy is not dependent on feelings of happiness. Finding joy may make us happy, but being happy does not guarantee that we find joy. Happiness is a passing emotion. It comes, and it goes; it rises, and it falls; it shines, and it fades. Joy

11. Karl Barth, *Church Dogmatics* II/1 (London: Bloomsbury, 1957), 374 (emphasis added).

has durability. The presence of Jesus does not pass, even if it may sometimes feel that way. We are not called to be happy; we are called to be joyful.

Jesus Is Our Joy

Joy is not something that can (or should) be understood apart from suffering. As Jennings points out, joy is the key point of resistance *within* the struggle. It is not the prize we gain when we overcome suffering. Joy is integral to suffering. In James 1:2 the apostle tells us to "Consider it pure joy, my brothers and sisters, whenever you face trials of many kinds." "Pure joy" comes when one is present with and participating in Jesus and his works. One of the many lessons that we learn from the cross of Jesus is that suffering is an aspect of the joy of Jesus's presence. To be with Jesus—our great joy—is not to be without suffering. The writer to the Hebrews reminds us of the presence of joy in the suffering of Jesus when he encourages us to fix "our eyes on Jesus, the pioneer and perfecter of faith. For the joy set before him he endured the cross, scorning its shame, and sat down at the right hand of the throne of God" (Heb. 12:2). It seems clear theologically that joy contains and sometimes necessitates suffering, sadness, and disappointment. When we speak and sing of joy in our worship, I am not always certain that this is the kind of joy that people ecstatically raise their hands and claim as their soul's desire.

Joy is thus seen inevitably to be an eschatological concept. Jesus says: "Very truly I tell you, you will weep and mourn while the world rejoices. You will grieve, but your grief will turn to joy. A woman giving birth to a child has pain because her time has come; but when her baby is born she forgets the anguish because of her joy that a child is born into the world. So with you: Now is your time of grief, but I will see you again and you will rejoice, and no one will take away your joy" (John 16:20–22). Joy is here, but not yet in all its fullness. Joy is not the absence of sadness or suffering; it is our awareness of the enduring presence of God in all things and at all times. Joy is the settled assurance that God is with us and for us in all circumstances and at all times. It is the bold confidence that ultimately everything is going to be all right, accompanied by the determined choice to praise God in every situation in the present.

All of this is well and good. But what if you find yourself unable to hold on to the great joy that is Jesus? What happens when you encounter the deep, dark abyss of depression, a place where happiness and joy vanish and Jesus seems to hide or simply disappear? The primary problem for Christians living with deep depression is not just an abundance of sadness (if in fact sadness is the issue at all). Rather, the problem is how to deal with an experience of the deep loss of joy. In teasing out this observation, we must listen carefully to the experiences of those who are forced to inhabit the world of depression and to wrestle with joy.

DEPRESSION AS ANTIFEELING

The first thing to observe about depression is that it is not really a feeling. Though we use language like "feeling depressed," that is not an accurate description. David put it this way: "Depression is not a feeling, it's almost an antifeeling. And that's why it's so frustrating when people say, 'What have you got to be sad about?' or just pull yourself out of it. And you're like, but that's not how it works. Depression strips away your ability to emote, and when I say emote, that's not expressive emotion, that's internal emotion. It is possible to be able to look as if you are expressing emotion but actually not be able to articulate it within yourself."

Depression is the opposite of feeling. That being so, responses that suggest that Christians shouldn't be *feeling* sad and unhappy may be based on two false assumptions:

1 Happiness is equal to joy.

2 Depression has primarily to do with emotions such as sadness and a correlating lack of happiness.

If depression is in fact antifeeling, this changes the ways we think about it. Many people may be able to identify with feeling sad, but how many can identify with feeling nothing?

Depression and Sadness

Depression is much more than sadness. Indeed, the language of sadness may not be the best way to articulate the experience. Explained Shane: "You can feel sad as an effect of depression. I sat and cried because of how I felt, not because I was sad. I was sad because of the way I was feeling, not because I was sad. In and of itself depression made me sad. Sadness is actually a positive description of an emotional state, and for me depression is a negative corruption of emotion. Sadness is something that you know will pass. Depression is something you know will never pass."

The suggestion that sadness may be a release is counterintuitive. To suggest that it could be a desirable alternative seems to make no sense to those who have not shared this experience. And yet, Shane continued, "Depression is really muted. It's an inability to feel sadness, you know? It's not that its beyond sadness, because when I think of the phrase 'beyond sadness' that's . . . it's like on the same road—you pass sadness and you go further. I think they're two different roads entirely. Yeah, sadness is—when you're depressed all of your emotions are very muted. You can't really feel angry, you can't really feel sadness, you can't desire anything (which is what I mean when I say I long for sadness). So, sadness is a wonderful healing feeling that I've rarely felt."

Sadness has an end. You grieve, things change, you move on. Major depression has a completely different dynamic. It is *enduring.* "It's like eternally grieving for something and never quite being sure what that something is." There are some things in life that we want to be durable—to go on forever. We want our earthly loves to go on forever, or our earthly lives. We want the love of God to go on forever. Durability is a wonderful gift, but it can also be a dreadful curse. Sadness will end, but depression endures. It feels like grief without resolution, woundedness without the possibility of healing, tears without the possibility of being dried. Even God seems to abandon us: "I don't know where God goes. I guess he doesn't go anywhere, but it sure as heck feels that way. When you cry out to God and get nothing but silence . . . that's a pretty lonely place to be."

This kind of experience resonates closely with Jesus's experience on the cross. But it is important to note what Jesus says. Jesus does not cry: "My God, my God, why does it *feel* like you have abandoned me?" The abandonment that Jesus felt was very real. After the fact, we might want to get around the mystery of how God can abandon God by psychologizing and reducing Jesus's experience to a perceptual mistake that can be seen for what it was in the light of the resurrection. Such a description may turn out to be true. Nonetheless, the psalmist's words "Darkness is my only companion" awkwardly challenge such a reading of Jesus's cry of dereliction. In the next chapter, we will return in more detail to the significance of God's hiddenness in the midst of depression. For now, its reality in the life of the believer is the thing to hold in mind.

The Removal of Joy

Depression is not an absence of happiness. Nor is it the presence of sadness. It is an antifeeling that results in an ongoing struggle to find and hold on to joy: "Depression for me was an overwhelming absence of things. Feeling like I will never feel joy again. That's not an uncommon experience for me even now, despite the medication and everything. Just a removal of joy. It's just a privation. I can understand why suicide comes in, because just feeling like you don't feel anything is just awful. . . . An absence of joy and an absence of rest."

When you are depressed, you can't sleep. When you can't sleep, you can't rest. When you can't rest, then day, night, present, and future seem to merge in a way that makes life seem pointless. If life is nothingness, what is the point? "It's a kind of active nothingness rather than a passive nothingness. You can imagine a kind of comatosed state where you think 'there is nothing here!' But it's not like that. It's kind of an active nothingness, and it feels like it is consuming everything else. It's actively consuming these things; taking whatever bit of positivity or joy and perverting it all; turning it around. All medication seemed to do was make the active nothing passive nothing, and I wasn't sure if that was helpful." Depression is unimaginable. It has to be experienced to be understood.

Tempted by Inauthenticity

Bearing in mind that a significant number of the psalms are psalms of lament, which seem to be intended to articulate precisely these kinds of experience, one might assume worship to be an event where the nothingness of depression was recognized, articulated, and brought into the healing presence of God: "How long, Lord? Will you forget me forever?" cries the psalmist! However, as Jen points out, that is not always the case: "It was difficult. Our church is charismatic, evangelical. I love Jesus, so that is just fine. But, there's a lot of happy-clappy-ness, which when you're depressed and crying, is just awful. Yeah, yeah. But I mean Sundays in church were excruciating—just turn up, worship, listen to the preacher, and then run away. Or cry during the ministry time. Just dealing with people was so overwhelming."

What must it be like to feel nothing when *everyone* around you is feeling (or appearing to feel) happy and seems to assume that being in the presence of the Lord requires a certain kind of feeling, a certain kind of emotion, a certain kind of happiness? The temptation toward inauthenticity becomes almost overwhelming: "You can live authentically with depression. We need to find language to talk about depression that is spiritually meaningful for people rather than the falsities of happiness. False happiness is a terrifying thing if you are depressed, because it is something you actually learn to mimic to survive. And if you start mimicking your spiritual life, then you are in real trouble."

Jesus is our joy. But if we, even for a moment, lose sight of Jesus in the midst of our darkest storms, and then have to pretend that we haven't, joy quickly turns to hypocrisy, deception, and despair. Feeling that one has to mimic one's spiritual life in order to fit in with what other human beings think is the emotional norm can only be destructive. I imagine many of us can identify with having to fake spiritual happiness at times. What might it be like to feel you have to do that at all times?

Lament and Authenticity

It is good to be happy. But what is required is a liturgical imagination that seeks to capture the fullness of the emotions that are present within the body of Jesus. Such an imagination recognizes that the liturgical space of worship is formative of the body. As we engage in the practices of worship, as we pray, sing, participate in the Eucharist, celebrate, lament, and hope, so our bodies and our minds are shaped, formed, and transformed by the Spirit. If we are only formed by happiness and a theology of glory, then that is all our minds will be able to comprehend. But if we are shaped by the fullness of the liturgy that emerges from the fullness of Jesus's body, we will be enabled to see the world very differently, including those aspects of the world that we describe as mental health challenges.

Authentic worship requires honesty. The chief end of human beings is not to be happy. It is the glory of God. The chief end of worship is not feeling better or even feeling closer to God. Rather, the goal of worship is to form people who have learned the subtle nuances of the vocation of loving God even when they can no longer feel God or indeed anything else. Such a task is not something one does alone. It is a task of the body. Developing such a liturgical imagination requires learning the power of lamentation. Jen continues: "But thankfully our worship leader is . . . he's a guy who really believes in 'let's have worship which talks about how rotten life can be.' Which I really like. And so, in the midst of this happy-clappy-ness, he'll often have a Sunday of lament where we'll all just wail and go 'life is awful!' Which really freed me up. It was incredibly helpful."

Lament demands a mode of liturgical inclusivity that does not insist that happiness and a lack of anxiety are the hallmarks of the presence of God. Lament puts the lie to those who insist that "praying harder" will bring blessing, with blessing defined as a release from our present sufferings. Jesus's lament from the cross: "My God, my God, why have you forsaken me?" drew neither release nor answer. Lament allows honesty and mystery: "Life is horrible, and I have absolutely no idea where you are, God." But lament does not belong only to those who are suffering. Lament is a practice that the body of Christ must learn together in times of happiness and tragedy so that it can deal faithfully with times of sadness, brokenness, and disappointment. There are plenty of things in the world to lament. The door to the school of lamentation is wide open. The fact that many of us are not thoroughly schooled in the language of lament is a judgment on the thinness of our worship practices. We need to learn how to lament for and with our brothers and sisters in Jesus so that, when it's our turn to suffer, we (all of us together) know how to embody the language of lament.

Lament is something we do together. So also, and perhaps oddly, is joy:

> But then saying that, actually it was also really helpful to be in a congregation of people who were still worshiping God, still being happy-clappy, still being hopeful when I was just like this, I just can't do this. Because it meant they were like, "Well, you can't do it, but we can do it for you." Which I just really appreciated. People would be standing alongside me in prayer; like during the worship time they'd have a hand on my shoulder while they were just fully singing, worshiping, and rejoicing. And I was just a wreck, crying, but I found that incredibly profound because it's that sense of someone willing to be alongside me, and yet they were not forgetting the truth that I couldn't grab ahold of at that point.

The body of Jesus is marked not by its uniformity of experience, feeling, or bodily presence but primarily by its diversity and by the enduring presence of Jesus, our joy. It is in our diversity that we discover what it is like to be with Jesus. If Jesus is our joy, then that joy is inevitably and inextricably imbedded and embodied within Jesus's body, that place of reciprocity, mutuality, and burden bearing. When our brother or sister in Jesus struggles to hold on to the great joy of Jesus, other brothers and sisters hold it for him or her, not in a way that is judgmental—"If you can't feel Jesus in the way that I do, then you are spiritually less than I am. You'd better work out what sin you have committed!"—but in a spiritually gentle way that says, "OK, for now it feels like Jesus has abandoned you. Jesus knows what it feels like to be abandoned. At this moment in time, you don't feel the way I feel, but I desperately want to help you hold on to the possibility that God exists, and the possibility that God loves you, and the possibility that joy might be closer than you think. I know that's not how you feel, but it remains a possibility, and I want to hold that for you. But I want to sit with you in this darkness (as best I can), and I want to say to you that I love you and that God loves you and that we can wait together. The storm will pass. Let me hold joy for you for a little while." When this happens, as Maggy observes, the possibility of hope emerges:

I can always remember God, I can't always feel God. My first psychiatrist, who was a brilliant woman, and very holistic—like, everyone in the world should have this psychiatrist!—she said to me, "Just remember that you know the possibility of feeling better exists. And know that the possibility exists." Not that I do feel better, not that I necessarily will feel better soon, but the possibility exists that I will feel better. And that's how I feel about God. The possibility that I will feel the presence of God exists. It may not exist in the moment, but the possibility exists.

Like the friends who opened up the roof and lowered the paralyzed man down into the presence of Jesus (Mark 2:1–12), worship holds open the possibility of God. Holding it open for others is the task of Christian friendship.

Joy as Resistance

Perhaps now we can better understand Willie Jennings's words we quoted above: "Joy is an act of resistance against all of the forces of despair. Joy is a work that can become a state which can become a way of life." Joy stands against the despair of depression but refuses to blame the individual for his or her situation. Joy recognizes the despair that emerges from depression and calls upon Jesus's body on earth to form itself as a joyful community that can hold joy for those for whom, at times, experiencing joy feels like an impossibility. Bearing witness to joy requires a liturgy that creates spaces of resistance and facilitates radical liturgical inclusion. Joy requires that we worship in quite specific ways.

At this point, we need to return to one aspect of depression and explore it more fully. It may be the case that Jesus is our joy, but what happens when Jesus seems to go missing? Where is joy when we cannot find joy? Where exactly does God go when we are depressed? What does it mean to cry with the psalmist: "*Darkness is my only companion*"?

5

Finding God in the Darkness

Testifying to the Presence of an Absent God

> About three in the afternoon Jesus cried out in a loud voice, "Eli, Eli, lema sabachthani?" (which means "My God, my God, why have you forsaken me?").
>
> —Matthew 27:46

In his book *The Spirituality of the Psalms*,[1] Walter Brueggemann draws attention to how the psalms are intended to structure and form our experiences of the world in ways that enable us to remain faithful throughout the vicissitudes of life. He notes that some of the psalms, particularly the lament psalms, are intended to function therapeutically in enabling people who have experienced deep trauma, suffering, and injustice to articulate their pain and find new ways of perceiving their situation and understanding the world. Brueggemann schematizes the psalms according to a threefold pattern meant to facilitate different ways of looking at, perceiving, and responding to tragic situations and feelings of alienation from God. The schema runs from *orientation* to *disorientation* to *reorientation*:

1 *Psalms of orientation*—Orientation is found particularly in the royal psalms (e.g., Pss. 2; 18; 20; 21; 45) but also elsewhere, such as in Psalms 8, 23, 24, and 33. These psalms assume and proclaim that the world is good and stable; God is in God's heaven, and the covenant is being faithfully upheld. Psalms of orientation speak to a way of being in the world that is safe and homeful. Homefulness, Brueggemann says elsewhere, "stresses both being with and belonging with God

1. Walter Brueggemann, *The Spirituality of the Psalms* (Minneapolis: Augsburg Fortress, 2002).

89

and being with and belonging with the neighbor in community."[2] Homefulness is precisely what is lost when one encounters tragedy and suffering.

2 *Psalms of disorientation* or lament—The majority of the psalms are lament psalms. These psalms speak powerfully of the disorientation that is the lot of human beings at various times and seasons, and for some, for most if not all times and seasons. Periods of disorientation can be devastating and completely bemusing. The old maps just don't fit; the old coping mechanisms simply don't help the psalmist to cope. "Why me, oh Lord? How long!" The old visions seem to make no sense anymore. The psalmist no longer sees the world in the ways he used to. When disorientation hits, you don't sing Psalm 23:

The Lord is my shepherd, I lack nothing.
     He makes me lie down in green pastures,
he leads me beside quiet waters,
     he refreshes my soul.
He guides me along the right paths
     for his name's sake. (vv. 1–2)

Instead you turn to Psalm 137 and you cry:

By the rivers of Babylon we sat and wept
     when we remembered Zion.
There on the poplars
     we hung our harps,
for there our captors asked us for songs,
     our tormentors demanded songs of joy;
          they said, "Sing us one of the songs of Zion!"
How can we sing the songs of the Lord
while in a foreign land? (vv. 1–4)

The suffering of exile requires a certain kind of language. The psalms provide just such a language.

3 *Psalms of reorientation*—Brueggemann's third typology relates to a movement from disorientation into a new mode of life. He describes

2. Walter Brueggemann, *The Practice of Homefulness* (Eugene, OR: Cascade, 2014), ix.

this movement as *reorientation*. There are two ways this movement occurs. In most but not all the lament psalms, there is (eventually) a profound change in the way the psalmist perceives the situation. For no obvious reason, something changes in his way of viewing the situation, and he moves from the language of lament to the language of joy and worship:

> But I trust in your unfailing love;
> > my heart rejoices in your salvation.
> I will sing the LORD's praise,
> > for he has been good to me. (Ps. 13:5–6)

What initiates this change? The psalmist remembers God's *hesed*—God's unending and faithful love. The psalmist looks out at the same situation, but he sees it quite differently. The pain of the suffering event is not taken away, but it is reframed in the light of the revelation of God's gracious, loving presence. As he takes a second look at the situation by allowing the lens of the love of God to change the way he sees things, he understands and responds differently. Grace and redemption did not enter the situation; they had always been there. The psalmist, for whatever reason, hadn't been able to recognize them.

In this chapter, we will explore some of the ways Brueggemann's typology of psalmic suffering can help us understand the experience of people living under the description of major depression.

ORIENTATION

One of the most difficult things in relation to living with enduring depression is its cyclic nature. It is possible to go through all of Brueggemann's schema in a single day! This makes the point of orientation fragile and tentative. Coreen describes it in this way:

> My normal, the point where I think that everything is more or less normal, you know, when I know that God is still with me, is kind of weird. Depression is a wee bit like an abyss. You know, a deep dark pit that you can't ever get out of. So, you have to sit there and just wait. When I'm in there I need medication. It sometimes lifts me up and out of the pit, and eventually I get to the point where I can cope, and I am able to be normal. That is great! But it is always like this very tentative kind of healing, very much like you're on this very, very fragile ground. So, when I'm ill, I'm in the pit. But when I am well,

I imagine myself sitting on the edge of the abyss, knowing that I could tumble in at any time. So, my normal is probably not like your normal (laughs).

For Coreen, an Irish businesswoman who had lived with depression for most of her adult life, the place of orientation had an impending sense of disorientation built into it. She never really felt certain that "God was in God's heaven and all will be well," even when she was well. God was, of course, in God's heaven, but her place before God's throne always felt wobbly. The presence of God is very real and very important to Coreen. But whether it can be trusted to stay that way is a question always on her mind.

DISORIENTATION

When the shakiness of her orientation begins to slip into darkness, things start to change. The usual points of orientation begin to fall away, slowly dissolving into nothingness. When this happens, the first thing that shifts is her language. Depression is powerful, overwhelming, and very difficult to articulate. In many ways, it defies language. Coreen tries to articulate her feelings in this way:

It's almost as if my body starts to close down. I stop being able to concentrate, and I guess because I'm not concentrating I forget stuff, so I have chunks of memory loss. Normally when I get a bit spiritually down, I turn to Scripture or remember a passage that helps me. But when I am moving into depression, I can't remember anything and even if I did I'm not sure that I can make any real sense of it. I find it difficult to articulate things. My fiancé can tell when I'm getting bad because I stop being able to form sentences properly. Which makes it very difficult for me to tell people what's going on. And the more I withdraw, the more I can't tell people what's going on.

Language becomes stretched and forced into odd and dissonant shapes that wrap around her experience as she struggles to capture and articulate what she feels acutely but has trouble saying out loud.

It's hard. My feelings are a kind of range between gray and black, although I guess feelings aren't really colors, but that is the only way I can describe it. It feels something between numb and just raw pain, and ironically, it's like both can happen kind of at the same time. I'm completely numb and yet in real pain. And just everything is completely overwhelming, everything is very far off and distant and . . . at the most intense points, it's a kind of visceral experience of isolation. I remember being in a room with some of my closest friends and just being in real pain. I was screaming out inside, but no one could hear me. Feeling it physically and yet not being able to express it, or if I did, it appeared to be quite incomprehensible. From appearances, my life would have no reason for sadness or for upset. And so not being able to explain yourself, not being able to give just cause seems to make no sense, not to me, not to anyone! It just sucks the energy out of you, and I didn't feel like there was any point to doing anything anymore.

As the darkness descends, her prose shifts into metaphor, a mode of language that speaks about something in a way that is not literal but still enables the hearer to grasp what is going on by comparing it with something familiar:

It just feels very nebulous, like it's just this big nebulous, black, bleak, horribleness. I grew up on the [Scottish] Island of Orkney, and it's kind of like a wintery December day in Orkney, there's just unrelenting wind, rain, and you're powerless against it. It's like a storm that just overwhelms you. It's like you're like going through treacle; like you can't move, and you use so much energy trying to move that you just get exhausted. I mean I used to lie in bed all day, and all I would be thinking all day was "I've got to get out of bed." But the amount of energy that it took to actually get out of bed . . . it was like, "I've got to get out of bed! I've got to get out of bed!" That would be all I'd be trying to do because I had to get out of bed to do something. But it was actually impossible. You know in your head what you should be doing; you know that actually lying in bed is not the best thing, but physically you feel like you've got lead weights on your body and you're actually stuck there, it's like somebody's pushing you down on to the bed and you just can't physically get up. I remember walking around the village and feeling completely separate from it; I was just functioning. I would say it was like I was living, but I wasn't alive.

Pain and Numbness

This strange combination of numbness and pain is disconcerting and discordant. How can two polar opposites be present simultaneously? Coreen continues: "It doesn't ever seem to make any sense. I think, I mean I know there are points where I was just numb and wasn't feeling pain. And then there were other points I was just in pain and not feeling numb. But I think it's like your brain feels gray and like it's flatlining, but your emotions feel pain. Which perhaps doesn't make any sense, but my response to the world around me was numb, but my response to my internal world was pain."

This tension between inner pain and numbness toward outer life makes it difficult to grasp any potential goodness in life. People can talk all they want about someone being loved and valued, but if you can't feel that or if your inner pain makes it impossible even to consider such a thing as being possible, words make little difference.

> What it feels like for me is that there is a separation between my inner life and my outer life. There is an internal narrator and an internal judge (my inner troll) and an incessant internal negative commentary that separates me from any goodness I may find in my external life where the love, where the friendship, where the connection is. And that gulf just widens in depression, so that I feel like I'm trying to reach from a deep interior place outside to all the places of love and goodness in my world and I can't quite get there. I am stripped bare of any notion that I can identify myself with my thoughts or with my feelings, because those two areas of me become so unreliable as reporting tools on the nature of my life. I basically have to rely simply on faith at that point.

When everything within Coreen is saying that life is negative and everything outside of her seems gray, black, and alien, the only thing to hold on to is faith and the hope that her way of processing the world may not be the only way. However, eventually even the hope of faith becomes problematic.

Abandoned by God

The descent into darkness has a profound physical, psychological, social, and relational impact. However, the spiritual dimensions are perhaps the most disturbing. The feeling of God's presence sometimes seems to vanish. James explains:

> God is nowhere to be found. Depression isolates me from people. Although I believe in a sovereign God who can connect with a person—it seems to isolate me from God as well. That feels awful. I came to faith as an older man, and it was a very slow process. My mum's a Christian, and I really

didn't come to faith until about fifteen to twenty years ago, so it was halfway through my life. And when I did, it was a very cognitive process for me. So I've never been a heartfelt Christian, and that's unfortunate because I think as I came to terms with the fact that God was not going to heal me of this affliction, at least I would like to know his presence in the midst of it, and I can't, because depression strips you of that one relationship that you should be able to rely on. And it strips you of the buoyancy that is talked about in Scripture that allows us to get through things. It strips away everything.

The experience of depression strips away the things that Scripture informs us should bring us joy and security. "If you can't feel the presence of God, then that's devastating. Throughout Scripture, the presence of God is considered the rock, you know, that's your foundation. I mean from Job to Jeremiah to what Christ talks about, and if you can't have that, it's really disenchanting, it's really bewildering." James's whole being resonates with the psalmist's cry:

> Save me, O God,
> > for the waters have come up to my neck.
> I sink in the miry depths,
> > where there is no foothold.
> I have come into the deep waters;
> > the floods engulf me.
> I am worn out calling for help;
> > my throat is parched.
> My eyes fail,
> > looking for my God. (Ps. 6:1–3)

Depression is a bewildering affliction that tears away all your certainties about God, self, and others and replaces them with . . . nothing. The prophet Isaiah's haunting statement, "Truly, you are a God who hides himself, O God of Israel, the Savior," takes on a whole new meaning.

Affliction and the Silence of God

In her book *Awaiting God*, the philosopher Simone Weil reminds us that the great enigma of human life is not suffering but affliction. She describes affliction as "an intensity of suffering that empties out our sense of self, destroys all our hopes, shatters our sense of being at home and safe in the world. In the realm of suffering, affliction is something apart, specific, and irreducible. It is quite a different thing from simple suffering. It takes possession of the soul and marks it through and through with its own particular mark, the mark of slavery. . . . There is no real affliction unless the event which has gripped and uprooted a life attacks it, directly or indirectly, in all its parts, social, psychological, and physical."[3]

Affliction is not simply a mode of suffering. Affliction is "inseparable from physical suffering and yet quite distinct."[4] Weil uses the example of toothache. The suffering that toothache brings is horrible but transient; it does not mark our souls.

> Affliction is an uprooting of life, a more or less attenuated equivalent of death, made irresistibly present to the soul by the attack or immediate apprehension of physical pain. If there is complete absence of physical pain there is no affliction for the soul, because our thoughts can turn to any object. Thought flies from affliction as promptly and irresistibly as an animal flies from death. Here below, physical pain, and that alone, has the power to chain down our thoughts; on condition that we count as physical pain certain phenomena that, though difficult to describe, are bodily and exactly equivalent to it. Fear of physical pain is a notable example.[5]

Stephen Plant points out that for Weil, physical pain "included several kinds of experiences in which the body is outwardly undamaged. . . . For example, fear of torture should be regarded as causing physical pain, even though the body remains untouched. Similarly, when a loved one dies, even though there is no bodily wound, the grief that follows is experienced as though it was physical pain, with difficulty in breathing, a sensation of unfulfilled need, even of hunger for the person who has been lost."[6] In this sense, depression is physical pain: "My whole body aches. It's just such a deep pain—a feeling of grieving without end. I want to sleep because it is just too painful to be awake. I can't feel God; I can't feel myself; I can't feel anything."

Affliction is a condition of the soul insofar as it seems to consume every aspect of one's life, leaving one with a deep sense of nothingness, a deprivation rather than a present thing. Affliction forms an ever-deepening abyss that can never be filled. Affliction is ultimately defined by its totalizing dynamic. It

---

3. Simone Weil, *Awaiting God: A New Translation of* Attente de Dieu *and* Lettre a un Religieux, trans. Bradley Jersak, 2nd ed. (Scotts Valley, CA: CreateSpace, 2013), 30.

4. Weil, *Awaiting God*, 31.

5. Weil, *Awaiting God*, 32.

6. Stephen Plant, *Simone Weil* (London: Fount, 1996), 47–48.

affects every aspect of a person—relationships, social behavior, psychological activity, spirituality—everything.

The psalms of orientation were intended to enable people to gain and sustain a sense of homefulness. When we feel at home, we experience God's presence, and we live under God's peace. Affliction is the *exact opposite* of homefulness. Affliction engulfs one's very soul and makes a person feel eternally homeless. Affliction shatters one's sense of homefulness and makes peace a dream that cannot even be imagined. With the psalmist, the afflicted cry out:

> Your wrath has swept over me;
>> your terrors have destroyed me.
> All day long they surround me like a flood;
>> they have completely engulfed me.
> You have taken from me friend and neighbor—
>> darkness is my closest friend. (Ps. 88:16–18)

Sitting at the heart of the experience of affliction in depression is the silence of God. Karen experiences her depression as an unbearable sense of perpetual mourning within which God often remains absolutely silent: "It feels like you're always mourning for something, but you don't know what it is that you are mourning for, so it can never end. How can you find resolution when you don't know what or who has died? You ask God to take it away, and God says . . . nothing." In the darkness of affliction, God is silent: "I remember being really low and one night telling God that if he didn't intervene, I was going to end it, because I'd had enough. And nothing happened, and there was no sense of intervention. And yet actually I guess God did intervene because I didn't take my own life."

Karen cries out for relief. God is silent. But looking back, she discovers that perhaps God was not as silent as she had thought he was when she was in the thick of it. Perhaps God did intervene, even if not in the way she expected or desired. Either way, God's silence remained mysterious and fearfully troubling.

Affliction and Suicide

As one reflects on the experience of affliction, one begins to understand somewhat the depths of the alienation and desolation that depression can bring, and why the desire to end it all can creep to the surface of people's thinking. This is not to attempt to justify the act of suicide, but understood in the light of affliction, suicide simply becomes more understandable. Laura puts it this way: "Depression is just exhausting. It's grinding. Day after day after day. You begin to think 'Well, if God has gone; if God has left me, and my friends and my family think I am a waste of time, and if I am going to feel this miserable forever, then . . .' Well, you know? It just seems like the right thing to do. I know it's not! But I just get so tired."

This mental and physical exhaustion and the sense of abandonment begin to open up previously unthinkable options for her: "The more I withdraw and the more I can't tell people what's going on . . . it's like my inner being is screaming out to be heard and understood, but I have no way of doing that. And I have had a number of times when I've been suicidal, where there's an element of—I go kind of almost passive suicidal—so if I die I don't really care, to a very active thinking, right: it becomes, the way I describe it, it's as if the instinct to survive flips, and it becomes the instinct to die." When this begins to happen, even the normally safe space of the Scriptures can become a place of danger.

Peter Herman, in a fascinating article titled "Jesus Doesn't Want Me for a Sunbeam: Thoughts on Depression, Race and Theology," talks about how his experience of depression resulted in the development of a "suicidal hermeneutic," that is, a way of reading Scripture in the midst of deep depression that casts a particularly negative light on its meaning and implications. He offers the example of Mark 8:34-36: "He called the crowd with his disciples, and said to them, 'If any want to become my followers, let them deny themselves and take up their cross and follow me. For those who want to save their life will lose it, and those who lose their life for my sake, and for the sake of the gospel, will save it. For what will it profit them to gain the whole world and forfeit their life?'" (NRSV). Normally we might interpret this passage as a call to forgo the riches of this world and follow Jesus. But when he is depressed, Herman interprets this passage in a quite different way:

> The cross isn't something to be borne during my life—life is the cross. The act of being alive—breathing, eating, speaking with others—is a burden. I don't want to save my life; my life is my cross. Even though I know that there is a world of difference between martyrdom and suicide, I find myself wondering whether Mark's Jesus is letting me know that it might be OK to let go of that cross. After all, I suffer by living, and Jesus promises to end suffering, doesn't he? This question suggests a somewhat unorthodox reading of these texts—a hermeneutics of suicide is not listed in theology textbooks or preached from the Sunday pulpit. Yet this theological perspective has marked my twenty-five-year struggle with major depressive disorder.

Herman reflects on how these days his suicidal thoughts come and go and are more of a nuisance than a threat. However, it has not always been that way, and it may well not be that way in the future:

> In the quiet hours of the day, there is an inaudible yet persistent voice that answers Jesus's suggestion that I must hate life itself with "Yes, I do hate life. I hate it so much. Life itself is my cross. Let me lay it down, Lord. Please, let me lay it down." I argue back against this urge. I resist. I rationalize. I take the pills. I go to the sessions. And then that internal monologue is quieter, but it's still there. I doubt it will ever be silent. "He called the crowd with his disciples, and said to them, 'If any want to become my followers, let them deny themselves and take up their cross and follow me. For those who want to save their life will lose it, and those who lose their life for my sake, and for the sake of the gospel, will save it. For what will it profit them to gain the whole world and forfeit their life?'" ([Mark] 8:34–36 NRSV). When my depression is heightened and my internal struggle especially fraught, my hermeneutic of suicide dominates my encounters with Scripture.[7]

Scripture is fundamental to Christian spirituality. Contextual theologians have long informed us (quite correctly) that the interpretation of Scripture is deeply influenced by culture and context. As we strive to understand the gospel and God's mission, recognizing the contextuality of our interpretative endeavors is of great importance. Everyone interprets from somewhere rather than nowhere. Herman points to the shadow side of contextual interpretation in the context of depression.

Richard Baxter on the Blessings of Not Reading the Bible

Interestingly, Herman's wrestling with Scripture in the midst of depression finds a potential solution from a somewhat unusual source, namely, the Anglican priest and Puritan Richard Baxter. For Baxter, as a Reformed pastor and theologian, Scripture was fundamental and totally indispensable. The Bible is God's word, and disciples are to make sure they live lives that are deeply bibli-

---

7. Peter Herman, "Jesus Doesn't Want Me for a Sunbeam: Thoughts on Depression, Race and Theology," *Other Journal: An Intersection of Theology and Culture*, April 6, 2017, https://theotherjournal.com/2017/04/06/jesus-doesnt-want-sunbeam-thoughts-depres sion-race-theology/.

cally informed. Bearing this in mind, we discover something quite remarkable in his pastoral reflections on how to deal with depression faithfully:

> Meditation is not a duty at all for a melancholy person, except for the few that are able to tolerate a brief, structured sort of meditation. This must be on something furthest from the matter that troubles them, except for short meditations like sudden, spontaneous prayers said out loud. A rigid and protracted meditation will only frustrate and disturb you, and render you unable to perform other duties. If a man has a broken leg, he must not walk on it until it is set, or the whole body will suffer. It is your thinking faculty or your imagination that is the broken, hurting part. Therefore, you must not use it to reflect upon the things that so trouble you.[8]

In 2 Timothy 3:16–17, the apostle Paul informs us that "All Scripture is God-breathed and is useful for teaching, rebuking, correcting and training in righteousness, so that the servant of God may be thoroughly equipped for every good work." The power of Scripture lies in the way it leads us toward God and toward good works. When we experience depression, our interpretative faculties can become so clouded and deceptive that we can be tempted to use them not to justify good works but to define good things (like living) as bad and to act accordingly. Baxter does not act judgmentally toward people in such situations. Rather, he acts pastorally and recognizes their interpretative difficulties and the way they can actually act against the intention of Scripture to bring us closer to God and neighbor. In the same way that a man should not be forced to walk on a broken leg, so a person living with depression should not be forced to engage in a practice that can actually cause the person harm. In order for Scripture to do its good works, it is sometimes necessary to lay it to one side until one is well enough to receive and enjoy its benefits. This is not to degrade or downgrade the centrality of Scripture for the life of a Christian.

> Perhaps you will say, "That is profane, neglects God and the soul, and lets the Tempter have his will!" But I answer, "No, it is simply to refrain from what you cannot presently do, so that by doing other things that you can, you may later do what you cannot do now." It is merely to postpone attempting what (at present) will only make you less able to do all your other duties.

8. *Depression, Anxiety, and the Christian Life: Practical Wisdom from Richard Baxter*, revised, updated, and annotated by Michael S. Lundy (Wheaton, IL: Crossway, 2018), 86.

At present, you are able to conduct the affairs of your soul by sanctified reasoning. I am not dissuading you from repenting or believing, but rather from fixed, long, and deep meditations that will only hurt you.[9]

Reading Scripture is a practice designed to help people learn how to enjoy God's glory. Along with the vital habit of reading Scripture, it seems that we also need to learn the equally vital habit of knowing when not to read it. We read Scripture together as the body of Christ. If one of our brothers and sisters cannot do that for a season, then the body reads on that person's behalf. Learning the skill of using Scripture pastorally is a vital aspect of ministry that is not always given the consideration it deserves.

Faith as a "Trap"

Herman highlights that it is not just Scripture that can play an ambiguous role in the lives of those living with depression. Faith can also play itself out in ways that are double-edged. Robert is forty-two years old. He is a laboratory technician and a musician, and is married with two children who are now grown up and live in the city close to him and his wife Cheryl. Robert lives under the description of "double depression": "Double depression is a complication of a psychiatric illness called dysthymic disorder, or dysthymia. Dysthymia is a chronic, depressed mood accompanied by just one or two other symptoms of clinical depression (such as low energy or low self-esteem) that lasts at least two years in adults."[10] Robert's normal mood is equivalent to what others might think of as clinical depression. He has lived with depression since he was twelve years old. Robert, like Peter Herman, sometimes feels suicidal. However, he talks about the strange frustration of feeling suicidal and at the same time recognizing that his faith simply won't allow it to be an option:

> For me in an odd way faith became a trap, because I knew [suicide] was wrong, and I knew my Bible and I knew Jesus loved me. I knew that he

9. *Depression, Anxiety, and the Christian Life: Practical Wisdom from Richard Baxter*, 86.

10. Double depression refers to a major depressive disorder (MDD) superimposed on dysthymia, a chronic, low-grade depressive disorder. Hellerstein and Eipper suggest that around "three quarters of patients with dysthymia have or will experience a major depressive episode and, thus, suffer from double depression." D. J. Hellerstein and J. W. Eipper, "Dysthymia and Chronic Depression," in *Clinical Handbook for the Management of Mood Disorders*, ed. J. J. Mann, P. J. McGrath, and S. P. Roose (New York: Cambridge University Press, 2013).

died for me, but it was like a trap because all I wanted was to die. I knew the consequences of taking your own life from a biblical perspective. That's my belief system! You know, so basically, I'd be going against my own belief system. In my belief system the consequence of suicide would be damnation, I suppose. Hell. (pauses) I know that sounds very old-fashioned. You shouldn't take your own life, it's up to God when you're going to die, is my belief. So, I'm trapped into life. I'm trapped! What do I do? You know, if I go that way . . . I end up in hell, and yet at the same time, I'm actually living in hell! One is permanent, the other is eternal. So, what do you do? You try and keep living. I have to say I had amazing help from my doctors. My psychiatrist was an American woman, and she basically got me through. But she couldn't get to the core, she couldn't actually get to the bit that needed healing. It was like the sticky plaster [or Band-Aid] over the top. But then again, God wasn't much help either. He just doesn't show up sometimes.

Robert has lived with this condition for over twenty years. He was no stranger to the abyss of affliction. Suicide sometimes seemed like the best response to his deep, afflicted disorientation. But he does not yield and says that he never could. However, it is not the *love* of God that prevents James from taking his own life. Rather it is the *fear* of God. For the lamenting psalmist, recognizing the loving presence of God became a turning point that led him into praise. But for Robert, recognizing the presence of God didn't so much lead him to praise as trap him into life. It didn't take him out of the pit, it simply located him within the pit in a way that paralyzed him. The presence of God saved his life and continued to protect him, but it didn't make him feel any better. It just prevented him from taking a course of action that he felt held the possibility of release. It is good that he was alive, but he desperately needed help to move from simply being alive to actually living life. Robert needed to find a point of reorientation.

REORIENTATION

Robert found his point of reorientation in a way that, at least initially, doesn't appear to be particularly spiritual. For Robert, there were three levels to his movement into darkness.

John Swinton: Do the psalms help you connect with God in the midst of your darkness?

Robert: It depends on the level of darkness. Yeah, it depends on how bad it is. If you were to break it into thirds, the upper third being the least severe, I would say that during those times—when I am feeling that upper third— are times when I can usually connect with the psalms and really read them and think, Yeah! This is what I'm experiencing. Because depression can sort of bring on a mental fog. It reduces my ability to cognate and to think clearly, so when it's really, really bad—that lower third—it's very difficult to connect with text, I think. I'm not confused to the point of not knowing my name, you know . . . but more complex metaphor is more difficult to connect with.

John Swinton: So, what do you do in terms of holding on to your spirituality when you are in level 3?

Robert: During those times, I do read the psalms and I do go to church. To be honest, those upper third times are my happier times. I'm still what somebody else would consider moderately depressed, to the point where they would probably seek medical attention. But those are my better times. So that's when I'm going to church and taking it in and agreeing [with God] in my spirit, as it were.

John Swinton: And what about when you are in the lower third? Is there anything that you can do there when you are really at the bottom?

Robert: Drugs! [Psychiatric medication] Yeah, literally when I'm there, I'm in a real scary [place]; it is scary. When I'm in my darkest places, there is no God; there's no help, or at least there has not been when I've been there. And my greatest fear when I'm in those places is that I might die without knowing God more.

John Swinton: Medication then in some senses has a spiritual role in getting you out of that place?

Robert: Absolutely! Only because . . . Ahhh . . . how do I put this? . . . I need a good metaphor for it . . . it's like, as a Christian I'm supposed to climb a ladder and I can look down this long wall and there's thousands of other Christians climbing their ladders. That is the spiritual effort/journey/ direction, and I can't climb the ladder, and then someone comes along with a lift or [elevator] and carries me to the top of the wall. I'm now on the top of the wall. It is the spiritual wall. It's real. I just didn't get there the way everybody else gets there.

It is Robert's medication that helps him find a spiritual place, which he simply could not inhabit without its assistance. For Robert, the taking of medication is much more than an engagement with pharmacological products. Taking medication functions as a deeply spiritual act. It is a part of a process in which he can reconnect with God, self, and others. Robert's closing remark—"It's real. I just didn't get there the way everybody else gets there"—is important. There is no way for him to climb the ladder on his own. His biology simply won't allow him to. His medication steps in to help lift him from deep disconnection with God to a place where he feels reconnected.

Medication as a Spiritual Practice

We do need to be careful with this metaphor. Christian spirituality, like depression, is not just about feelings. As we have seen, the object of the spiritual life is not to feel better or to feel happier, desirable as these experiences may be. The object is to encounter joy: to be with Jesus—something not defined by the presence or absence of feelings but by the presence of Jesus. If pharmaceutical intervention becomes a substitute for joy, then we have a significant theological problem. As my friend and colleague Gerry McKenny put it when I presented Robert's situation at a conference at Duke Divinity School, "Does that mean that we can have a pill for Jesus?" His concern was a fair one. As Barshinger, LaRowe, and Tapia once framed it: *"Can a pill do what the Holy Spirit could not?"*[11]

Nevertheless, Robert's problem was not a resistance to the workings of the Holy Spirit or an attempt to substitute chemicals for the Spirit's work. He had a recognizable form of mental health challenge that not only plunged him into the depths of depression but actively separated him from the love of God. The evidence for the precise etiology of depression may be mixed and varied, but few would argue that people pretend to be depressed or that the experience of depression is unreal or inauthentic. The experience is very real, and the consequences of that experience are very real and not bound by the will of the sufferer. Robert's desire was not to *enhance* his spirituality through chemical means. Antidepressants are not like mescaline.[12] Taking them to help escape

11. C. E. Barshinger, L. E. LaRowe, and A. Tapia, "The Gospel according to Prozac: Can a Pill Do What the Holy Spirit Could Not?," *Christianity Today*, August 14, 1995, 34–37.
12. Mescaline is a naturally occurring psychedelic known for its hallucinogenic effects

the pit of depression is not the same thing as taking something to experience a spiritual high. For Robert, psychopharmacology was a necessary aspect for healing and maintaining his spiritual well-being. There are two aspects of this suggestion that we need to draw out, one theological, relating to who and what we are as human beings before God, and the other spiritual, relating to the kinds of practices that emerge from such a theological position.

The Biology of the Soul

In our discussion on affliction, I mentioned that affliction affects the human soul. There is an important connection between the nature and significance of the soul and the faithful taking of medication. In teasing out such a suggestion, we might begin with the question: *What is the soul?* Human beings are inexorably biological creatures. Our biological nature, however, must be carefully framed. In the Genesis account of creation, God creates Adam out of the dust by blowing God's *ruakh* into the dust. God breathes God's *ruakh* into Adam's nostrils, and "man became a living soul" (Gen. 2:7 KJV). The meaning of the Hebrew word *ruakh* is "breath" or "wind" or "spirit." God "gives breath [*ruakh*] to all living things" (Num. 27:16). Before God blew God's *ruakh* into the dust, there were no bodies (Gen. 2:7). When God blew God's *ruakh* into the dust, bodies came into existence. We come from the earth, and we live on the earth in bodies that are fundamental to our ways of being in the world. Matter matters! As Christians, we recognize that we are creatures and that our bodies are wholly contingent upon the creating and sustaining power of God. First there was God, then there was creation, then there were bodies. The movement of God brings about the movement of bodies. This is a crucial observation. *Human biological existence is inevitably, thoroughly, and unavoidably theological in its origin and intention.* God is not in any sense apart from our biological existence. God is the very sustenance that holds it in place. We don't have a realm "over here" that is biological and another "over there" that is theological. The two are one: the biological *is* theological.

In his paper "Finding God in Prozac or Finding Prozac in God: Preserving a Christian View of the Person amidst a Biopsychological Revolution," Michael Boivin notes that, "according to Old Testament thought, persons do not 'have' bodies but *are* bodies such that all the important theological dimensions of

---

and in particular for enhancing religious experience. See Mike Jay, *Mescaline: A Global History of the First Psychedelic* (New Haven: Yale University Press, 2019).

personhood (that is, soul, spirit, will, conscience, mind, heart) emerge or emanate from our physical beings."[13]

We are our bodies, as we are our souls. What we encounter here is a picture of a human being as, at precisely the same time, thoroughly biological and deeply soulful. Our bodily existence is soulful existence; our soulful existence is bodily existence. Within such an anthropology, the fact that emotional and spiritual well-being may be deeply affected by changes in or to our biology is neither surprising nor reductionist. Such changes operate within a theological framework. The biological dimensions of spirituality and soulfulness do not in any way detract from their theological significance. Pharmaceutical intervention, soulfully aligned, is a practical theological enterprise that relates primarily to facilitating the positive movements of the soul toward its true desire, that is, reorienting our bodies in such a way that we can be open to the glory of God. To suggest that experiences of God are related to brain states is not in and of itself a problem as long as we bear in mind this theological context.

The Chief End of Medication

Biological existence is thus seen to have a purpose and a trajectory. The Westminster Confession of Faith states that the chief end of human beings is to glorify God and enjoy God forever.[14] Human life before God is thus seen to have a quite particular intention and direction. Engaging in practices such as offering medication to alter people's experiences goes on within a *theological* context, with the efficacy and intention of the outcome ultimately determined by its contribution to the nurturing and realigning of the human soul toward God's glory. When the chemicals that compose medication touch the cells of the human being, they engage in deep spiritual activity and in a real sense encounter the pull and presence of God's *ruakh*. For a drug to function faithfully, it must affect the human body in a way that enhances the intentions of the *ruakh* (which is why there is a difference between heroin, alcohol, and antidepressants, at least when the latter are faithfully prescribed). If a drug

---

13. Michael J. Boivin, "Finding God in Prozac or Finding Prozac in God: Preserving a Christian View of the Person amidst a Biopsychological Revolution," *Christian Scholar's Review* 32, no. 2 (January 2002): 159–78. For a further development, see Michael J. Boivin, "The Hebraic Model of the Person: Toward a Unified Psychological Science among Christian Helping Professions," *Journal of Psychology and Theology* 19, no. 2 (June 1, 1991): 170.

14. Douglas F. Kelly, "The Westminster Shorter Catechism," in *To Glorify and Enjoy God: A Commemoration of the 350th Anniversary of the Westminster Assembly*, ed. John L. Carlson and David W. Hall (Edinburgh: Banner of Truth Trust, 1994).

blocks or prevents the soul from communing with God, it inhibits faithfulness. However, if it aids in the process of communion with God and the enjoyment of God, it may be functioning faithfully. The criterion for judging whether a drug "works" is therefore not only or even primarily the alleviation of symptoms (although this may well remain an appropriate goal) but the way it affects the person's soul.

Such a perspective offers a significant repositioning of the psychopharmaceutical enterprise. Within such a frame, pharmacological intervention can be seen not simply as a therapeutic intervention designed to alleviate symptoms and ease distress but as a theological enterprise that can aid in the realignment of the souls of those who suffer the affliction of depression. Of course, such interventions could be abused and the drugs taken for pleasure and selfishly oriented spiritual excitement. But I think we call that idolatry: substituting the capacities of the drug for the real presence of God. Easing pain in the context of cancer care is rightly seen as an act of compassion, even though heroin and morphine can be devastating when taken out of context. It is not clear to me why ameliorating the pain of affliction as experienced within depression cannot similarly be perceived as a theological act of compassion.

Medicating as a Spiritual Practice

The implication of this line of theological thinking is that our understanding of pharmaceutical healing needs to be redirected. We need to stop seeing the practice of giving medication as a purely technical, biological, and therapeutically oriented task within which God is perceived as optional and healing deals simply with symptom alleviation. What is required is a theological interpretation and a spiritual practice in which God becomes central and healing comes to be understood in terms that include the human desire to connect with God. In this way, the faithful giving and receiving of medication might be considered a spiritual practice designed to facilitate reconnection with self, God, and others. Psychological pain separates us from all these sources of healing. Medication faithfully prescribed can reconnect us in a way that is deeply spiritual.

The fact that medication is intervening to bring about biological change that has spiritual significance is but a slightly different example of what occurs in everyone's spirituality.[15] All of us get to the top of the wall by differ-

15. We will discuss this in more detail when we come to the issues around bipolar disorder in later chapters.

ent means. As soulful biological creatures, our access to God is always and inevitably mediated by and through our neurology. Part of Robert's path to God came through changing the biochemical components of his body via the use of psychotropic medication. This may be different from other ways of beginning our spiritual journey, but it is no less theological in its reorientation and outcomes.

A Revised Theology of Suffering

Reorientation does not mean going back to the way things were before. The resurrection did not mean that the passion and the crucifixion never happened or can ever be forgotten. Surely, at least a part of the significance of the scars on Jesus's resurrected body is to remind us of the cost of our redemption. Suffering changes things.

One significant change that comes in the light of the affliction of depression is the way in which God comes to be perceived. The psalms of glory speak of a God who is in control; a God who will bring happiness, peace, prosperity, and settledness; a God who will take away our suffering and dry all our tears. It is true that in the eschaton this is exactly what God will do: "He will wipe every tear from their eyes. There will be no more death or mourning or crying or pain, for the old order of things has passed away" (Rev. 21:4). But the God of the present who emerges from the disorienting affliction of depression is different from the God of the royal psalms and, indeed, from the way people used to believe in God. As Anna points out, God doesn't save you from suffering. God didn't take Jesus off the cross:

> I guess initially a few years ago I probably had this idea that God sort of protects you a bit more, whereas now actually I realize that God doesn't save you from the really bad stuff. God didn't take Jesus off the cross. The presence of Jesus in my suffering is incredibly healing—just to know that I'm not alone in this. One of the things that my spiritual director reminds me of is that even when I can't feel the presence of God, that doesn't mean that God is not present. It is not up to me at all times and places to be able to feel the presence of God. What I have to do is simply to remember that God is in all times and places. If I based it on what I can feel, I would have killed myself a long time ago. But when I base it on what I believe to be true and know that it's not always going to feel this bad—there are vicissitudes even in the course of a day—then I can remember that God is present, and not to be alone in this is hugely healing for me. When I can remember that

God has infused the universe, even the one that feels so empty to me, it is a powerful reminder. It doesn't give me hope. I can't feel hope. That is for others to do.

Anna's reorientation comes through her remembering God, recognizing God's place in suffering, and not assuming that the binary of being healed and not being healed is the only way to look at her situation. In this sense, she echoes the psalmist's recognition of God's *hesed*:

> But I trust in your unfailing love;
>> my heart rejoices in your salvation.
> I will sing the LORD's praise,
>> for he has been good to me. (Ps. 13:5–6)

The psalmist remembers God and, in remembering, finds relief. This reframing enabled her to cope and to understand something new about God. "God didn't take Jesus off the cross." Jesus's suffering was like hers: mysterious, deep, painful, and without immediate release. Even in those dark places where God seems to be hidden, she finds Jesus is with her. This theological paradox—God is hidden, but Jesus, who is God, is with her—is something she needs to learn to live with, not something she needs to explain. As a Christian, she finds the paradox difficult to explain. As a person living with major depression, the paradox is difficult to live with.

Being Certain of What You Hope for but Cannot See

Anna entered the reoriented world with a different view of God and a different form of trust: "It's affected my theology in that I think I find it a little bit harder to, not to trust. . . . I don't know if I would say I find it harder to trust God, but I find it difficult to have a certain kind of trust. There's no longer, like, whenever people have theological platitudes that essentially, like, God will just make everything OK if we trust him, I definitely don't have that sort of a theology anymore."

Trust in God shifts and changes as the rawness of the experience of depression reshapes and re-forms it. The naïve platitudes that used to make sense—"pray a little harder, it will all be fine"—no longer do so. When you have experienced the abandonment of God, when your cries into the night have gone unheard, your trust in God shifts; it doesn't disappear, but it does change. No longer do you expect God to come racing in to save you. You still believe that all will be well in the grander scheme of things, but for now, the presence and the absence of God need to be held in a creative tension that may be frustrating but is exactly according to Scripture. Depression is not caused by faithlessness. Quite the opposite: it reveals something very important about faith. As the systematic theologian and biblical scholar John Colwell put it: "Faith is trusting God in the darkness, it is not a quasi-magical means of turning the darkness into light. It's not that I don't believe that God can and does turn darkness to light—ultimately he will, but here and now he calls us to trust him, even in the darkness. . . . Faith is no more a magical power than it is a feeling; *faith is a settled trust in God even in the continuing darkness and silence, even when we cannot see and cannot hear.*"[16]

Faith is not something we do alone. It is a gift of the Spirit; it is something that the church does together. Like joy, we hold faith for one another until the darkness passes, even if we have to carry on and prepare for the next cloud of darkness that will inevitably follow. Robert articulates this powerfully:

> The Scripture that is the hook that I hang myself on . . . Sorry! that's a suicidal metaphor, that's not what I meant! The Scripture that I hang my faith on is where the apostle's Christ is talking about being born again. And they say, he looks at them and he can tell by their faces that they're horrified—but I think, he was also talking about eating my flesh and drinking my blood—and they say, I think it's Peter who says where else are we going to go? You have the words of life. And that's what I come down to: there's something in me that agrees with those words of life, that finds them philosophically the end-all, be-all. And I can't shake them. And that's my faith: really, at the end of the day, in the darkest, darkest times, when I can say those things—that's my faith.

Finding God in God's Absence

One last point of reorientation relates to changes in how we understand the presence and the absence of God. One of the most disturbing things for Chris-

---

16. John Colwell, *Why Have You Forsaken Me? A Personal Reflection on the Experience of Desolation* (Milton Keynes, UK: Paternoster, 2014), Kindle locations 2152–2153 (emphasis added).

tians living with major depression is the sense that sometimes God seems to be completely absent. People process this absence in various ways, as we have seen. However, in closing our discussion on depression, it will be helpful to encourage those living with depression to recognize that while some aspects of depression are deeply spiritual, the sense of God's abandonment is not an indication of errors or sins on their part. Feelings of abandonment are actually a surprisingly common experience encountered by the people of God throughout history.

There is a strange, enigmatic, and deeply disturbing tension within Scripture between the presence of God and the absence of God. At times God is very much present with God's people:

> Where can I go from your Spirit?
>> Where can I flee from your presence?
> If I go up to the heavens, you are there;
>> if I make my bed in the depths, you are there.
> If I rise on the wings of the dawn,
>> if I settle on the far side of the sea,
> even there your hand will guide me,
>> your right hand will hold me fast.
> If I say, "Surely the darkness will hide me
>> and the light become night around me,"
> even the darkness will not be dark to you;
>> the night will shine like the day,
>> for darkness is as light to you. (Ps. 139:7–12)

Sometimes God is present and appears to be ever present. And yet, at other times God seems remarkably forgetful of *God's people*:

> How long, LORD? Will you forget me forever?
>> How long will you hide your face from me?
> How long must I wrestle with my thoughts
>> and day after day have sorrow in my heart?
> How long will my enemy triumph over me?
> Look on me and answer, Lord my God.
>> Give light to my eyes, or I will sleep in death. (Ps. 13:1–3)

Reflecting on Jesus's cry of dereliction in Matthew's Gospel, Walter Brueggemann suggests that "Popular, easy, reassuring religion imagines God's constant attentiveness to us. But we know better. We know that to live in God's world is to live being abandoned, to face free-fall and absence and aloneness that go all the way to the bottom of reality. This Friday cry of Jesus calls us to relearn about faith and obedience and discipleship. Jesus is not the first one to know about being forsaken. He quotes a psalm. Old Israel knew, well before Jesus, about being abandoned by the God in whom they trusted."[17] The psalmist's lament—"Darkness is my only companion"—is a mode of prayer that was not alien to the people of Israel. The psalms of lament contain precisely the kind of language that articulates not just the presence of God but also God's absence. They are paradoxical prayers that testify to the presence of an absent God. More than that, they indicate that the experience of God's absence does not suggest sinfulness—"I wonder what I have done to deserve this?"—but actually reflects an experience that has been the plight of the faithful from the beginning. John Colwell, in his reflections on Jesus's cry of dereliction in the light of his own experience of bipolar disorder, puts the issue succinctly:

> I am calling for a renewal of the recognition that the psalms of lament, echoed in the cry of Jesus, are spiritually normative, that periods of felt abandonment are not to be shunned or misconstrued as spiritual failure. Let us pray that this darkness doesn't engulf us, in any of its forms, but if and when it does let us not misconstrue it as spiritual failure or mistake our feelings of forsakenness for the reality. As in the case of Job, there is probably vastly more occurring here than we can possibly comprehend and certainly more occurring here than we can immediately perceive.[18]

We have then a strange tension. The experience of feeling God's absence is, in some senses, part of our spiritual journey. And yet, the power of the gospel is that God has promised

> "Never will I leave you;
> never will I forsake you." (Heb. 13:5)

The apostle Paul is convinced that "neither death nor life, neither angels nor demons, neither the present nor the future, nor any powers, neither height

---

17. Walter Brueggemann, *Into Your Hand: Confronting Good Friday* (Eugene, OR: Cascade, 2014), 18.

18. Colwell, *Why Have You Forsaken Me?*, 2262–2265.

nor depth, nor anything else in all creation, will be able to separate us from the love of God that is in Christ Jesus our Lord" (Rom. 8:38–39). This difficult tension between the presence and the absence of God seems to find its paradigmatic revelation in Jesus's cry from the cross: "*My God, my God, why have you forsaken me?*" The question is not whether God hears our cries for help. Scripture is clear that

> The righteous cry out, and the Lord hears them;
> he delivers them from all their troubles. (Ps. 34:17)

The psalmist was praying to a God who heard him. The mystery is why God does not answer and deliver them from all their troubles. The answer to such a mystery very often never comes.

When God Goes Missing

Colwell's assertion that the absence of God may be spiritually normative is evocative, provocative, and slightly disturbing. At points in the lament psalms, the psalmist seems to resign himself to living into the fact of God's absence. So, when in Psalm 88 the psalmist says, "Darkness is my only companion," he seems to be articulating a kind of holy resignation that God is not going to rescue him. The darkness that he feels at this moment is not going to be lifted. How he is now is just the way things are. There is no recognition in this psalm of God's presence, and no recognition of the psalmist feeling God's unending *hesed*. There is only darkness, only lostness, only hopelessness. However, we should not mistake the psalmist's desolate cry for a cry of unbelief. Psalm 88 is a prayer to the living God, not a scream into the emptiness of the void. It is a prayer that bears witness to a God who is both very present and very absent. David knows exactly what that feels like: "There's some comfort in reading the psalms, because the psalmist talks about that distance from God. He annoyingly talks about the presence of God, and I can't really figure that out. But then again, in Scripture, the writers talk about being depressed, they talk about feeling completely alone and apart from God. I kind of go through a very prolonged version of that. I ask where God is, but he doesn't seem to have much to say." This is indeed an odd paradox. Like Jesus's cry of desolation, even this profound statement proclaiming God's absence is spoken with the assumption of God's presence. If this were not the case, both the psalmist's and Jesus's words would be pointless. The resurrection helps us realize that Jesus's words were neither meaningless nor pointless. Rather, and with a deep strangeness, his cry of desolation indicates that feelings of abandonment are not alien to being in the presence of God. God's absence may well be a rather disturbing dimension of God's presence.

Kathryn Greene-McCreight draws our attention to the words of Isaiah 45:15: "Truly you are a God who has been hiding himself, the God and Savior of Israel": "Even here, Isaiah does not say, 'Truly *he* is a God that hides himself.' Isaiah addresses God directly, even in God's apparent absence. He acknowledges that this absent God is still his own God and the God of his people. And Isaiah acknowledges that God is Savior, even in hiding. Truly, you are a God who hides himself, O God of Israel, the Savior."[19] The theologian and preacher Fleming Rutledge notes that "the fact that God hides himself in the midst of revealing himself is paradoxically a testimony to his reality. Presence-in-absence is the theme of his self-disclosure. God isn't hidden because we are too stupid to find him, or too lazy, or not 'spiritual' enough. He hides himself for his own reasons, and he reveals himself for his own reasons. If that were not so, God would not be God; God would be nothing more than a projection of our own religious ideas and wishes." Why does God act in such a way? Rutledge replies: *because God is God*: "The Lord hides himself from us because he is God, and God reveals himself to us because God is love (1 John 4:8). Does that make sense? Probably not—but sometimes Christians must be content with theological paradox. To know God in his Son Jesus Christ is to know that he is unconditionally love unto the last drop of God's own blood. In the cross and resurrection of his Son, God has given us everything that we need to live with alongside the terrors of his seeming absence."[20]

Such a response may be disappointing for those who wait for an ever-present God who will rush into history to save us. However, for those of us who worship the God revealed in Scripture, paradox, mystery, and absence may be unsettling, but they are not an indication of God's abandonment even when it seems hard to hold on to God's presence. It is also strangely reassuring to realize that we share the experience of God's abandonment with Jesus and the saints.

19. Kathryn Greene-McCreight, *Darkness Is My Only Companion: A Christian Response to Mental Illness*, expanded ed. (Grand Rapids: Brazos, 2015), 28.

20. Fleming Rutledge, "Divine Absence and the Light Inaccessible," *Christian Century*, August 27, 2018, https://www.christiancentury.org/article/critical-essay/divine-absence-and-light-inaccessible. This essay was originally published in Fleming Rutledge, *Advent: The Once and Future Coming of Jesus Christ* (Grand Rapids: Eerdmans, 2018).

Depression and the Absence of God

My reason for ending this chapter with this particular theological reflection is quite straightforward: it is a theological mistake to assume that the experience of abandonment and the absence of God is necessarily a sign of human faithlessness or sinfulness. The situation is much more complex and much too important for quick and easy reductionistic, theologically uninformed explanations that tend to add to people's distress rather than bring them healing balm. Living faithfully means learning to live well with unanswered questions and to avoid the modern temptation to turn such mysteries into puzzles.

Feeling God's abandonment is a disorientating aspect of being with God; it is deeply entangled with our discipleship, not apart from it. Strange as it may seem in some respects, darkness and feelings of God's abandonment are actually normal aspects of a biblical spirituality and of what it means to be in the presence of a God who sometimes hides. Of course, such experiences can be unhelpfully exacerbated when we enter into the dark world of depression, but that exacerbation does not place us outside the experience of the people of God. Instead, it offers a stark and prophetic reminder and warning for those of us who might mistake happiness and ecstatic experience for biblical faith.

In a dark and damp cellar in Cologne, Germany, a place where thousands of innocent Jews hid from the horrors of the Nazi regime, a poem was found inscribed on one of the walls. Translated, the words of the poem are these:

> I believe in the sun even when it is not shining.
> I believe in love even when I cannot feel it.
> I believe in God even when he is silent.[21]

In the midst of the unspeakable horrors of the Holocaust, someone had taken the time to think about hope. We have no idea why God goes absent. But we can be assured that God's presence will accompany us even when it is impossible to feel it. In the darkness of depression, when God seems to disappear, such a reorientation of the presence of God won't help us feel any better. It's a blessing that we receive retrospectively, if at all. Drawing from her own experience of depression, Greene-McCreight suggests that even in the midst of God's absence, there may be blessing, although it may only really become

---

21. Rutledge, "Divine Absence and the Light Inaccessible."

available after the fact: "Sometimes depression can be a blessing, because one can learn about God through his hiding. That usually only comes afterward, because during depression, as during the flood, the waters of death cover the face of the earth."[22] Perhaps what we need are spaces within which we have time and guidance to look back at our spiritual experiences of depression so that we can look forward with the possibility of hope.

22. Greene-McCreight, *Darkness Is My Only Companion*, 28.

PART IV

Hearing Voices

6

UNDERSTANDING PSYCHOSIS

Faith, Schizophrenia, and the Meaning of "Symptoms"

I remember telling my friend Paul, although he misunderstood me, "Paul, I've been diagnosed with schizophrenia," and he said, "Oh, I'm sorry to hear that. I don't know much about schizophrenia, all I know is that you've got two personalities." I said, "Oh no! It's not like that!" So I explained to him what it was and how I felt. He's always been very keen to help me. That's the kind of friends you need, isn't it? (smiles)

—Allen,

who lived under the description of schizophrenia

KATHLEEN COLDIRON BEGINS HER REVIEW OF ESMÉ WEIJUN WANG'S autobiographical collection of essays *The Collected Schizophrenias* with a powerful observation:

If there exists a mental-illness diagnosis as scary as the physical-illness diagnosis of cancer, schizophrenia may be it. To the general public, it's a monolith of a condition: the one where you hear voices in your head and talk to people who aren't there. That Beautiful Mind guy had it, and he invented Ed Harris completely, remember? But the words and stories of those who live with schizoaffective disorder offer proof that it's a spectrum illness, which manifests with great variety and defies stereotype. And though it's a serious diagnosis, many of those afflicted insist that they are not doomed.[1]

---

1. Katharine Coldiron, "Fractured Origins in Esmé Weijun Wang's 'The Collected Schizophrenias,'" *Los Angeles Review of Books*, February 5, 2019, https://lareviewofbooks .org/article/fractured-origins-in-esme-weijun-wangs-the-collected-schizophrenias/.

The Problem with Schizophrenia

Coldiron highlights the easily overlooked fact that schizophrenia is not a monolithic entity and that people experience it in quite different ways. Most important, she highlights that it is not a death sentence. People can and do live well with it, and some do recover. Schizophrenia is not like cancer or measles. It is a medical construct designed to make sense of a series of lived experiences that have become troublesome either to an individual or to those around her. However, it is a very broad and indistinct category.

In developing this point, Coldiron contrasts three autobiographical accounts of people living with schizophrenia: *The Quiet Room: A Journey out of the Torment of Madness*, by Lori Schiller and Amanda Bennett; *The Center Cannot Hold: My Journey through Madness*, by Elyn R. Saks; and Esmé Weijun Wang's *The Collected Schizophrenias*.[2] Each account is markedly different. Schiller hears horrible voices that shout at her relentlessly. Her experiences make her life totally miserable, even to the point where she tries to take her own life. She also suffers from certain forms of treatment (overmedication) and from unnecessary electric convulsive therapy, which is cruel and inhumane. Saks's book talks of extraordinary willpower wherein she hid profound symptoms and channeled her energies into becoming outstanding in academic pursuits in the legal and medical fields. Esmé Weijun Wang's experience is quite different, as it progresses, recovers, and regresses in ways that are deeply disturbing but at times spiritually revealing: "Wang's voices aren't much like Schiller's, and her delusional convictions (for example, that she is dead—also known as the Cotard delusion) are much more unusual. Saks is paranoid and manic while Wang leans to catatonia. Wang's book is less alarming than the other two, in part because her voice is so measured and intelligent. The fact is, *the three women have different illnesses*, even though their umbrella diagnosis is the same—schizoaffective disorder varies as much as its patients do."[3] All three live under the description of schizophrenia, but they all have quite different experiences, so much so that Coldiron surmises that they may actually have three different conditions.

Historically, the precise nature and boundaries of schizophrenia have al-

2. Lori Schiller and Amanda Bennett, *The Quiet Room: A Journey out of the Torment of Madness* (New York: Warner Books, 2011); Elyn R. Saks, *The Center Cannot Hold: My Journey through Madness* (New York: Hachette Books, 2008); Esmé Weijun Wang, *The Collected Schizophrenias: Essays* (Minneapolis: Graywolf, 2019).

3. Coldiron, "Fractured Origins in Esmé Weijun Wang's 'The Collected Schizophrenias'" (emphasis added).

ways been unclear. In her excellent book *Mind Fixers: Psychiatry's Troubled Search for the Biology of Mental Illness,* historian Anne Harrington describes the situation as "diagnostic chaos."[4] She observes that while schizophrenia has tended to be perceived as a poster-child disorder for those who accept the biological explanation of mental health challenges, the evidence for its existence as a biological entity, and indeed the evidence for its existence at all, has always been controversial, fragmented, and constantly changing. What is true historically remains the case today:

> At a conference in Worcester, Massachusetts, in 1990, and titled "What Is Schizophrenia?," the first speaker paused at the podium to ask for the next slide. It would, he said, show a list of "established facts" about the disorder. The screen then went blank, prompting wry laughter to ripple through the auditorium. A full generation after that, there was a lot more research, a lot more data, many more claims, but no more certainty. In 2008 a group of researchers launched a multipart project designed to identify and critically assess all "facts" currently established for schizophrenia. They identified seventy-seven candidate facts. Each was graded on a 0–3 scale for reproducibility, relevance for understanding schizophrenia, and durability over time. Some turned out to be more robust than others, but none got full marks. More important, even the most robust individual facts pointed in a range of different directions; they did not, as a group, lead logically to any coherent explanation of schizophrenia. As these researchers reflected in 2011, the field seemed to be operating "like the fabled six blind Indian men groping different parts of an elephant coming up with different conclusions." In fact, they admitted, in the current state of knowledge, one could not rule out another possibility: "there may be no elephant, more than one elephant, or many different animals in the room."[5]

For some, such as the neuropsychologist Simon McCarthy-Jones, the controversies that surround this diagnosis spell the end of schizophrenia as a meaningful concept: "Arguments that schizophrenia is a distinct disease have been 'fatally undermined.' Just as we now have the concept of autism spectrum disorder, psychosis (typically characterised by distressing hallucinations, delusions, and confused thoughts) is also argued to exist along a continuum

---

4. Anne Harrington, *Mind Fixers: Psychiatry's Troubled Search for the Biology of Mental Illness* (New York: Norton, 2019), 139–40.

5. Harrington, *Mind Fixers,* 181.

and in degrees. Schizophrenia is the severe end of a spectrum or continuum of experiences."[6]

So acute is this issue that in Japan psychiatrists recently renamed schizophrenia "integration disorder."[7] Since the name change, the number of people recognizing that they have the condition has increased. People with "integration disorder" are more likely to consent to or even seek treatment than those with the more stigmatized diagnosis of schizophrenia.[8] Elsewhere, there is a growing push to think of schizophrenia in a way similar to autism, as a "psychosis spectrum disorder." These moves have partly to do with the malignant social psychology that accompanies the diagnosis of schizophrenia, to which we will return later, and partly to do with the lack of available evidence to convince people that we are dealing with a monolithic entity.[9] The issue is not helped by what the philosopher Jonathan Glover has described as the problem of *wandering diagnoses*: "the problem of 'wandering diagnosis' [reflects the fact that] symptoms can change in ways that suggest that one disorder is morphing into another and perhaps back again. 'It did look like bipolar disorder at first, but now it looks more like schizophrenia. Perhaps it is schizoaffective disorder. We will see more clearly as it runs its course.' Wandering diagnosis raises questions about the distinctness and usefulness of the diagnostic categories."[10]

And so, someone like Alice, whom we shall meet more fully later in the book, has had a challenging journey in her movement toward schizophrenia:

> I kind of got diagnosed with everything. I mean my last major diagnosis was early onset schizophrenia, but I had been through bipolar, I had been through borderline personality disorder, I had been through manic depression. I had run the whole gamut really, because no one understood what was going on with me, partly I think because a lot of it was also related to

6. Simon McCarthy-Jones, "The Concept of Schizophrenia Is Coming to an End—Here's Why," *Independent*, September 4, 2017, https://www.independent.co.uk/life-style/health-and-families/healthy-living/concept-schizophrenia-coming-to-end-psychology-genetics-psychiatry-schizophrenia-a7925576.html.

7. Sato Mitsumoto, "Renaming Schizophrenia: A Japanese Perspective," *World Psychiatry* 5, no. 1 (2006): 53–55.

8. Mitsumoto, "Renaming Schizophrenia," 54.

9. The term "malignant social psychology" was coined by the psychologist Tom Kitwood in relation to the way people with dementia can have their personhood undermined by subtle (and not-so-subtle) slights and negative assumptions that assume that they are no longer fully present as persons. Tom Kitwood, *Dementia Reconsidered: The Person Comes First* (Buckingham, UK: Open University Press, 1997).

10. Glover, *Alien Landscapes?*, 90.

what was going on at home, so it was kind of hard to separate the threads out of what was abuse and what was mental health. So, kind of the last diagnosis I got was early onset schizophrenia. They still say I have PTSD and anxiety issues and things like that but, you know. (laughs) So that's kind of . . . I mean I've done everything. It's really funny actually, watching movies and they're like, "he's crazy and he's on all this medication," and I'm like, oh I've been on that. (laughs) I know that medication! So yeah . . . (giggles).

To be clear, the issue is *not* the reality or validity of people's experiences. The problem is the parameters of the diagnosis, the lack of supporting evidence for a monolithic entity, and the negative social persona that the diagnosis of schizophrenia has drawn to itself.

I raise these critical issues at the beginning of our discussion of schizophrenia for three main reasons: First, to enable readers to see and understand that when we talk about "schizophrenia," we are talking about a wide range of experiences that do not necessarily or naturally fit together. Schizophrenia is not like those forms of physical illness that have clear causes, uniform manifestations, and fixed verifiable forms of treatment. People living under this description may share features, but there is a variability and a malleability that is important to keep in mind as we reflect on their experiences.

Second, the diversity of experiences draws attention to the varied and deeply personal ways in which those who live under the general description of schizophrenia experience the world. Some people are haunted by horrible voices and are tortured by paranoia and unhelpful delusions. Others live well with their voices and visions and have no desire to have them taken away. Some people cycle from depression to elation (so-called schizoaffective states); others remain emotionally neutral, and the emotions of still others become flattened. Some become cognitively disoriented; others do not.

Recognition of this diversity helps us think slightly differently about schizophrenia. Schizophrenia seems to be a continuum of experiences rather than a single thing. We will learn relatively little by focusing on the general category of schizophrenia. A more fruitful approach will be to develop a more nuanced understanding of the various experiences that make up the category. Jonathan Glover draws out the importance of this point: "Particular symptoms are more fine-grained than diagnostic categories—'having delusions' rather than 'schizophrenic.' Some symptoms are more fine-grained than others—'hearing voices' rather than 'having delusions.' Knowing what the voices say is more fine-grained still. And obviously some narratives are more fine-grained than others. 'Violent and emotionally labile' is less informative than 'He was emotionally warm arriving at his mother's house, saying how much his old room meant to him, and telling her about his new job, but only an hour later he was crying and he killed her cat.'"[11] In this way, we can assess the variety of basic experiences that constitute the category "schizophrenia" in a way that helps us get into the personal as well as the biological dimensions of people's experiences—the lived body as well as the material body. The lived body—the body as it encounters and engages with the world—is the realm of the spiritual and, as such, vital for current purposes.[12]

Participation in that continuum is not confined to those people whose apparently unconventional experiences bring them into contact with professional mental health care. Many people without a diagnosis of schizophrenia encounter the kinds of things that people living under the description experience. This is particularly so in relation to hearing voices, which we will explore in some detail in the next chapter. It's not that we are "all a bit schizophrenic"; it's that none of us is "schizophrenic." The category is too fragile and fluid to be a sufficient mark of identity. The experiences that come under the general banner of schizophrenia are much less "other" than many of us might assume.

Third, schizophrenia has become a highly stigmatized diagnosis. In the United States and elsewhere, people are often portrayed as having a "hopeless brain disease that is worse than cancer." However, as McCarthy-Jones correctly points out, "this view of schizophrenia is only possible by excluding people who live well with their schizophrenia and those who have positive outcomes."[13] The problem is that the negative persona of schizophrenia can become an ideology, that is, a doctrine that defines the condition and within which transgression from the doctrine can mean exclusion from the conversation. Some who recover from schizophrenia are effectively told that "it mustn't have been schizophrenia after all."[14] For schizophrenia to be a truly hopeless condition, recovery and hope must be removed from the criteria. As

---

11. Glover, *Alien Landscapes?*, 91–92.

12. Glover, *Alien Landscapes?*, 91.

13. McCarthy-Jones, "The Concept of Schizophrenia Is Coming to an End—Here's Why."

14. H. Writer, "Recovering from Schizophrenia Not Rare," Healthy Place, last updated June 11, 2019, https://www.healthyplace.com/thought-disorders/schizophrenia-articles/beautiful-but-not-rare-recovery.

McCarthy-Jones points out, recovery properly framed and understood is in fact possible at a number of levels.[15]

In the following chapters, I will use the term "schizophrenia" as a holding category for a number of experiences that require clarification and exploration, not necessarily as part of a monolithic diagnosis but as important and meaningful (if sometimes deeply distressing) personal experiences that must be understood and responded to in particular rather than general ways. In what follows, I begin by presenting an overview of the general parameters of psychotic experience by exploring what it feels like to live with schizophrenia. I will focus on the impact of these experiences on people's faith lives. In the following chapter, I will pick up on Glover's suggestion regarding the importance of more nuanced understandings by focusing on the experience of hearing voices. Chapter 8 will burrow down even further and explore the importance of the meaning of voices for a nuanced understanding of what people are going through and what might help as we accompany them on their journey. In chapter 9, I will do something similar with the issue of delusions, something that is shared by those living under the description of bipolar disorder.

Understanding Psychosis

"Psychosis" is a broad term that incorporates a variety of experiences that run across diagnoses. People with schizophrenia and people with bipolar disorder can experience psychoses, as can those living with major depression, fevers, infections, and so forth. Our primary focus here will be on people living under the description of schizophrenia, but it is important to note the diverse and shared nature of psychotic experience. Broadly speaking, the types of experiences of people living under the description of psychosis in general, and schizophrenia in particular, are as follows:

- Voices and visions: hearing, seeing, or feeling things that others do not (sometimes described as hallucinations)
- Holding strong beliefs about things that others do not share (sometimes described as delusions)
- Disorganization in thought, speech, or behavior

15. McCarthy-Jones, "The Concept of Schizophrenia Is Coming to an End—Here's Why."

- Disordered thinking such as moving quickly between unrelated topics, making strange connections, or mixing up words
- Difficulty concentrating
- Feelings of emotional flatness, apathy, lack of speech (sometimes described as negative symptoms)
- Unresponsiveness (sometimes described as catatonia)

Some people live with all or most of these experiences for long periods of time. Others have some of these experiences, some of the time. Others have some or all of them for a relatively short period of time and never experience them again. Whatever the duration, each of these experiences has both clinical and spiritual significance. It will be helpful to expand a little on some of these experiences and to draw out some of their spiritual implications.

Hearing Voices

This phenomenon entails hearing a voice, either internally or externally, that is not heard by others. It is often associated with people with psychotic disorders and is often perceived as paradigmatic of schizophrenia and as a primary mark of "madness." Yet voice hearing is actually a relatively common occurrence. Brent's voices started when he was in his early twenties. He was two years into his university course focusing on English and philosophy when suddenly his world turned upside down: "There was one particular night when I woke up in the middle of the night and I could hear voices inside my head. Just a weird chatter to begin with and then louder, louder voices that really had a go at me! They told me I am wicked and not worth spending time with. It was quite a shock really!" Brent's voices were terrifying, grinding, commanding, controlling:

> They tell you to do things. So, sometimes I would be walking down the road and they would shout, "STOP!" So, I'd have to stop and stand there until they said, "GO!" So, I have to stand there, sometimes for ages. It's really embarrassing. . . . Or they tell me to go to a place and tell people things, sometimes good things (or so I think) but often not such good things. But mostly the voices just tell me that I'm rubbish. I can resist them, but sometimes I get so tired that I think, "Oh well. I will just do what they say."

Brent felt baffled, bewildered, and helpless, but above all, he felt afraid. The grinding criticism and the incessant calls to kill himself were terrifying and especially draining. Though he was exhausted, he oftentimes could get no sleep.

Sometimes his voices morphed into spiritual beings.

There was one night, I thought a demon appeared to me in my room. I could see it, and I was scared. So, I phoned up my mum, and she said: "You phone up Dr. Shervington, and see if you can get an appointment." So, I phoned him up, and he said, "Yes, come in right away!" So, I went and told him, and he came up and saw me. He kept me in hospital, and then he saw me something like once a week for a couple of months. I was put on medication, but the tablets he gave me, I can't remember what kind, made me very stiff. So, I found it difficult to get up the stairs. I needed to hold on to the hand rail, sort of pull myself because my legs were so stiff. They managed to sort that out, but things just got worse! I was convinced that this demon was going to kill me.

Once he even heard the voice of God:

And I've only heard this once, but it was October last year: I thought I heard the voice of God speaking inside my head. And he was telling me to do things. So, I went out and did them right away because I said to myself, well, you can't say to God, "you've got to wait," or something like that, you know? If God says to do something, you've got to do it! And be pleased about it! The voice spoke with God's authority, and he said who he was, and it was just like, oh, that's good, God spoke to me! I was very pleased. That was good. I felt special. I could hear God's voice telling me that I was the Messiah, and things like that.

At other times, God's presence was darker: "I was saying to myself, oh, you're not a good person, are you? No, you're going to hell when you die. And all this. And I just felt like God had done this to punish me for this terrible life I lived." And yet, in the midst of this cacophony of horrible voices, other things were going on:

Well, sometimes it was really obvious, sometimes I would be like lying in bed with my hands over my ears, just screaming for stuff to shut up and go away. And then I would just be at my wits' end, basically, and I would be going, "God, you need to help me, you need to help me, I need to sleep." And it would just be, just this hush, and this kind of "I've got you," you know? That didn't happen often, but every now and then, and in those moments, I knew he still remembered me. My life seemed like the surface of the sea in the storm, but God was the undercurrent that was peaceful.

In the midst of such storms, Brent sometimes finds something to remind him that God remembers him. It's fleeting, but the memory is important. When he feels as if he is drowning, he can hold on to those moments as possibilities for hope.

But there was something else going on. Something dissonant but intriguing. Voices can be horrible, but they can also be supportive:

But it's funny, people ask me, "Do you hear voices?" assuming it is a bad thing. It is! And it's scary. But it's not as straightforward as that. I began to hear a nasty voice, but I also heard a nice voice. I still do. The nice voice I don't mind, because it says nice things; it sticks up for me against the nasty voice. The nasty voice is just like . . . well . . . nonstop criticism. Day and night, it tells me how bad I am; it tells me to kill myself, and things like that. I could hear them inside my head arguing, one telling me I'm good, the other that I am really terrible.

In the midst of this barrage of negativity, Brent found an ally: a welcoming voice that was supportive, caring, and kind; a friendly voice that gave him hope. He lived in a strange tension between voices that taunted him and voices that encouraged him. We will return to this strange and unsettling ambiguity that sits at the center of voice hearing.

Holding Beliefs Those around You Do Not Share

Having beliefs that others do not share has important implications for Christians living with psychosis. Jane articulates her experience in this way:

So, I think one of the very strange things going through it [an acute psychotic experience], as a Christian, was that the delusions that I was experiencing were very much rooted in quite spiritual things. My thoughts were very concentrated on God and the Bible, and what was happening prophetically was, you know all of that, in a very distortive way. I constantly thought I was getting messages from God, which was troubling and tiring. So, because I didn't know I was unwell, I didn't have insight and was believing that it was all real; it was very, very strange. I was walking through these thoughts and thinking God was going to send me to hell, and thinking all sorts of strange things, like that God was telling me to do certain things to win his approval. I definitely felt special. I reckon God was indeed with me, but something in that experience was distorted. I do think God was in that, but I couldn't work it out until I felt better.

The idea of feeling special was encouraging and, in principle, life enhancing, but there was a shadow side to Jane's feelings of specialness:

And, on top of that, there was such a strong theme of self-sacrifice throughout the delusions, so it was really like actually, you know, I felt like I had to die, I had to be the one to die, and that would be pleasing to God if I died. But another side of me was saying something else. The moral framework that I had within me was somehow coming against that. And however you want to frame it, I believe that God was helping me at that point, not to do whatever my mind was saying. Yes, my Christian formation had a huge bearing at that time, not to do that.

In this situation, Jane's faith was protective. She felt that she had to die in order to protect her family, but her Christian formation held her back. This protective dimension certainly helps, but still, the intensity of these experiences remains deeply and enduringly troublesome. The ordinary practice of worship seemed thin and unenticing:

The numbness really continued for a long time, and I got really frustrated by it, because I would go every Sunday to church. I would stand there. I'd be exhausted as well, just concentrating was really hard. It was like . . . it just, there just was no connection, like I had no real connection with God. I knew he was there, but it wasn't like . . . I don't know, I don't know. It's really hard to explain. Like if I could engage in worship and respond to God and enjoy that on a Sunday morning or whatever, and there's a connection that I get. So . . . but it was just like that didn't exist for about a year after my first episode. I can't explain it, it's a bit strange.

Here we find resonances of the experiences that people living under the description of depression encounter, but for different reasons:

Part of it, I wondered, was maybe the medication, but I just wanted to have my old self back. And I just thought this is awful, you know, standing here and worshiping him and feeling nothing. Everybody else is just praising God, and I wanted to be part of that really. So I went to a prayer meeting. I got prayer a few times, and then I went to one particular meeting one night. I was so frustrated, I just said, please, someone pray for me. I'd had enough of this numbness, and my friend who's the leader of the church and another friend prayed. And then within a week that numbness had receded and naturally things got much better, which was great. And I was able to relate to God in a way that perhaps I had done before, which was really positive, I thought.

Prayer seemed to help, but there seemed to be nowhere within the established mental health services where this kind of experience could be discussed and worked through: "I think because I'd had very intense spiritual stuff, there was nowhere afterwards to work that through. So, you couldn't do that in the NHS, so I had to sort of compartmentalize the stuff that I'd experienced; some things I could discuss with my nurse, but there was other stuff which I had no one to talk to about."[16]

Jane was fortunate to have a psychiatrist who understood how important Jane's faith was to her and also took seriously the content of her unconventional beliefs. "Because I said, look, what was that all about? And he said often when you have these delusions you really . . . it's what's important to the person that is coming out. So, while it's distorted thinking, it's obviously important to you, the God bit. And so that was all coming out in a really strange way. And I think, after having such intense, strange thoughts, actually I was so numb afterwards that I couldn't relate to God in a normal way."

Jane's psychiatrist recognized that some of her interpretation of her experiences was distorted, but he acknowledged that positive and potentially helpful spiritual dimensions may be mixed in with the more difficult interpretations. How we might understand, discern, and tease out these differences is something we will return to later in the book.

Difficulties with Thinking and Concentrating

Very often the more energetic dimension of the experience of schizophrenia— hearing voices, seeing things others don't see, and believing things other people

---

16. The NHS stands for the National Health Service. It refers to the government-funded medical and health-care services that everyone living in the UK can use without being asked to pay the full cost of the service.

don't believe—draws our attention. For John, the positive, more florid aspects of his mental health experiences were easier to cope with than the negative ones:

> I have become quite good at coping with some of the positive symptoms of schizophrenia. When I hear voices, I have certain ways in which I can cope with that. But what I've since discovered is that it's the negative symptoms of schizophrenia that cause me the most problems. I have not had an acute episode for many years, but I haven't got rid of those negative symptoms. It's those negative symptoms in conjunction with my faith, that's probably been most challenging. I found my faith to be very helpful with the positive symptoms for sure, because I could just give it all to God, as some Christians would put it. With the negative symptoms it's been a far tougher journey, that still goes on to this day. Sometimes I can just be so tired, and sometimes it can be my motivation, concentration that are the biggest things to suffer. My ability to focus on a task for a good amount of time suffers. And therefore I can feel guilty, like I'm not doing enough. What does God think about this? Yeah, working through those things has been a tricky thing really.

Part of the issue for John relates to the impact of his medication. He is often very drowsy, and although he holds down a good job, he gets exhausted very easily. But it also relates to a general sense of lethargy and negativity that seems to accompany his mental health challenges. This sense of negativity in thought and action has changed the way he processes some aspects of his faith life, and the theological and spiritual practices that accompany it. These changes are not necessarily lesser, but they are certainly different. This has led to a different approach to theology and faith. One thing he has still to do is unlearn certain kinds of theology and relearn certain central things:

> I guess, because of the way my brain processes stuff, to this day almost, it's hard to let go of things that are unhelpful. Some of the theology which I kind of took in hook, line, and sinker as gospel truth to start with without questioning it, without critically assessing it, I had to rethink. For example, the idea that I was ill because God was judging me or that my mental illness was caused by demons. That was tough because I've had to unlearn stuff which became sort of hardwired into my brain over the course of my life and which caused me problems, particularly in the early stages of the illness.

We are not talking about people becoming unorthodox. Just as we need a mental health hermeneutic in relation to Scripture reading and interpretation, we also need to remember that theology is a human creation with the primary goal of helping people to love God and glorify God forever. We need to think about theology and Scripture in flexible and contextual ways that enable people to achieve these goals. The voices of people living with mental health challenges are as important as the voices and interpretations of those who are not. Within the body of Jesus, theology needs to care for the needs of all disciples. Many of us strive to make theology complex and complicated.[17] For John, the key was to keep things simple:

> Pain happens in life, as the bumper sticker says, it's true. It happens, and I can accept that. So my question to myself was in the light of that, how am I going to live my life? It's only in recent times that I've come to the conclusion really, that the old Golden Rule in the Bible has really helped me in terms of it being, treat people as you would like to be treated. And that's about as in-depth as I want to get with it really, because I can go off on too many tangents and too many pathways which are unhealthy, and I just think, treat people like you want to be treated. And that's to me, when Jesus says it sums up the law and the prophets, I think, well, if it's good enough for him, then it's good enough for me. Now you [John Swinton] are a theo-logian, so you might not like that! (laughs) But if it keeps me in touch with Jesus, I'm OK with that. When I'm really ill, I need that simplicity. Actually, when I am well, I need it too.

Loving God, self, and neighbor is not complicated.

NUANCING OUR UNDERSTANDING

As mysterious as schizophrenia may appear to be, people's experiences and responses are nonetheless understandable. Why? Because they are people! People's understanding and interpretation of the world may not always be logical, at least according to conventions, but if we think seriously about the meaning of the experience for the individual, some of this might become more understandable. Now, some readers may be thinking, "The people you have

17. That is not to say that exploring theology as a complex and dynamic enterprise is not appropriate. I am a professional theologian, so I value complexity. Nevertheless, very often it is the simple things that have tremendous power: "But God chose the foolish things of the world to shame the wise; God chose the weak things of the world to shame the strong" (1 Cor. 1:27).

engaged with here are clearly suffering from a mild version of schizophrenia. The people I know have quite different experiences." That may confirm my point about the diversity within the diagnosis, but it doesn't alter my point that people are people and that love, acceptance, friendship, and belonging form all our heart's desires. However, the suggestion that some people's schizophrenia is more severe than other people's schizophrenia is valid but more complex than it might at first seem. Is this because of the severity of the condition in and of itself, or might other factors exacerbate the severity of people's experiences? Is schizophrenia simply a naturally occurring spectrum within which some people's experiences are inevitably worse than others, or might there be something else going on?

7

HEARING VOICES

Moving beyond "Symptoms" toward Meaning

> Still, we have the theoretical idea of the two histories, each complete in its own terms; we might call them the physical history and the personal history. . . . Each story will invoke its own explanatory connections, the one in terms of neurophysiological and anatomical laws, the other in terms of what is sometimes called, with apparently pejorative intent, "folk psychology," i.e., the ordinary explanatory terms employed by diarists, novelists, biographers, historians, journalists and gossips, when they deliver their accounts of human behavior and human experience— the terms employed by such simple folk as Shakespeare, Tolstoy, Proust and Henry James.
>
> —P. F. Strawson[1]

NOW THAT WE HAVE A CLEARER UNDERSTANDING OF THE EXPERIENCES that make up the category of schizophrenia, having focused on how it affects people's faith lives, we can further nuance our understanding by focusing on one aspect of the experience of schizophrenia that is in some senses iconic: hearing voices. All the experiences narrated thus far are worthy of a more detailed examination. However, we cannot achieve everything in a single text. Focusing on voice hearing will provide insight and an approach that has the potential to help us understand and respond to those living under the description of schizophrenia with accuracy, compassion, and faithfulness.

It is clear that psychosis in general and schizophrenia in particular are complex, personal, and spiritually significant. The experience regarding psychosis

---

1. P. F. Strawson, *Scepticism and Naturalism: Some Varieties* (New York: Columbia University Press, 1985), 56

that seems most baffling is hearing voices. In the eyes of many, this is truly the kind of experience that marks out people living under the description of schizophrenia as "radically other" than the rest of "us."

Hearing Voices

It may therefore come as a surprise to some to discover that it is estimated that between 5 and 28 percent of any general population hear voices that other people do not.[2] Famous historical figures such as Mahatma Gandhi, Winston Churchill, the prophet Muhammad, and Jesus heard voices. In his autobiography, Martin Luther King recalls the impact that voice hearing had on his life and work. Late one night the telephone rang. "An angry voice said, 'Listen, nigger, we've taken all we want from you; before next week you'll be sorry you ever came to Montgomery.' I hung up, but I couldn't sleep. It seemed that all of my fears had come down on me at once. I had reached the saturation point." King got up and started to pace the floor. He began to think how he might get out of his situation without appearing to be a coward. He prayed:

> The words I spoke to God that midnight are still vivid in my memory: "Lord, I'm down here trying to do what's right. I think I'm right. I am here taking a stand for what I believe is right. But Lord, I must confess that I'm weak now, I'm faltering. I'm losing my courage. Now, I am afraid. And I can't let the people see me like this because if they see me weak and losing my courage, they will begin to get weak. The people are looking to me for leadership, and if I stand before them without strength and courage, they too will falter. I am at the end of my powers. I have nothing left. I've come to the point where I can't face it alone."

But then something happened. He heard a voice:

---

2. "Hearing Voices," Mental Health Foundation, accessed October 28, 2019, https://www.mentalhealth.org.uk/a-to-z/h/hearing-voices; S. de Leede-Smith and E. Barkus, "A Comprehensive Review of Auditory Verbal Hallucinations: Lifetime Prevalence, Correlates and Mechanisms in Healthy and Clinical Individuals," *Frontiers in Human Neuroscience*, July 16, 2013, http://journal.frontiersin.org/article/10.3389/fnhum.2013.00367/full; Vanessa Beavan, John Read, and Claire Cartwright, "The Prevalence of Voice-Hearers in the General Population: A Literature Review," *Journal of Mental Health* 20, no. 3 (2011): 281–92.

It seemed as though I could hear the quiet assurance of an inner voice saying: "Martin Luther, stand up for righteousness. Stand up for justice. Stand up for truth. And lo, I will be with you. Even until the end of the world." I tell you I've seen the lightning flash. I've heard the thunder roar. I've felt sin breakers dashing trying to conquer my soul. But I heard the voice of Jesus saying still to fight on. He promised never to leave me alone. At that moment I experienced the presence of the Divine as I had never experienced Him before. Almost at once my fears began to go. My uncertainty disappeared. I was ready to face anything.[3]

Voice hearing has a recognizable history within Christian tradition; it has been clearly documented in Chris Cook's excellent book *Hearing Voices, Demonic and Divine*. Prophets, priests, saints, martyrs, and even Jesus himself heard voices at certain points in their lives.[4] It seems clear that the phenomenon of voice hearing is not unique to psychotic experience and does not inevitably cause distress. So, what might be the difference between a positive voice such as what King encountered and the kinds of deeply negative voices that people living under the description of schizophrenia experience?

WHEN GOD TALKS BACK

In her book *When God Talks Back: Understanding the American Evangelical Relationship with God*,[5] the anthropologist Tanya Luhrmann narrates the fruits of her extensive ethnographic study of the Vineyard Christian Fellowship communities in Chicago and Northern California. Vineyard communities are charismatic churches that have a central focus on the Holy Spirit and the gifts of the Spirit. Members speak in tongues, believe in miracles, pray for healing, and seek after God in tangible, experiential ways. Luhrmann spent four years in these communities, observing, reflecting, and participating. One of the most interesting phenomena she encountered was the idea that God spoke back to people when they prayed, read Scripture, and engaged in spiritual practices. Luhrmann was fascinated by this apparently countercultural phenomenon.

3. *The Autobiography of Martin Luther King, Jr.* (London: Abacus, 2000), 77.
4. C. H. Cook, *Hearing Voices, Demonic and Divine: Scientific and Theological Perspectives* (London: Routledge, 2018).
5. Tanya Luhrmann, *When God Talks Back: Understanding the American Evangelical Relationship with God* (New York: Knopf, 2012).

How could apparently intelligent middle-class people hold to something so "unscientific" as a belief that God was talking to them?

Luhrmann's answer to this question is interesting and quite startling. She hypothesizes that people are taught to discern the voice of God, that is, to distinguish some thoughts as coming from God and others that are their own. By absorbing their minds in spiritual practices such as prayer, meditation, Scripture reading, and more formal spiritual journeys such as Ignatian spirituality, they reattune their minds in a way that enables them to discern that some thoughts are from God and others are their own. Through this process, they develop a new theory of mind. Westerners might assume that the mind is a closed entity and that everything that goes on within it relates to the workings of the individual holder of that mind. Mind is an intracranial affair. However, Luhrmann's hypothesis is that Christians learn to understand a different theory of mind wherein they recognize alien thoughts and words from God as being present, deeply significant, and separate from other thoughts. This is not to suggest that the presence of God is purely a psychological phenomenon. It is not an argument against the *actual* presence of God in the life of Christian devotion, nor is it a reduction of the phenomenon of hearing the voice of God to purely psychological processes. It is simply to observe something of the psychospiritual (and neurospiritual) procedures in which humans engage, wherein the voice of God is foregrounded and experienced as present, personal, and intentional. The suggestion that Christians develop a new theory of mind has particular significance when we reflect on those voices that emerge under the description of psychotic experience.

HEARING VOICES ACROSS CULTURES

One of the interesting things about voice hearing is that while there is continuity of the general phenomenon across cultures, there is considerable variation cross-culturally in relation to the actual experience of voice hearing. Ethan Watters has observed that recovery rates for schizophrenia tend to be higher in developing countries than in the West.[6] There seems to be something about Western cultures that makes living under the description of schizophrenia particularly problematic. The nature of that problematic is particularly enlightening for the purposes of this study.

---

6. Ethan Watters, *Crazy like Us: The Globalization of the Western Mind* (New York: Little, Brown, 2011), chap. 3.

Alongside her work with American evangelical Christians on the voice of God, Tanya Luhrmann has also done important cross-cultural work focused on hearing voices in the context of schizophrenia. This research has implications for the ways we understand and describe voice hearing. Luhrmann's study compares hearing voices in the United States (San Mateo, California), India (Chennai), and Ghana (Accra).[7] What Luhrmann discovers is challenging and, I think, illuminating. She highlights the fact that the nature of and response to voices differ significantly across cultures.

Hearing Voices in America

In the West (specifically, in the United States), her interviewees often experienced voices as harsh, judgmental, violent, and threatening. We saw some examples of this earlier in John's experience. Voice hearing among people living with schizophrenia is assumed in the United States to be a manifestation of a deeply negative pathological condition, and, as such, the correct method of eradication is assumed to be primarily via psychopharmacological medication. The people living with schizophrenia in the United States that she interviewed held a quite specific perspective on their experiences of voice hearing, which reflected this negative pathological persona: "In general the American sample experienced voices as bombardment and as symptoms of a brain disease caused by genes or trauma. They used diagnostic labels readily: all but three spontaneously described themselves as diagnosed with 'schizophrenia' or 'schizoaffective disorder' and every single person used diagnostic categories in conversation."[8]

The American participants clearly found their identity in the medical model of schizophrenia. They assumed that their voices were unreal thoughts that emerged from a disrupted relationship between their thoughts and their minds. No one in her American sample reported their experiences as predominantly positive, although half reported some positive dimensions to them.[9]

People tended to be aware of "textbook" definitions of schizophrenia and used the term "schizophrenic" as a way of finding a place within that framework. People considered themselves "patients," assuming that hearing voices was a clear sign of madness. They also felt a deep shame, which caused them to

7. T. M. Luhrmann et al., "Differences in Voice-Hearing Experiences of People with Psychosis in the USA, India and Ghana: Interview-Based Study," *British Journal of Psychiatry* 206 (2015): 41–44.

8. Luhrmann et al., "Differences in Voice-Hearing Experiences," 42.

9. Luhrmann et al., "Differences in Voice-Hearing Experiences," 42.

conceal their experiences. After all, nobody wants to be known as crazy! Voices were a source of great unhappiness, and denial was often the best strategy in relation to others, if not to themselves. Their experience was thus deeply negative and seen to be indicative of "insanity." "Losing one's mind" is a label that has particular weight within a hypercognitive culture that values deeply clarity of thought and soundness of mind. The cultural weight of these experiences is immense. The voices themselves were generally unknown to the hearers: they were the voices of strangers intruding on their lives, entering into their minds without permission. All the subjects heard horrifying voices, telling them they were worthless and that their lives were not worth living. Indeed, one person even referred to her "suicide voice."

As I read these reports, I couldn't help wondering whether my friend Allen, to whom this book is dedicated and whom we met earlier, had heard just such a voice. He was one of the first people I interviewed for this book. I'd known him for fifteen years, and he was a dear friend. On March 21, 2017, he took his own life. He jumped from the top floor of a multistory car park. It seemed that on that fateful occasion, the commands of the nasty voices prevailed. They prevailed, but they did not win. I remember sitting at Allen's funeral and looking out at the hundred or so faces that made up the congregation. Some knew Allen's battles only too well from personal experience. Together we sat, we sang, we lamented, and we remembered Allen. We thanked Jesus for hope in the midst of apparent hopelessness. I remember reflecting on the apostle Paul's words: "Nothing in all creation will ever be able to separate us from the love of God that is revealed in Christ Jesus our Lord." Allen is with Jesus in that place where there is no more suffering, no more pain, and no more tears. We miss him, but we remain hopeful.

Hearing Voices in Chennai, India

One might be tempted to assume that this is the standard pattern for all people living under the description of schizophrenia. But it is not. The people Luhrmann interviewed in Chennai, India, had a significantly different experience:

> More than half of the Chennai sample . . . heard voices of kin, such as parents, mother-in-law, sister-in-law or sisters. Another two experienced a voice as husband or wife, and yet another reported that the voice said he should listen to his father. These voices behaved as relatives do: they gave guidance, but they also scolded. They often gave commands to do domestic tasks. Although people did not always like them, they spoke about them

as *relationships*. One man explained, "They talk as if elder people advising younger people." A woman heard seven or eight of her female relatives scold her constantly. They told her that she should die; but they also told her to bathe, to shop, and to go into the kitchen and prepare food.[10]

Even when individuals in Chennai heard aggressive or critical voices, they also reported hearing "good" voices that told them to ignore these negative influences. People tended not to use the term "schizophrenic."[11] Instead, local explanations tended to prevail. Voices didn't necessarily mean that someone was "insane" or "crazy." Rather, the local explanation often framed the issue in terms of "spiritual attack" by either witches or spirits. Being the victim of a witch or a spirit carried less stigma there than having a diagnosed mental health challenge.

Hearing Voices in Accra, Ghana

In Ghana, a similar shift in culture and interpretation seemed to benefit people living with schizophrenia who heard voices: "Fully half of the 20 described their current voice-hearing experience as entirely or primarily positive. A man admitted with terrible burns because a 'bad' voice had told him to grab a live electrical wire said that, 'Mostly, the voices are good.' A man admitted for the first time in 2007 said: 'They just tell me to do the right thing. If I hadn't had these voices I would have been dead long ago.' It sometimes took time for participants to admit that they heard bad voices as well as good ones."[12]

In Accra, positive voices were found to be central to the experience; in the United States, they are treated as an aside, peripheral to their primary condition. In Accra, people even said that the voices had "kept them alive." Like the people in Chennai, using spirits and demons as an explanatory framework seems to be beneficial: "Although many of the Accra participants understood that hearing audible voices could be a sign of psychiatric illness, their social world accepts that there are human-like non-embodied spirits that can talk. 'Voices [are] spirits,' one man explained. Only two people used diagnostic labels (schizophrenia)."

This is interesting. Problematic as the ascription of the demonic is (some-

---

10. Luhrmann et al., "Differences in Voice-Hearing Experiences," 43 (emphasis added).

11. Others have noted the tendency in Southeast Asia not to use diagnostic categories; see, for example, A. Sousa, "Pragmatic Ethics, Sensible Care: Psychiatry and Schizophrenia in North India" (PhD diss., University of Chicago, 2011).

12. Luhrmann et al., "Differences in Voice-Hearing Experiences," 43.

thing we will explore in more detail toward the end of this book) in the contexts of India and Africa, the ascription of the demonic seemed to serve a quite different function. It is worth reflecting on what that function might be.

Spirits and Demons

In her ethnographic work on schizophrenia in Zanzibar, the anthropologist and occupational therapist Juli McGruder reveals interesting similarities to Luhrmann's data from Accra and Chennai.[13] She points out that demon possession, while sounding rather odd to Western ears, actually serves a positive function. As she worked with people living with schizophrenia and their families, she came to understand belief in the demonic in ways that differed from her normal Christianized perspective. In Zanzibar, belief in spirit possession emerged from a complex combination of traditional Swahili culture and Arabic beliefs in jinns and was common and prevalent and not necessarily seen as extreme. Within this belief system, spirits routinely inhabit human bodies and are not considered uniformly good or bad. They can cause difficulties, but there is always an available way of dealing with them.

A spirit might be picked up accidentally or through witchcraft.[14] Spirits are not exorcised in the Christian sense. Rather, they are coaxed out with food, song, and dance. Importantly, these conditions are assumed to be transitory; the person is not presumed to be trapped in or lost within an illness that has no cure and over which the person has absolutely no control. The belief in spirits puts distance between the condition and the person. This frame of reference and interpretation offers the person and his or her family a broader range of interpretive possibilities and a wider range of options for intervention and growth than is available in Western cultures.

McGruder's point is not that such local understandings and practices should supersede other forms of intervention or etiological theories. She is saying that dealing with spirits in this manner kept people within their social group, thus increasing their relational prospects and broadening their horizons to include alternative possibilities and positive futures: "Importantly, the idea that spirits could come and go allowed the person with schizophrenia a cleaner bill of health when the illness went into remission. An ill individual

---

13. J. H. McGruder, "Madness in Zanzibar: An Exploration of Lived Experience," in *Schizophrenia, Culture, and Subjectivity: The Edge of Experience*, ed. R. J. Barrett (Cambridge: Cambridge University Press, 2004), 255–81.

14. McGruder, in Watters, *Crazy like Us*, Kindle location 2125.

enjoying a time of relative health could employ the spirit-possession story to, at least temporarily, retake his or her responsibility in the kinship group."[15]

People are thus encouraged to avail themselves of different types of opportunities when they start hearing voices. They aren't taken out of the concern of the community and handed over to specialists. The blessings and burdens of God and the spirits are beyond the control of the family, so guilt and blame are not pertinent. McGruder makes this astute observation: "When humans do not assume that they have complete control of their experiences, they do not so deeply fear those who appear to have lost it."[16] In a Western context, where clarity of thinking and control of one's self and one's destiny are paramount, the loss of control that often accompanies schizophrenia is feared. This was not the case in a culture that had different priorities and assumptions about the nature of human flourishing.

What Makes the Difference?

Returning to Luhrmann's work, we might ask the question: *What might make the difference between these cultures and Western cultures?* The answer to such a question is obviously complex, but we can draw out three possibilities that are helpful: a wider range of options for interpretation and treatment, a different way of identifying people, and a different theory of mind.

One of the main differences was hinted at in the conversation around spirits and demons: in the non-Western cultures, people have more options to deal with the voices they hear. A dynamic similar to the one we explored in relating severe mental illness to biological explanations seems to be at work here. Rather than being riveted to a single trajectory, which seems to make people's plight hopeless and completely outside their control, people in the countries discussed seem to have a much wider range of options in terms of explanation, interpretation, and action.

The people in Chennai and Accra seemed to have developed a different and more positive form of identity than those living in America. Reflecting on the ways in which people tend to think about schizophrenia, Luhrmann notes that we may not know what schizophrenia is, but we certainly know that it is not us! It is interesting that the people Luhrmann studied in India and Africa, unlike people in America, rarely referred to themselves in terms of their med-

15. McGruder, in Watters, *Crazy like Us*, Kindle location 2125.
16. McGruder, in Watters, *Crazy like Us*, Kindle location 2147.

ical diagnosis. They did not hold that particular term—"schizophrenia"—as central to their identity.

Amy June Sousa, in her ethnographic exploration of psychiatric treatment in North India, discovered a practice she describes as "diagnostic neutrality":

> When doctors do choose to discuss a diagnosis with a family, they try to emphasize a condition's treatability. This lack of diagnostic focus, which I will call "diagnostic neutrality," is a treatment tool that psychiatrists use, often unwittingly. By deemphasizing diagnoses, doctors prevent the development of negative stereotypes that encumber social recovery in other cultural contexts. In this way diagnostic neutrality may thwart social processes that have transformed schizophrenia into a devastating diagnosis elsewhere. The North Indian families who participated in this research did not treat relatives with schizophrenia as though they had immutable biological conditions. They imagined schizophrenia as a cluster of symptoms that would remit with medication and time—as not who a person is, but rather a condition a person temporarily has.[17]

In this way, people became less vulnerable to hopelessness and despondency. All of this allows for a diversity of interpretations and potential interventions and relational possibilities. Interestingly, Sousa ends her chapter by saying that "schizophrenia is neither a way to be a person in North India, nor a way to identify oneself as a person."[18] This takes us back to Ian Hacking's idea of making up people. It would appear that, at least in that part of North India, it wasn't possible to be a schizophrenic. That kind of person simply didn't exist.

Finally, it seems clear that, similar to the Vineyard Christians, the people in Africa and India were working with a different theory of mind from that of the American participants. Luhrmann notes that "When the research team asked American patients whether the voices were 'real,' the question was easy for US subjects to answer; they recognized the distinction between 'real' voices and voices 'inside your head,' in part because the mind was understood to be a closed space. Having some other agents in your mind was clearly a sign of illness or dysfunction, so the voices were 'extremely disconcerting.'"[19]

17. Amy June Sousa, "Diagnostic Neutrality in Psychiatric Treatment in North India," in *Our Most Troubling Madness: Case Studies in Schizophrenia across Cultures*, ed. T. M. Luhrmann and Jocelyn Marrow (Berkeley: University of California Press, 2016), 43.

18. Sousa, "Diagnostic Neutrality," 55.

19. Luhrmann et al., "Differences in Voice-Hearing Experiences," 43.

The theory of mind that people in the United States employ for living with schizophrenia made the overall experience much more terrifying and threatening than it was in the other two contexts, where culturally the mind was considered to be much more open and porous. Schizophrenia also had a different meaning. Diagnostic neutrality meant that the fearfulness of the diagnosis was minimized. Consequently, the range of options open to people living under the description of schizophrenia was much broader.

A PATHOGENIC CULTURE

It seems clear then that schizophrenia is complex and unsettled and that the experience of hearing voices is not inevitably pathological. It is also apparent that there is something about Western cultures that shapes and forms the experience in profoundly negative ways. We are all always and inevitably affected by culture. Anthropologist Janis Hunter Jenkins notes that "culture provides its members with an available repertoire of affective and behavioral responses to the human condition, including illness. . . . It offers models of how people should or might feel and act in response to the serious illness of a loved one. Individuals in a given place and time will react to illness similarly, in other words, because they share the same limited repertoire of cultural scripts for how to play their part. The different ways that cultures communicate expectations for behavior are often quite subtle. Seemingly small differences, such as the disease's name, can make a difference."[20]

We have seen that, in Western cultures, the description "schizophrenia" has accrued particularly negative connotations. These connotations create or configure people living under this description in negative ways and put their lives on a trajectory of hopelessness that deeply affects their recovery. The core experiences that some people choose to describe as pathological are exacerbated and made socially and psychologically toxic by a pathogenic culture that chooses to describe schizophrenia in thin, negative, and negativizing ways and responds to the experience in ways that at one level appear to be helpful but actually close down people's social opportunities. To argue that schizophrenia is just like cancer and diabetes is problematic because it locates all the problem within the individual. Such identifications frame people's experiences primarily as symptoms of some form of underlying pathological process. People are

20. Janis H. Jenkins and Marvin Karno, "The Meaning of Expressed Emotion: Theoretical Issues Raised by Cross-Cultural Research," *American Journal of Psychiatry* 149 (1992): 9–21.

surrounded by voices, but their own voice is silenced by the overwhelming power of the negative cultural narrative of schizophrenia. "She hears voices! She must be mad!" (with "mad" seen as equal to "not worthy of being listened to"). "It's only her schizophrenia talking." "Perhaps it's a demon." People thus find themselves discredited, not only as stigmatized people but also as people who actually *know* things that others should take seriously. When this happens, people's expectations (personal and cultural) become narrow and thin. People's lives are reduced to a single trajectory, and, implicitly or explicitly, primary if not sole responsibility for recovery is placed on the technical skills of the mental health professionals who very often simply don't have the capacity to deal with the weight of mental health challenges in society.

Epistemic Injustice

The ethicist Miranda Fricker describes this kind of silencing as *epistemic injustice*.[21] Fricker argues that what is and is not accepted as knowledge is a matter of justice. Some people can experience significant injustice in relation to their capacity as *knowers*, that is, as people who claim to know things about the world and strive to articulate that knowledge credibly within the public square. So, for example, imagine a boardroom meeting with five men and one woman. The woman makes a suggestion, and no one responds. A few minutes later a man makes the same suggestion, and everyone thinks it is a great idea! The woman has been wronged in her role as a knower, as someone who has information or perspective that is worth knowing.

Epistemic injustice functions at two levels. *Hermeneutical injustice* occurs within the experiences of groups that, because of prejudices and epistemological imbalances, have been unable or less able to participate in the processes involved in generating new knowledge and publicly available concepts.[22] Within such a context, people lack the kinds of social resources necessary to articulate their experiences authentically and openly. The suggestion that we may create and inhabit pathogenic cultures is indicative of a mode of hermeneutical injustice that provides the social and linguistic constrictions that are built into certain understandings of schizophrenia. The general tendency is not to take seriously the experience of people living under this description.

Testimonial injustice occurs when an individual's statements and interpreta-

21. Miranda Fricker, *Epistemic Injustice: Power and the Ethics of Knowing* (London: Oxford University Press, 2009).

22. Fricker, *Epistemic Injustice*, 147-76.

tions are given significantly reduced levels of credibility because of the listener's prejudice toward the social group to which the speaker belongs.[23] When someone encounters attitudes that infer that "what you say can't be taken seriously because you are mentally ill," that person experiences testimonial injustice. The process runs something like this:

- Jane has schizophrenia.
- Persons with schizophrenia are not credible reporters of their own experiences (**stereotype**).
- Jane is not a credible reporter of her own experience (**prejudice**).
- I will listen, but I won't believe or act on what she says (**discrimination**).
- Derek has depression.
- Depression is caused by sin (or perhaps the demonic) (**spiritual stereotype**).
- Derek is not a credible reporter of his experience (due to sin or demon possession) (**prejudice**).
- I will listen, but I will pray for his release (**spiritual abuse**).

Hermeneutical injustice provides the context for testimonial injustice, as people are generally less inclined to believe even their own testimony in the light of prevalent cultural hermeneutical practices and assumptions. Such hermeneutical injustice puts people at a disadvantage in the interpretation of their social experience, as personal interpretations are excluded from hermeneutical consideration. Fricker's central point is epistemological: *people are wronged as knowers*. Particular individuals or groups of people are assumed to be the *receivers* of knowledge but not the *givers* of knowledge. In terms of mental health, people's attempts to redescribe their situation is downgraded because of the way a particularly powerful cultural description negatively positions their experiences hermeneutically.

Within such a situation, people tend to lose their voices, not in a clinical sense but in a very literal social sense. The narratives and interpretations that individuals place on their own experiences become downplayed and subsumed to the language of symptoms and problems. Psychopharmacology becomes the "obvious" solution rather than one aspect of an array of healing possibilities. Before long we have created a culture that assumes that feelings of hopelessness and futurelessness are symptoms that emerge from the condition rather

23. Fricker, *Epistemic Injustice*, 17–30.

than the social context within which the condition is experienced. But there is another way of looking at voice hearing.

Making Up People: The Voice Hearer

Recall Hacking's idea of making up people. This idea applies in an interesting way to the experience of voice hearing. Angela Woods, reflecting on voice hearing from the perspective of the medical humanities, argues that one way some people have tried to destigmatize schizophrenia is by creating a new way of being a person: the voice hearer.[24] Voice hearing can certainly be described in terms of neuropsychology. However, the statement "I am a voice hearer" has deeper and more complex meaning.[25] In like manner to Hacking's idea of "making up people," Woods notes that "before 1987, there were no voice hearers."[26] By this she does not mean that the phenomenon of voice hearing is new. Voice hearing has been recorded across cultures and throughout history: "Socrates, Moses, Margery Kempe, Joan of Arc, Virginia Woolf and Gandhi are among the most famous figures to have been identified as voice-hearers, and remind us that these experiences were until recently at least as strongly associated with spiritual enlightenment, saintliness, creativity and philosophical insight as with madness and disease."[27] Her point is that it was not possible to adopt the identity of voice hearer until certain events occurred in 1987. The option to become that kind of person did not exist. In 1987, Patsy Hague, who lived under the description of schizophrenia, persuaded her psychiatrist, Marius Romme, that her voices were meaningful and what was required was not their eradication but help in making sense of them. She gave Romme a copy of a book by American psychologist Julian Jayne titled *The Origins of Consciousness and the Breakdown of the Bicameral Mind*. The book argues that at times in the development of human beings, voice hearing was considered normal. This gave Patsy hope in a situation that had previously been framed as hopeless.

She was angry that Romme seemed to assume that the voices were meaningless. For her they were meaningful; it was the content that distressed her rather than the phenomenon itself. She wanted Romme to ask her what the voices were saying. She said to Marius, "You believe in a God we never see

24. Angela Woods, "The Voice Hearer," *Journal of Mental Health* 22, no. 3 (2013): 263–70.
25. Angela Woods, "The Voice Hearer," 263.
26. Angela Woods, "The Voice Hearer," 264.
27. Angela Woods, "The Voice Hearer," 264.

or hear, so why shouldn't you believe in the voices I really do hear?" "Marius like many other psychiatrists had always dismissed voices as being part of the delusional and hallucinatory world of the psychiatrically ill. It made sense to Marius because it was certainly the case in our society that to believe in the existence of God, in spite of the lack of any physical evidence, is acceptable and no one who believes in this is thought of as mad, yet the same acceptance is not extended to those whom psychiatry regards as hallucinators."[28]

Eventually Romme became persuaded that the key to dealing with voices was to learn how to manage them and live with them rather than eradicate them. In 1987 Patsy finally persuaded Romme to think differently about voices. Woods notes that "1987 was also the year that they [Patsy and Marius] appeared together on Dutch television to publicise this new approach to voice-hearing and to seek responses from the general public. After the screening, hundreds of people phoned in to the programme, 450 of whom reported hearing voices. The world's first hearing voices congress was held in Holland later that year, and from there an international voice-hearing movement spread first to the UK, which now has a network of over 180 hearing voices groups, and then to Europe, Australia, America and beyond."[29] This was the beginning of a new movement, the Hearing Voices Network, which now has groups across the world and focuses on helping its members manage to live with voices and sharing strategies for living well with them.

Woods suggests that Patsy's story has become a founding myth that is told and retold in various contexts and that establishes the experience of hearing voices not simply as a symptom of schizophrenia but as a meaningful human experience that forms part of a person's identity. "The voice hearer" emerges from, and is a rejection of, a related but very different identity—"the schizophrenic." In this way, we move away from the term "schizophrenia" and its spoiled identity and toward a new identity that is meaningful and less stigmatized.

Central to this way of thinking is the distancing of voice hearing from the diagnosis of schizophrenia. Eleanor Longden's experience of hearing voices illustrates this well: "'I went in to the hospital a troubled, confused, unhappy 18-year-old and I came out a schizophrenic. . . . I came to embody what psychosis should look and feel like.' Eleanor describes her first meeting with post-psychiatrist Pat Bracken as a turning-point in her self-understanding.

28. "Patsy Hague: Inspiration," Intervoice, accessed October 28, 2019, http://www.inter voiceonline.org/about-intervoice/patsy-hague-inspiration.
29. "Patsy Hague."

Bracken 'didn't use this terrible mechanistic, clinical language but just couched everything in normal language and normal experience,' inviting her 'to see [her]self—not as this genetically determined schizophrenic who was biologically flawed and mentally deficient like a degenerate.'"[30] In this way, reframing voice hearing moves her from an identity as a "schizophrenic" to an identity as a "voice hearer." The former smacks of hopelessness. The latter empowers and confers identity and hope.

Voice Hearing and Epistemic Generosity

The language of voice hearing and the idea of the creation of the identity of voice hearer help us move away from some of the deeply negative cultural connotations of the diagnosis of schizophrenia. The kind of identity that Woods points us toward is highly politicized in that it tends to be adopted as a stance against psychiatric descriptions. Some are comfortable with this, and others are not. My sense is that trying to force people to adopt an identity they do not desire is unhelpful. There is great power in being able to name oneself as opposed to being named by others. The idea of the voice hearer allows for this and also opens up a range of possibilities not necessarily open to those living under the description of schizophrenia, at least in Western contexts.

Problematic as the term may be, some people do desire to keep the identity of schizophrenia, and that should be respected. To do otherwise is simply to create a different kind of stigma. It is perhaps better to keep open the possibility of multiple identities. Woods quotes and affirms Elisabeth Svanholmer when she writes:

> Am I a recovered mental patient? Am I a schizophrenic? Am I a voice hearer? Yes and no. To me, these are all just words, labels. They describe something superficial. I am recovered and recovering. Being me and being human is a process of constantly experiencing, reacting and changing. The diagnosis "schizophrenia" has opened doors within the social and psychiatric system in Denmark and it has helped me understand and respect my sensitivity.... For me to think of myself as a "voice hearer" is just as much of a diagnostic approach; this label is just more specific and less influenced by years of taboo and stigma. As a voice hearer, I have been able to work with my problems in a way that makes sense to me.... I am gifted, sensitive,

30. Eleanor Longden, in *Living with Voices: 50 Stories of Recovery*, ed. M. Romme et al. (Ross-on-Wye, UK: PCCS Books, 2009), 143–44.

schizophrenic, a voice hearer, or a mentally disabled person, depending on who I am talking to and how they perceive the world.[31]

Perhaps we need a form of *epistemic generosity* that allows for diversity of experience and counters the injustice of having negative identities forced upon us. As long as we (all of us together) allow people to have identities that are multiple, this seems to me to make perfect sense. However, as we have seen, not everyone is willing to offer such generosity.

There are a tendency and a temptation to assume that the stories told by people living under the description of schizophrenia are simply symptoms of an underlying brain disorder. As such, they have no real meaning in the individuals' story or the stories of those around them. The reframing discussion around the identity of "voice hearer" frees us to listen to people's voice-hearing experiences without simply assuming that they are nothing other than the product of a culturally difficult diagnosis. Regardless of whether it provides an enduring positive identity, this way of thinking teaches us to listen differently, to step beyond epistemic injustice and into a different realm where all of us together see and hear one another's voices differently, more meaningfully, and more faithfully.

31. Elisabeth Svanholmer, in Romme et al., *Living with Voices*, 147–52.

8

A Strange Kind of Loneliness

Alice's Story

> There is little study of what schizophrenics' voices say to them, which would make people's experiences more valid and meaningful and also lend itself to a more human account of mental illness. People's experiences of hearing voices are often silenced, which can only augment ignorance and fear, both in society and in the mental healthcare system. To make matters worse, it is almost impossible to talk with other people and relate the pain that voices inflict when they are raging inside you and shouting you down.
>
> —Benjamin Gray[1]

ALICE IS IN HER EARLY THIRTIES. SHE CURRENTLY WORKS IN A LIBRARY, but her real passion is to become a mental health advocate and to help churches develop faithful understandings of mental health issues and, in so doing, become places of love and belonging. She is a passionate Christian but has always struggled to gain acceptance in the church. She admits that some of that is because she can be a bit difficult at times, but that is not the only reason. She has frequently been rejected by Christians not because of her behavior but because they have discovered that she lives with schizophrenia. Reactions to this description have often been profoundly troubling. Alice has lived with voices since she was twelve years old:

My earliest recollection of hearing voices would have been at age twelve. Where I was sitting out in the back garden and I heard a voice that was outside of myself, talking to me. It wasn't very nice. In fact, it freaked me

---

1. Benjamin Gray, "Hidden Demons: A Personal Account of Hearing Voices and the Alternative of the Hearing Voices Movement," *Schizophrenia Bulletin* 34, no. 6 (2008): 1006-7.

out! Growing up in the church that I had, my initial response was, "Well, this is obviously just demonic. I just need to pray more." I assumed that it was wrong and that "obviously" it showed that I was going through some spiritual stuff. "We won't tell mum and dad that then!" and you know, it was that whole kind of guilt associated with it, that this is "only spiritual," I'm not going to talk about it, I'm not going to say anything.

Alice's first response was to assume that her voice hearing had a spiritual root in the demonic. We will return to the demonic later in the book, but here we note how some Christians have a tendency to turn to the demonic to explain unusual experiences. That may be helpful if you live in Accra or Zambia, but it is less helpful if you live in downtown London. This negative spiritual interpretation initially caused a good deal of distress and isolation. Her family members were very religious, and the idea that her experience could be framed as demonic would have been deeply distressing for them. She couldn't share her new experience with her family for fear of rejection and, perhaps, confirmation of her own deep, dark fear that what she was experiencing *was* in fact demonic. At first the voices were simply irritating: "The voices became more annoying than anything, because they wouldn't shut up. Sometimes I just really wanted to sleep, and they just didn't. And it was just this constant barrage of people talking and information and babies crying. I had this baby that would cry in the background—psychotherapists would love to look into that one; you know, my inner child is screaming for relief!—and all those kinds of things. When I got used to it, it was more frustrating than anything. At first it was quite scary and upsetting, but then it just became annoying."

But as time moved on, the voices became more difficult, darker, more sinister, more dangerous: "I would see dark figures over my shoulder and the voices would shout at me, telling me I am useless and worthless and sometimes they would tell me to hurt myself. They didn't tell me to hurt other people, but I have a few scars to remind me of what they told me to do to me."

Tied in with the distress that came with the voices was the impact they had on Alice's spiritual life, both internally and externally. Internally she struggled with the way her difficult experiences tempted her to discredit her own spiritual experience: "My life seemed like the surface of the sea in the storm, but God was the undercurrent that was peaceful. And so, I did have some kind of recognition of what it was that I was feeling. But . . . I mean even then . . . because everyone was telling me you're nuts, you learn to not trust everything you feel. So even the peaceful, the happy or the joy, well that could be manic, that could be psychosis, that could be . . . it's not real." God was present as a potential source of joy and peace, something she recognized even in the midst of her wildest storms. However, because of the nature of her experiences, she, at least at points, felt that she couldn't trust her own perceptions. Her assumptions about the nature of her "condition" discredited the feeling of the presence of God.

Externally, this feeling of spiritual uncertainty was amplified by the fact that her voice was often discredited in the public arena:

> People assume that nothing you're feeling or experiencing is real. "It's just the schizophrenia talking!" When that happens, even the things that you want to be real you write off as, no, they can't be. But when you are looking back, you go, "no, that actually was God! I wasn't crazy!" (laughs) But nobody believes me. I mean if you [John Swinton] went into a church and said, "Oh, look, God's been speaking to me about such and such," people would go, "Oh, John, the big theologian and professor! (laughs), tell us more!" If I went into a church, even if I wasn't going through my more difficult periods, and said, "Oh, God's been speaking to me!" they'd be like, "Oh dear . . . here she goes. And what has God been saying to you, dearie?" So, yes, it's not hard to write off people pretty quickly when it comes to God and everything else.

Alice's spiritual fragility and vulnerability to being silenced as a knower are apparent. She is uncertain about her own spiritual experiences but aware that if she articulates them, she may well be discredited and her testimony reduced to a mere symptom.

> And I felt God very strongly with me saying, you know, you've seen so much bad, let me show you the good. And since then I've had some incredible spiritual experiences where I have seen stuff, but there's always been, it's not just the dark figures on people's shoulders anymore, there's always the glory of God outshining that stuff, you know, like . . . it's like I had been blind to that side of it. But it's really hard to talk about this stuff and not sound like I'm still crazy, so I'm really careful about what I say and what I think. Because I don't want people going, "That's it, you're still schizophrenic. Wrap you up and take you off to the loony bin." Because it's not like that at all anymore; it's a very different experience now.

The third dimension relates to the spiritual meaning ascribed to her experiences by fellow Christians. "I had a lot of prayer from very well-intentioned people, about demonic stuff, and was told that I didn't have enough faith, so I wasn't being healed, all that kind of crap that you hear at churches. All the time, it makes me so angry! But it's hard being told that you're filled with evil, you know? Or that everything that you're hearing and seeing is of the devil. Particularly as some of that stuff actually brings you peace. That's really hard." Alice loves Jesus. She sees some of her experiences as spiritually difficult but other aspects as beneficial. However, some of her closest friends, who should have been allies, opted for what they considered the "more obvious" description of her situation: the demonic. In so doing, they reinforced her own self-negativity and created a difficult and complex distance between Alice and God. "*If I am truly filled with evil, then I can't be with God.*"

So, she finds herself in a rather painful situation: she loves Jesus, and her brothers and sisters who also love Jesus claim that she is filled with evil. What might it feel like for a brother or sister in Christ to be told that they are filled with evil and for it to be assumed that some of their most meaningful experiences are the work of the demonic? It's pretty difficult to defend yourself when your testimony is so profoundly spiritually discredited. There is a strange parallel here between certain forms of the medical story that proclaim that voices are "only symptoms" and the theological story that proclaims that "it's really demons!" Both narratives seem unwilling to listen to what it *means* for someone in Alice's position to encounter voices that are deeply meaningful and perhaps even positive. People seem keen to explain the phenomenon but less interested in understanding it.

ARE VOICES INEVITABLY BAD? A STRANGE KIND OF SILENCE

We heard Alice state that "*some of that stuff actually brings you peace.*" This is a curious statement. What could there be in her seemingly wild and confused experiences that brought her peace?

Before we address that question, we need to discuss one rather unusual aspect of Alice's story. After many years of wrestling with schizophrenia, when she was in her early twenties, Alice's voices and other accompanying unconventional mental health experiences left her. Why this happened is a mystery to her and to others, although a significant number of people diagnosed with schizophrenia do recover.[2] Alice put the disappearance of her voices down

2. Anne-Kari Torgalsbøen, Susie Fu, and Nikolai Czajkowski, "Resilience Trajectories to Full Recovery in First-Episode Schizophrenia," *European Psychiatry* 52 (2018): 54–60

to a group of elderly women in her church who gathered together regularly to pray for her, not, so they thought, that she be cured but simply to pray for her. Yet, from Alice's perspective, the disappearance of her voices was the outcome of supernatural intervention. However, her psychologist told her that she had been misdiagnosed. The presumption seems to have been that if she had genuinely recovered, she couldn't have had schizophrenia in the first place. Somewhere within these two descriptions of Alice's situation lies the truth.

Loneliness

Putting to one side the exact nature of the causes, Alice's voices and accompanying experiences were no longer a part of her life. One might assume that she would be delighted about this, and at one level she was. But she was ambivalent: "One of the big things I found really hard when I first was healed was that I was really lonely. It was suddenly really quiet, and I didn't have anyone to talk to in the middle of the night. And so that was really hard. I went through this whole grieving process for things, for people that weren't real. Which was really difficult, because who do you go to for that? 'Hey, I'm really grieving over a friend that never actually existed.' (laughs) Kind of hard." How exactly does one articulate a feeling of loss and grief for people who never existed without people assuming that your grief is "obviously a symptom of your illness"? The removal of Alice's voices led not simply to relief (although clearly that was an aspect for which she was thankful) but also to *loneliness*.[3] For Alice, standard accounts of what it means for a treatment, or a healing, to "work" stood in tension with some important aspects of her experience.

> I think that one of the things I found difficult was that [the psychiatrists] would be like, "your voices are bad, so we're going to give you medication to get rid of the voices." But [I would say] Yes! Sometimes the voices are terrible. But not all the voices are bad. Can we keep the nice ones? And so I understand why a lot of people don't take their medication, because it's actually sometimes a lot harder to be without your friends and to be with your enemies as well; it's better to have them all than to have none. What they don't take into account is that this is somebody's narrative and these are characters in their narrative. And you can't just . . . it's like taking away

3. In relation to the administering of psychotropic medication, there would be logic in recognizing that while this may be necessary and helpful for some, it may also have side effects that are important but easily overlooked, this kind of loneliness being one.

their family, you know? It's like you can't do that and not have any reper-
cussions of that. You can't.

Alice makes an important point. For many people, the experience of voices
is challenging, frightening, and undesirable, and they do consider medication
a helpful way of coping with the suffering that comes from voices. However, as
we discovered in our discussion of "the voice hearer," there is another side to
the experience of voice hearing. For some people, voice hearing is meaningful
and relational. Voices are *always* characters in a narrative, a personal and com-
munal story within which people try to make sense of their lives (for better or
for worse) and to live well according to the experiences they encounter. Some
of these relationships are clearly very difficult and require professional help,
but not necessarily all of them. Failure to frame the issues within this narrative
framework risks failing to look seriously at the relational nature of people's
voice-hearing experiences.

Missing Anne: A Strange Kind of Loneliness

The importance of recognizing the narrative and relational dimensions of
voices comes to sharp focus as we listen to Alice's encounters with Anne.
Anne was a consistently friendly and beneficent voice who stood by Alice in
the midst of other voices that were the exact opposite. For Alice, Anne was
very real and also very unreal at precisely the same time. Alice can live with
this unusual tension, but when she tries to articulate it to others, problems
arise: "I told someone once in a moment of weakness about my girlfriend
Anne who would hang out with me in my sad moments, and they said, 'Oh
she's a demon, Alice, you shouldn't talk to her.' And I'm like, 'She's the only
person who sticks around long enough to see me cry.' I'm like, where are you?
If there were a real person there, maybe I wouldn't need her, would I? So, what
are you going to do? So yeah, it is really difficult when people say that kind of
thing. It is hard."

Alice's friend may well have cared a lot for Alice. But when it came to
her voices, things became complicated even if her intentions were positive.
Anne, on the other hand, understood Alice's situation. Alice's "real life" friend
struggled to understand her situation. Her confusion caused her to fall back
on an explanatory framework with which she was familiar and that provided
an explanation for Alice's situation that seemed to comport with her belief
structures. Her intention was to help. The outcome was not so helpful. Her
description was intended to be spiritually discerning and pastorally thera-

peutic, but it had the result of demonizing (literally) an important source of Alice's support. It's not that Anne had to be "real." As the sociologist William Isaac Thomas famously put it: "If men define situations as real, they are real in their consequences."[4] Ontology was really not the point. The point was the way in which Anne functioned within Alice's social-support network: "Anne was an actual person to me, even though she wasn't a person. And I knew she wasn't real, I knew not to talk to her in public, but she was someone I could confide in and talk to. She was the person who was always there when I was upset. She was probably the biggest loss to me. She wasn't there after that (her healing); I had to do it alone, I had to figure out how to do life alone. I mean, she wasn't always the best influence, you know, but she was there. And that's really hard to explain."

Indeed, it is hard to explain. But difficulty in articulation does not invalidate the significance of Anne's presence. When Anne was no longer available, Alice was left with a strange kind of loneliness. She knew that Anne was not real, but she also knew that she had been a meaningful presence. What looked like healing and release had side effects. Alice reflected on the implications of her situation for other people living under the description of schizophrenia: "I would meet people when I was in hospital, and a lot of them, in their sane moments, and you can always tell when someone is having a lucid moment, would talk about how lonely they were, and how much their medication just made them feel so isolated and lonely. And it's like if you're used to years of being surrounded, to take away that community is crazy; it's crazy. It doesn't actually address what that community was there for in the first place." Discerning the underlying psychological reasons for someone feeling this way is the task of the mental health professionals. Understanding and responding to feelings of loneliness is a task for the church.

A Strange Kind of Community

The problem with Alice's loneliness was that once the voices left her, she had nothing to fill the gap. It is interesting to reflect on the tension between Alice's loneliness and emptiness and the fullness of life she felt when she was in a psychiatric hospital. Some of her most meaningful times were when she was with people who saw the world differently.

---

4. W. I. Thomas and D. S. Thomas, *The Child in America: Behavior Problems and Programs* (New York: Knopf, 1928), 571-72.

When I was in hospital, I met some really interesting people. I met Jesus at one point; he's a fifty-year-old moldy man from London. Being Jesus seems to be a common mental health issue; it's really interesting. But, yeah, he was Jesus or an Old Testament prophet; [it] depended on the day. But I met a guy in his sixties who thought I was his mum. And I met a whole lot of interesting people. I met a lady who thought her face was falling off and all this kind of stuff. It's so fascinating what people's brains can do to them. It's just . . . and I think for all of us, because we were all in it together, there's a sense of community that is definitely I find I've missed, a lot. And we're the nuttiest community out there, and we used to just sit around in a circle and smoke up a storm and swear and drink and whatever, but we understood there was no need to explain if you start talking to a corner. Everyone would just go, "Ah, she's off her meds again!" No one would care! There was a real sense of family. And I haven't found that again.

I wonder why Alice, a lover of Jesus, has not found such a community within the body of Jesus, the one who sits with and befriends tax collectors, sinners, and prostitutes; the one who touches lepers and sits with people who are assumed to be demon possessed. Jesus, the one who introduces himself to the Samaritan woman and "defiles himself" by drinking from her cup. Jesus, who draws to himself a rather bizarre group of followers whom he claims he will disciple into the ways of the kingdom. A ragtag group of followers who will transform the world and defeat the earthly powers that think they own the world but will soon discover that they do not. Jesus, who died and came back to life and now reigns in heaven.

True, Alice's strange community has odd beliefs. True also that her voices are unconventional, although not perhaps as unconventional as we might have thought before we reflected on voice hearing. Nonetheless, one might expect that a community built on unconventional relationships and unusual beliefs might at a minimum empathize with her need for epistemological generosity, understanding, acceptance, and community. Sadly, it seems that this may not be the case. They always presume that the problem is her schizophrenia. It may be that at least some of her problems lie elsewhere.

Theological Implications

Thus far we have suggested that rather than looking at schizophrenia as a single monolithic condition, it might be better to adopt a perspective that seeks to explore the various experiences that constitute the diagnosis as individual and deeply meaningful experiences that can bring great distress but do not inevitably do so. Our focus on voice hearing has helped make the point that the presence of voices is not necessarily the problem. Many people hear voices, and it makes little difference to their lives. The issue that concerns mental health professionals emerges from the *distress* these voices may cause them. It is the issue of distress that forms the realm of the mental health professionals' remit.

However, we have seen that at least some of this distress is culturally bound, and some of it can actually be caused by the *eradication* of voices. This affects the meaning and impact that medication has for the personal experiences of individuals. If mental distress is the focus of professional mental health care, then we must understand the breadth of experience that those living under the (fragile) description of schizophrenia actually encounter. Alice's story has begun to show us what that might look like. The alleviation of psychological distress is very important. We just need to be careful that we understand what that means.

In closing this chapter, we will draw together some central theological issues that can help us understand and care more deeply and faithfully.

A Theology of Naming

One thing that has become clear is that the diagnosis of schizophrenia is culturally highly problematic. Regardless of the experiences that the diagnosis attempts to capture and respond to, there is something about the term that has become difficult for Westerners. That difficulty affects individuals in significant ways. Previously we explored the idea of the more positive identity of "voice hearer." This has positive potential, but there is another way we might name people living under the description of schizophrenia, and that is *friend*. Before teasing out this suggestion, we need to think our way into what God calls human beings to do.

The Genesis account of creation is a tremendously powerful story that informs us of a creator God who brings the world into existence and promises to love it. The word of God brought the world into existence, and the love of God sustains and holds it in its place. God creates a whole wealth of beauty—animals, plants, seas, rivers, and mountains. In the first creation account, God gives human beings responsibility for the world by giving them *dominion* over it—a call to crush it down and hold it in its place: "Then God said, 'Let us make mankind in our image, in our likeness, so that they may rule over the fish in the sea and the birds in the sky, over the livestock and all the wild animals, and over all the creatures that move along the ground'" (Gen. 1:26). Humans are to hold the world in its place. But in the second creation account, we get a slightly different story. God tells Adam to care for and tend the world: "The LORD God took the man and put him in the Garden of Eden to work it and take care of it" (Gen. 2:15). The world is wildly out of control, but our response to this should be caring and tender. That is a powerful metaphor for being alongside of people living with psychotic disorder. People may be wildly out of control, but our response must always be caring and tender. This is a creation principle, which is critical if we are to develop a kinder, gentler mode of mental health care.

A responsibility that sometimes gets overlooked comes in Genesis 2:19–20, where Adam is given another vital responsibility: *to name things.* "Now the LORD God had formed out of the ground all the wild animals and all the birds in the sky. He brought them to the man to see what he would name them; and whatever the man called each living creature, that was its name. So the man gave names to all the livestock, the birds in the sky and all the wild animals."

Part of Adam's responsibility to care and tend for the world was to name things faithfully and properly. Adam sat down, and as each creature came forward, he gave it a name. So the long-necked four-legged creature came forward, and Adam named it a giraffe. The long-toothed hairy-headed animal came forward, and Adam named it a lion. The smooth, thin, wriggly creature came forward, and Adam named it a worm. Once the creatures were named, that was what they became. There were no lions before Adam named them. There were long-toothed hairy-headed animals, but lions came into existence only when Adam gave them that name. They found their place within creation as they received their particular name. God gifted them their existence; Adam gave them their name.

That being so, a primal responsibility of human beings is to name things properly. The way we describe and name things is a matter of faithfulness. We have seen that stigma takes away one's name and replaces it with a caricature or a stereotype based on a person's diagnosis. The name "schizophrenia" has become an aspect of a pathological culture that makes living well with experiences often described as schizophrenia very difficult. Stigma in all its forms is deeply sinful. It is a distortion of human beings' primal responsibility to name creation properly. As such, it needs to be countered at every level. In this chapter, we have argued that destigmatizing voices destigmatizes those who hear voices and allows us to see them and to name them in a quite different light. Taking seriously our vocation to name things means we monitor our language around diagnoses such as schizophrenia and refuse to allow that diagnosis to determine the person who bears it. *There are no "schizophrenics" in the kingdom of God; just people who love Jesus.*

A primary aspect of the church's response to the pathogenic dimensions of culture is to give people back their names. Enabling the possibility of people having a name of which they can be proud is central to facilitating a future that makes hope possible. It is interesting to reflect on Jesus's encounter with the Gerasene demoniac in the light of this suggestion. Jesus encounters a man who seems to be possessed by demons and who lives among the graveyards. He is violent toward himself and others. In Mark 5:9 Jesus does a rather unusual thing. He asks him what his name is: "My name is Legion," he replies, "for we are many." Putting to one side the issue of demons (which we will address later in this book), two things are important here. First, Jesus did not call the man possessed. He wanted to call him by his name. Second, the man did not reply by giving his name but rather named his condition. In this sense, he self-stigmatized, as opposed to Jesus, who refused to go with the man's stigmatic persona. Here we see Jesus moving beyond "diagnosis" toward the person by seeking to name him differently than the way society and indeed the man himself had done up to then.

In John 15:15 Jesus once again draws our attention to the importance of naming: "I no longer call you servants, because a servant does not know his master's business. Instead, I have called you friends, for everything that I learned from my Father I have made known to you." Here the disciples are given a whole new identity. No longer are they servants. Now they are friends of Jesus. Friendship is the nature of discipleship in God's coming kingdom. Perhaps the most radical way we can counter the pathological culture we have encountered in this chapter is quite simple: make Christlike friendships with people. Sometimes the simplest things in life turn out to be the most profound.[5]

---

5. For a further development of friendship in the context of schizophrenia, see John Swinton, *Resurrecting the Person: Friendship and the Care of People with Mental Health Problems* (Nashville: Abingdon, 2000).

PART V

REDESCRIBING BIPOLAR DISORDER

9

Bipolar Faith

Toward a Spirituality of Bipolar Disorder

> Religion, spirituality, and mysticism are all complex and contested concepts and it is often debatable as to whether any particular experience is "religious," "spiritual," "mystical," or some combination of the three. However, we must take seriously the attribution of experience to one of these categories by the person who has had that experience—even if we disagree. If two people on a walk through a beautiful sunlit pasture have differing experiences—the one saying it was mystical, and the other simply that it was beautiful—we do well to find out why they describe their experiences as they do.
>
> —Chris Cook[1]

"Bipolar disorder" is a term developed by mental health professionals to describe the experiences of those who go through severe disruptions of mood, thought, and behavior. The British Psychological Society outlines the main features in this way: "Many people experience periods of depression and also periods of elation and overactivity. For some people, these episodes are frequent and severe enough to be seen as a 'disorder'—bipolar disorder. The word 'bipolar' refers to the two extremes or 'poles' of mood: depression and 'mania.' Until recently the term 'manic depression' was also used. Each person's experience is unique and there is a continuum between the extreme mood states . . . and the normal mood swings that everyone experiences. Some people, but not all, find it helpful to think of themselves as

---

1. C. H. Cook, *Hearing Voices, Demonic and Divine: Scientific and Theological Perspectives* (London: Routledge, 2018), 148.

having an illness."[2] The swing between depression and mania is not necessarily sequential: "People do not necessarily swing from one extreme to another, but instead typically experience maybe one, two or three periods of significant mood problems over a two or three year period. Episodes may last several weeks and usually follow no particular predictable course—depression is not necessarily followed by a 'high'; it isn't inevitable that a period of mania will crash into low mood."[3] Losofa is originally from Trinidad but now lives in London. He is tall and well built and lifts weights as a hobby. Losofa is a family man who, at least when not struggling with aspects of his bipolar disorder, always puts his wife and two children first. He articulates the distress that accompanies bipolar disorder in this way:

> Yeah, I mean the highs for me were and still are both tremendously difficult (although it doesn't feel that way at the time). I know when it begins because I can't sleep; I get anxious and really unsettled. I start to get racing thoughts, an uncontrollable sense of energy, and basically quite a blatant disregard for boundaries. I've been high [in the elated phase of his bipolar disorder] when I've been driving a car, and that is not good news. I sort of lose the sense that I should be keeping to a certain speed limit or observing certain road rules. And just basically the high sort of ushers in a certain level of overconfidence in your ability. Some people spend a lot of money or sleep around, but I don't do that. I don't have any money to spend! (laughs) But unfortunately, when I'm high, I'm actually very difficult to contain, like people can't really get a word in. I like to sort of dominate discussions and conversation and basically, yeah, I'm sort of very difficult to be around. I also tend to wander. I once got completely lost walking the train tracks in Sydney, Australia. I thought I was gone. But God brought me back. When I'm not high, I'm mostly considerate and allow people to voice their opinions. I am always respectful of other people. So, its mixed, but I've lost a lot of friends over the years.

The highs can be wonderful! But coming down, not so much: "It's the coming down that is the worst. You see what you have done, how you have treated people, the mistakes you have made. If it wasn't for my wife, I don't know

2. British Psychological Society, *Understanding Bipolar Disorder: Why Some People Experience Extreme Mood Status and What Can Help* (Leicester, UK: British Psychological Society, 2010), 11.

3. British Psychological Society, *Understanding Bipolar Disorder*, 11.

what I would do. It's kind of, well, I don't know . . . shameful? Having bipolar is not shameful in itself; it's just an illness. But the things I do . . . sometimes . . . I do feel ashamed."

All of us understand the experience of mood changes, and all of us understand the feeling of shame and regret. What makes bipolar disorder different is the level of distress and disruption that occurs in response to people's actions during their elevated state. After the high is when things get difficult, which contributes to the depth of the lows that often follow the elation. The painful rhythm of high and low is difficult to live with sometimes. Losofa's lament, "I've lost a lot of friends over the years," indicates something of the relational tragedy of his situation.

The Biology of Spirituality

Jackson is forty-five years old. He lives in Seattle, Washington, where he has worked as a car mechanic for twenty-two years. Like Losofa, he lives with bipolar disorder. Both Jackson and Losofa were glad to have a diagnosis (unlike Monica Coleman, discussed earlier, who was very reluctant to accept diagnosis and medication). Jackson's diagnosis helped him explain some things to himself and others and, in so doing, brought some healing release. However, accepting his diagnosis and having to take medication had not been easy for him:

> I think that probably one of the things I struggled with early on was accepting the diagnosis as being helpful. I've had some really difficult experiences, and I could never really make much sense of them. But I think after the many relapses that I've had since the first episode, I've resigned myself. . . . I've basically come to view it in a positive way as the best approach to take, not only for me but also for the family and loved ones around me; my friends who are supporting me. It's not quite "take the meds and everything will be fine!" But you know what I mean. I need it.

Bipolar disorder is one mental health challenge for which there is strong evidence for a biological origin.[4] Recognizing this is key, not just in terms of

---

4. For some helpful overviews of the science of bipolar disorder, see Kay Redfield Jamison, *Touched with Fire: Manic-Depressive Illness and the Artistic Temperament* (New York: Free Press, 1993); Jamison, *An Unquiet Mind* (New York: Vintage Books, 1995). Jamison has also written a very helpful book on suicide that will help readers more fully understand

treatment but also because it raises important theological and spiritual questions. We touched on this in our discussion about biology and medication. Jackson brings another dimension to the conversation. Without his medication, his spirituality suffers: "I still suffer from having my spiritual beliefs follow my moods, which are sometimes wildly swinging, and even within a day they can swing from extreme highs to extreme lows. It's difficult to hold on to God in the midst of that sometimes. Solid spiritual ground can be hard to find." There is a deep and soulful (in the sense outlined previously) connection between his biological state and his spirituality:

> What always challenged me was that maybe some of my core beliefs, even my spirituality, is in itself biological. My brain is where my spirituality comes from. It's a bag of salt water with proteins and DNA in it, that does complex reactions that leads me to have all the spiritual experiences. So, I guess it's inevitable that when my chemistry is out of kilter, I get spiritually sick as well as physically. Some people think it can be dangerous to mix spirituality with mental illness, but every waking moment until I die I'm going to be mixing my spirituality with my mental illness, so hopefully it's not all bad.

Jackson's medication is necessary for his spiritual stability. As we discussed previously, as a biological creature, he required biological intervention to deal with a biological issue. Put slightly differently, as soulful creatures, we require soulful interventions, which include forms of intervention that affect our body-soul in quite profound ways. For the reasons previously discussed, that does not reduce our spirituality to chemical interactions. It simply indicates something of the nature of our embodiment. *There is no shame or theological contradiction in taking medication.*

However, Jackson's emphasis on the biology of his spirituality does raise the issue of meaning: Does the fact that the experiences connected to bipolar disorder have a biological basis mean they are meaningless, that is, simply symptoms to be gotten rid of? Jackson's answer is illuminating: "I think the experiences I have had are meaningful to me. The sum of my experiences and my genetic code make me who I am today. Every experience was a biological one, and that reductionist categorization does not reduce the meaningfulness of the experiences." His unconventional and often very difficult mental health experiences may have been the product of biology, but they were also deeply meaningful to him and formative of him as a person. Biology provides

---

this tragic area of human experience: *Night Falls Fast: Understanding Suicide* (New York: Vintage Books, 1999).

an *explanation* for his experiences, but it does not capture the fullness of his experience. It's important to be clear on what this means.

The Problem with Neurological Explanations: Moving beyond Neuromania[5]

Previously we looked at the way in which explanations can be reductionist, in that by explaining something in a particular way, other ways of looking at it are downgraded and subsumed to that single explanation. We can see the problems with such explanations in the area of neurobiology. Neurology is posited as an explanation for a wide range of phenomena, including morality, art, and even love.[6] Such explanations attempt to reduce complex human phenomena to a single explanatory framework.

In his fascinating (and often very amusing) book titled *Aping Mankind: Neuromania, Darwinitis, and the Misrepresentation of Humanity*, the English philosopher Raymond Tallis offers a helpful critique of this approach. Tallis points out the ways in which neurology has become the new "theory of everything." He names this tendency to use neurology as an overarching explanatory framework for everything "neuromania." In Tallis's thinking, neuromania is a delusional condition that makes four key assumptions:

1   Human consciousness is identical with neural activity in the human brain.

2   I am my (you are your) brain.

3   The brain explains every aspect of awareness and behavior.

4   To understand human beings, you must peer into the intracranial darkness using the techniques of neuroscience.[7]

5. This section originally appeared as John Swinton, "Medicating the Soul: Why Medication Needs Stories," *Christian Bioethics: Non-Ecumenical Studies in Medical Morality* 24, no. 3 (December 2018): 302–18.

6. Darcia Narvaez, *Neurobiology and the Development of Human Morality: Evolution, Culture, and Wisdom* (New York: Norton, 2014); Jean-Pierre Changeux, "Art and Neuroscience," *Leonardo* 27, no. 3 (1994): 189–201; S. Zeki, "The Neurobiology of Love," *FEBSPRESS Letters* 581 (2007): 2575–79.

7. Raymond Tallis, *Aping Mankind: Neuromania, Darwinitis, and the Misrepresentation of Humanity* (London: Routledge, 2011), 237.

Tallis highlights neurological research into romantic love. The neurobiological exploration of romantic love goes something like this:

- Place head of subject (attached to body) in a functional MRI scan.
- Record responses to pictures of the beloved and pictures of mere friends.
- Subtract brain activity of latter from former.
- Repeat many times on many subjects.[8]

Through this process we discover that "Love (romantic) is due to activity in a highly restricted area of the brain: in the medial insula and the anterior cingulate cortex and, subcortically, in the caudate nucleus and the putamen, all bilaterally."[9] It is safe to say that this is not exactly how most people would describe romantic love!

Tallis's point is that neurology is clearly *necessary* for all human experience, but it is equally as clearly not *sufficient* to explain key experiences such as love. He suggests this about love:

- Love is not simply a property of part of a single organ (the brain).
- Love is not simply a property of an organism as a whole.
- Love belongs to a self that relates to and is part of a community of minds (or perhaps better, a community of people).[10]

Love is something that we do together. Love requires lovers. Trying to reduce humans and human experience to nothing more than a cluster of firing and misfiring neurons makes little sense, convinced as the proponents of such a view may appear to be. Neuromania is, to say the least, troublesome. Reducing human beings to one dimension of their bodies—their brains—creates a very thin view of humanness.

The Authenticity of Experience

Tallis's challenge is important and will become still more important as we explore, below, the nature of religious experience in the midst of elevated moods

8. Tallis, *Aping Mankind*, 73–76.
9. Tallis, *Aping Mankind*, 76.
10. Tallis, *Aping Mankind*, 92–93.

and delusional experiences. Jackson views all experience as meaningful, but not all of it as authentic:

> However, some of my experiences such as my delusions and hallucinations are meaningful in the way they caused me to develop as an individual, but by definition do not carry the weight of the nonpsychotic experiences in my life. They were madness, and for me to give them the same weight in informing my life view would make me less accurate of a product of my "true" biology. For example, I thought at one point I had died when I fell off a cliff at age eighteen. In my mania I thought I might be a living dead person. Once the mania passed, I was able to dismiss this concept, and even though my memories of being psychotic don't have exact identifiers as being irrelevant or nonmeaningful, I have to curate them in my memory as meaningless.

Jackson's position is complex. All his experiences are meaningful. But some he deems nonmeaningful in the sense that he realizes they are an aspect of the dimension of his experience he considers pathological. He realizes that the belief that he was a living dead person was not accurate, if for no other reason than that he now recognizes that he is alive. He had to go through a process of discernment to work out what was real and enduring and what was transient, real at the moment but recognized as unhelpful later on. The possibility of discernment in the midst of a high is not great:

> For me I haven't really been, to be honest, I don't think I've really been good at discerning the difference. And I think when you're undergoing, or when you're going through, the relapse or the episode, the ability to discern is actually for me nonexistent. But I think it's always in the aftermath and with discussing this with my wife or initially with my parents and siblings, and just hearing their feedback as to what took place and what was happening, it's only then that I can sit down and discern, I can see that that type of experience was a real spiritual experience or not.

This kind of retrospective assessing of what is and is not real within unconventional mental health experiences is important and requires people who are open to listening in quite particular ways. We will examine what such looking and discerning look like in the next chapter when we think through how best to deal with beliefs that some people consider to be delusional.

Enjoying the Highs

People living under the description of bipolar disorder are not always ill, and every aspect of their experience is not inevitably pathological. Even when a person is going through a manic phase, there may be aspects of that experience that are deeply meaningful and important, and that have enduring significance, even if the test of their authenticity and utility comes retrospectively when the acute phase of the experience has passed.

The thing that marks elevated or depressed moods as requiring intervention is the level of disruption and distress the mood causes either to an individual or to those around her. Put slightly differently, the line between mood *changes* and mood *disorders* is the level of distress rather than the nature of the experience. It is important to bear this in mind, particularly when we explore spiritual experience. Some aspects of people's experiences can be positive and, for some, even enjoyable.

Miriam lives with bipolar disorder. Some aspects of her bipolar disorder bring her real suffering: "A lot of people have really terrible and frightening experiences. I did, for example, believe I was in hell once, walking lost through Hackney on a freezing February night. . . . When I am low, I just feel I am in a big void. I have heard people say they meet God in their dark places, but I feel like I am completely on my own. I don't necessarily stop believing in God, though sometimes that is the case. I just feel like he is behind a big black cloud."[11] Both from the perspective of psychiatry and in terms of her spirituality, Miriam's bipolar disorder brings disruption and suffering into her life. When this occurs, Miriam is glad for the assistance of the mental health professions. However, not all her unconventional mental health experiences bring suffering or disturbance.

> I have also had some really beautiful experiences and visions—like seeing angels and sitting on top of a hill in Lancashire for four hours, totally believing I was in heaven. I once went to a service at Sheffield Cathedral. The only other people there were three women sitting on the other side of the chapel. A sunbeam suddenly shone down on them, through the beautiful stained-glass window, and I had an overwhelming feeling that they were God the mother, God the daughter and God the Holy Spirit. A psychiatrist

11. Jean Vanier and John Swinton, *Mental Health: The Inclusive Church Resource*, Kindle ed. (London: Darton, Longman & Todd, 2014), Kindle location 316.

would probably call this a delusion or a hallucination, but to me it felt much more like a metaphor and still feels very special and real. A gift from God. There is a fine line between mystical and psychotic experiences. I think that probably a lot of the saints and prophets of old would nowadays end up in the psychiatric system.[12]

This kind of experience is clearly unconventional, that is, it does not adhere to what is considered by the majority of people to be "normal" experience. Yet it is not disordered in the sense that it is causing her distress. It may be the case that psychiatrists can authentically describe such an experience as a delusion within their frame of reference, but Miriam, with equal authenticity, can describe it differently, as a meaningful spiritual experience. Unless she is in distress, there is no inherent need for the psychiatric description to prevail. Both descriptions contain truth. It is how we work with that truth that is key. Miriam's description may reveal important aspects that can become occluded if we lean too heavily on a description that focuses primarily or solely on pathology.

Learning from Suffering

Even though people's experiences may have been deeply troublesome, there can still be positive things to be learned. Losofa puts it thus:

I think my bipolar disorder has given me a heightened awareness of the reality of God in my life, that God is not distant or God is actually with me on a daily and continuous basis. And I think that has allowed me not to be, to not sort of view God as being so much transcendent and distant when I'm, when I live life on a daily basis. Religiously, I may not sort of conform to trying to sort of . . . how can I say it . . . maintain certain rituals and stuff because I know that I've had these experiences and I have this awareness that God is present, if that makes sense. Yeah, so regarding the ministry, I think it gives me a different type of lens to be able to appreciate peoples' behavior or . . . yeah, and maybe adds a different level of tolerance and understanding compassion that may not be there without experiences.

12. Vanier and Swinton, *Mental Health*, Kindle location 306–312.

Like many forms of suffering, bipolar disorder can open us up to a more empathetic understanding of other people and of God. Such can be the nature of suffering, although, of course, that is not always the case. However, the kind of suffering that accompanies bipolar disorder is complicated and worthy of further reflection.

10

BIPOLAR DISORDER AND THE NATURE OF SUFFERING

Delusions, Demons, and Truth Telling

> "What is truth?" retorted Pilate. With this he went out again to the Jews gathered there and said, "I find no basis for a charge against him."
>
> —John 18:38

THE ISSUE OF SUFFERING IS COMPLEX, DIVERSE, AND CONTEXTUAL. As one reflects on the literature emerging from, for example, the field of disability theology, one can see some reasons for that complexity. People are reluctant to use the language of suffering in relation to disability, often for good reasons.[1] There is no inherent reason why people should assume that those living with Down syndrome suffer because of their Down syndrome. They may suffer because of people's *responses* to their presence and their projection of their own fears, but there is nothing intrinsic to their disability that necessitates suffering. Likewise, people living with (as opposed to suffering from) dementia do not necessarily suffer. There is research that indicates that people with dementia even in its latter stages can live valuable and enjoyable lives.[2] The problem with the rhetoric of suffering in relation to human disability is that it tends to focus the conversation on that which is perceived as negative, and in so doing, it occludes aspects of human diversity that are clearly positive. It is therefore wise to monitor the language of suffering in relation to disability issues.

Yet, when we reflect on issues around mental health and mental health

---

1. Nancy Eiesland, *The Disabled God: Toward a Liberatory Theology of Disability* (Nashville: Abingdon, 1994); Amos Yong, *Theology and Down Syndrome: Reimagining Disability in Late Modernity* (Waco, TX: Baylor University Press, 2007).

2. John Swinton, *Dementia: Living in the Memories of God* (Grand Rapids: Eerdmans, 2012); Tom Kitwood, *Dementia Reconsidered: The Person Comes First* (Buckingham, UK: Open University Press, 1997).

challenges, the language of suffering, although not hegemonic, at least at times can be appropriate. As we have seen, experiences of being in the deep, dark pit of depression are much more than social constructs. They contain real suffering. Living with voices that constantly taunt and offend you, telling you that you are useless, worthless, and have no right to live, can clearly be a mode of suffering, although even here we need to be aware that some people perceive voice hearing quite differently.[3] The language of suffering, when used with discernment and sensitivity, can be helpful within a mental health context. Bipolar disorder should not be defined by suffering, but there is no question that it is deeply marked by it. But when viewed through a spiritual lens, some aspects of that suffering turn out to be surprising. In what follows, we will consider three aspects of suffering that people living under this description encounter in relation to

1   religious delusions,

2   the ascription of the demonic, and

3   the experience of being "told the truth in love."

If we bear in mind, in what follows, what we have previously learned about the hidden power of epistemic injustice, we will discover unusual and deeply challenging things.

CATHERINE'S STORY

Catherine is a forty-five-year-old woman, a medical doctor, and the mother of three children. She is an excellent pianist, "a keep-fit addict" (to use her own words), and an excellent cook. Catherine also lives under the description of bipolar disorder. Catherine does not describe herself formally as a Christian insofar as she has no formal affiliation with the established Christian church. However, somewhat unusually, many of her unconventional mental health experiences, particularly those aspects that some describe as delusions, relate to Christianity. Christianity is therefore important to her, but in a rather unusual way.

3. M. Romme and S. Escher, eds., *Understanding Voices: Coping with Auditory Hallucinations and Confusing Realities* (London: Handsell Publications, 1996).

Bipolar Disorder as Suffering: A Place Where God Is Not

The lows of her bipolar experience were quite devastating for Catherine:

> Being depressed? Yeah it is kind of like . . . I mean you can't breathe un-
> derwater, but, it's sort of like breathing underwater or just being lowered
> into a pit, like just going lower and lower and lower. Being around people
> is very difficult. . . . I interact a lot with people, I'm an extrovert, but it's just
> like when I'm depressed . . . everything is on mute or something. And then,
> it just takes such a tremendous amount of energy to do things, it's hard to
> describe, but just like putting the laundry in the washing machine is like a
> monumental task. And as somebody who's quite high functioning generally,
> it's just so strange.

Living life "on mute" is hard work. Simple things become major tasks. Finding God becomes difficult and sometimes impossible. Still, she finds some solace and a sense of solidarity in the psalms: "I mean I have read some things in
the Bible that are helpful. I mean like the psalms. Because some of the psalms,
the ones that are really like, 'God, why have you, where are you?' I feel horrible,
I'm in this pit, whatever that one is, [Ps.] 40? That's so helpful, because it's like
it's OK to feel abandoned." The psalms give Catherine a language to express
her pain and sense of abandonment, and, in an odd way, they provide a sense
of solidarity within the experience of feeling lost and abandoned. The psalms
help her hold on to the possibility of God.

Bipolar Disorder as Spiritual Elation

The darkness and spiritual confusion of Catherine's lows contrast quite strik-
ingly with the brightness and apparent spiritual clarity of her highs. Sitting
at the spiritual heart of many of her experiences of elation is the experience
of having beliefs and ideas that others find strange, technically described in
terms of *delusions*.[4] Many of these experiences relate to intense experiences
of the presence of God:

---

4. Readers will have noticed that I have tried throughout to avoid technical medical
language when talking about mental health challenges. However, when it came to the idea of
delusions, I found it difficult and overly clumsy to use alternative terms. I therefore decided
to hold on to the language of delusion but to offer it a degree of new content.

Yeah, like I have pretty classic delusions. I become so euphoric that it's hard to describe. Basically, the whole world is connected to me; God is right there, and I'm next to him, and we're looking down on the whole world. . . . I just get like the intense feeling that everything is sort of relating to me, and that's hard to describe, but that's not how you sort of normally feel. I just feel like all of a sudden, I'm a different person than I was before, and like God has chosen me to be his second person. And so, I need to help him to help others. It's generally very like positive, like I feel I'm able to do amazing things for humanity. . . . Yeah. God and everything I see has some sort of meaning.

In technical terms, a delusion is described as a solid fixed belief based on inadequate grounds that is not amenable to rational argument or the acceptance of evidence to the contrary. Sometimes it is defined as not being in sync with a person's regional, cultural, and educational background. However, such ways of defining delusions are problematic, not least because they make epistemic claims that cannot always be supported. How can one disprove a religious experience? Putting the epistemological concerns aside for now, at this stage in her experience, Catherine's beliefs are pleasurable and encouraging insofar as they give her a sense of being special and having a particular purpose in life.

EPISTEMIC INNOCENCE: MEDICATING A PROPHET

In an intriguing paper titled "The Epistemic Innocence of Motivated Delusions," Lisa Bortolotti points out that some experiences that professionals describe as delusions have psychological benefits: "One proposal is that some delusions defuse negative emotions and protect one from low self-esteem by allowing motivational influences on belief formation."[5] She describes these as "motivated delusions," that is, delusions that play a defensive function and help avoid or deal with loss of self-esteem or negative emotions. Bortolotti develops the concept of "epistemic innocence" to describe unconventional beliefs that, when adopted, deliver a significant epistemic benefit, a benefit unattainable were the delusion not adopted.

Writing in the *New York Times*, the psychiatrist Irene Hurford offers a helpful illustration of this. She recalls an event that changed her perspective on delusions in a profound way:

5. Lisa Bortolotti, "The Epistemic Innocence of Motivated Delusions," *Consciousness and Cognition* 33 (May 2015): 490.

In the middle of the night in my second year of psychiatric residency, 13 years ago, I was awakened to see a prophet. The man, in his early 50s, had been living on the streets. He was a college graduate from a middle-class family. But on Christmas Eve three decades earlier, the Archangel Michael had come to him in a vision and demanded that he spread God's word. "He told me I would suffer great pain," the man said. "His words are true. I suffer great pain." He lifted his shirt and showed me his chest, covered in Kaposi sarcomas, the stigmata of full-blown AIDS. He said he had come to the emergency room to preach. I encouraged him to check into the hospital for care. He refused, and I considered my options. I could allow him to leave, or I could admit him involuntarily. I knew, though, that if we gave him antipsychotic medication, he would realize that he was a homeless man with AIDS. Would he rather stay a prophet? Did he have the right to choose psychosis? Did I have the right to choose for him?

Hurford's dilemma was based around different aspects of compassion and a desire to care. On the one hand, as a psychiatrist, she had probably seen similar types of behaviors in other people. She knew this man's experiences could be described as a delusion. The compassionate thing to do was to forcibly take him into care and ensure that he got the most appropriate medication. However, in doing that, she feared that she might take away something that was functioning positively: an identity that was not marked by homelessness, hopelessness, and the pain of a terminal illness. Hurford does not try to resolve that dilemma. She just sits with the tension: "That night 13 years ago, I did hospitalize my patient who thought he was a prophet, and he received treatment that he had not consented to. I never found out what happened to him. I think about him often; I question my decision each time I do."[6]

The psychiatrist's difficult task is to walk that tricky line between the "obviously pathological" and the not so obviously meaningful aspects of a person's delusional experience.

The idea of epistemic innocence is helpful in understanding certain aspects of Catherine's experience. It would appear that something similar happens to Catherine at times (and I stress "at times," as there are dangers that must not be overlooked). Some of her apparently delusional experiences were psychologically constructive, although any benefits tended to be discovered *after the fact* rather than in the midst of the episode. It is true that most people do not experi-

---

6. Irene Hurford, "Medicating a Prophet," *New York Times*, October 1, 2016, https://www .nytimes.com/2016/10/02/opinion/sunday/medicating-a-prophet.html.

ence the sense of elation and specialness that Catherine does, which does mark out her experience as unconventional. Nevertheless, from her perspective, and to a certain extent, her experience can be seen as a positive, as something worth taking seriously as potentially more than mere pathology. At this point, her experiences do not present a disorder or danger, but that can change quickly.

Coping and the Mystery of Spiritual Emergence

Catherine's religious experiences occasionally helped her cope with difficult times: "When people go through hard times, they look for stuff, I mean, that's obvious, right? I mean, people need their faith sometimes when they are going through something difficult. But with me it's more like, I mean, certainly when I'm manic, but also when I'm depressed, I need something to hold on to. I do *really* believe in God then, and I pray and do things that I wouldn't normally do. And . . . so . . . I don't know."

Catherine's experience is both challenging and mysterious. Scripture tells us that God listens to the prayers of the righteous. In John 9:31 the apostle informs us that "We know that God does not listen to sinners, but if any one is a worshiper of God and does his will, God listens to him" (RSV). This passage reveals a paradox. Catherine does not describe herself as a Christian, and yet, at her most intensely spiritual times, she worships the Christian God with faith, and she prays to the Christian God in hope. Does the fact that she lives under the description of bipolar disorder and has experiences that prompt professionals to consider her ill annul her description of herself as a praying worshiper of Jesus? What might it mean that God hears Catherine's prayers? Wrestling with these questions would take a book by itself! But notice here how epistemic injustice threatens to silence and discredit her spiritual experiences and prevent such questions from even being asked. Catherine's "bipolar spirituality" causes confusion to herself, but also for her and her family:

> It's strange. I have no background in religion. The delusions didn't come from anywhere. And then afterwards I was, and sometimes I still am, just so mixed up about it. I talked to my psychiatrist a lot about it . . . he is a Christian . . . and other people, especially religious people, well, those that I can trust! I would ask them: "What does this mean?" Most of them (not my psychiatrist, who was great) were like, "Well, if you don't believe in God and Jesus, if something is just there when you're ill, then it's not real." I found that to be really upsetting, because my experiences were so intense and meaningful to me, so I was like, well, that's just your opinion. But how

do you know? Maybe God was talking to me then when I needed him. Who are you to say?

Catherine's point is a fair one. Who are "we" to say that God can be present only if someone does not have a description of bipolar and has a previous spiritual history within which God is not present in a form that is recognizable to particular forms of institutional religion? The issues are complex, but one dimension that doesn't get the attention it should is the matter of *orthodoxy*.

Orthodoxy or Heresy?

In a fascinating paper titled "Orthodoxy or Heresy? A New Way of Looking at Spiritual Care for People with Delusional Beliefs," mental health chaplain Janet Foggie offers a way of thinking through the epistemic tensions that are inevitably present when professionals encounter people who hold beliefs that others do not share. She begins by drawing an epistemic comparison with the development of doctrine in the church, noting that there has always been heterodoxy of belief within the church. The early church (like the contemporary church) consisted of a rainbow of beliefs about who Jesus was and what it meant to live as a Christian.[7] All the beliefs shared a common theme: a desire to understand who Jesus was and to live faithfully with him and those who chose to follow him. Foggie compares this plurality of beliefs with the diversity of beliefs held by the various participants within contemporary mental health care systems. She points out that there is a similar complexity of epistemological and belief systems. Even though everyone desires to get to the same end point—recovery—the various belief structures that occur have quite different ideas of how to get there. This epistemological diversity can be highly problematic for people living with what are described as delusional experiences.

Members of any interdisciplinary team are shaped and formed by the particular beliefs and values that form the boundaries and parameters of their professional status. Occupational therapists can see the value of nurses, nurses can see the value of psychiatrists, and so forth, because they share a basic paradigm of beliefs. The patient, however, does not belong to this group and has not been taught this language or been formed in these ways. Nor has the patient been taught to see the world of mental health challenges in the way those in the

7. Janet Foggie, "Orthodoxy or Heresy? A New Way of Looking at Spiritual Care for People with Delusional Beliefs," *Scottish Journal of Healthcare Chaplaincy* 10, no. 1 (2007): 23.

mental health professions are taught to see it. The beliefs of the patient group can thus be viewed as separate and distinct from the views of the medical professional. There is therefore a significant but often unacknowledged epistemic tension: "Like the strands of the earlier churches, the patients and doctors hold a different set of beliefs and use a very different vocabulary leading to the same goal, which is recovery, broadly defined. Before entering the mental healthcare system the patient would have had little or no knowledge of its belief systems, and the generally agreed beliefs that make each particular multi-disciplinary team work. The teams have to decide whether to convert the patient to their way of thinking (the most common outcome) or to fight the patient while the patient maintains their own beliefs intact."[8]

This tension becomes intensified when someone holds unusual beliefs: "The patient's complex and fluid beliefs of everyday life have been put under great stress by the disordered thinking he or she is now experiencing. The task of bringing that patient round to a new set of medical beliefs in order to communicate the details of a care-plan, prescription, diagnosis, if there is one, and plans for discharge, is immense and it is not surprising that in receiving communication of large amounts of alien material the deluded patient is lost and confused. This is worsened still further when those delusions are religious in nature."[9] Sylvia Mohr has noted that people living with religious delusions tend to do less well than those with other forms of delusion: "Patients who have persistent delusions with religious content . . . frequently feature antagonism with psychiatric care and get less support from their religious communities."[10] The reason for this, Mohr suggests, is that "Delusions with religious content were an obstacle to participation in religious activities with other people and support from a religious community . . . due to the dysfunctional behaviors related to their delusions. As a result, these patients kept their distance from both psychiatric care and religious communities."[11]

People with religious delusions tend to be ambiguous about professional services while also finding it difficult to gain acceptance in religious communities because their views are considered unorthodox. They therefore lack support from two main sources of healing that are potentially available in society. Foggie points out that a cornerstone for professionals working with people with unconventional beliefs is never to collude with

8. Foggie, "Orthodoxy or Heresy?," 23.

9. Foggie, "Orthodoxy or Heresy?," 24.

10. Sylvia Mohr et al., "Delusions with Religious Content in Patients with Psychosis: How They Interact with Spiritual Coping," *Psychiatry* 73, no. 2 (2010): 158–72.

11. Mohr et al., "Delusions with Religious Content," 167–68.

patients. She suggests that this might be a mistake, particularly if such non-collusion leads to a lack of sympathy, empathy, and understanding, which lack is compounded for religious people by the lack of knowledge certain sectors of professional mental health care possess regarding religion and spirituality.[12]

Foggie suggests that what is required is a different way of thinking about being with those who see the world differently and hold different beliefs from what are considered normal. Emmanuel Peters has observed that the line between normal and delusional thinking is hard to draw. He suggests that we think in terms of "a continuum of belief from 'orthodox' Christian faith to the New Religious Movements (such as Hare Krishna or Druids) through to schizo-typal delusional thinking."[13] The idea of a continuum does not exclude clinical recognition of difficulties based on the previously highlighted criterion of distress. What it does do, however, is allow us the freedom to respond differently to unusual beliefs.

RETHINKING RECOVERY: CREATING A CONTEXT FOR EPISTEMIC JUSTICE

Foggie's next move is important. She urges her intended readers (primarily hospital chaplains) to change their understanding of recovery,[14] from a model in which recovery refers to overcoming mental health challenges to a model that emphasizes learning how to live fruitfully with them. Recovery can mean different things to different people, but in this case it basically relates to realizing personal goals and developing relationships and skills that help people live well even though their mental health challenge will be enduring. This model positions the chaplain in a way that emphasizes the need to give up power and enter into the situation differently. The chaplain should take the side of the patient:

12. J. Neelman and M. B. King, "Psychiatrists' Religious Attitudes in Relation to Their Clinical Practice: A Survey of 231 Psychiatrists," *Acta Psychiatrica Scandinavica* 88 (1997): 420–24.

13. E. Peters, "Are Delusions on a Continuum? The Case of Religious and Delusional Beliefs," in *Psychosis and Spirituality: Exploring the New Frontier*, ed. Isabel Clarke (London: Wiley-Blackwell, 2011).

14. J. Repper and R. Perkins, *Social Inclusion and Recovery: A Model for Mental Health Practice* (Edinburgh: Baillière Tindall, 2003).

In my own working life and practice I have come to the conclusion that in order to work with a patient's religious delusions I have to lose my professional identity as one of them, the skeptical team, and become one of us, the patient belief group. I also have to prove my worth to the patient, allowing them to give me their view and not to contradict it immediately, to listen and ask questions that constantly remind the patient that it is OK, indeed normal, to have a religious faith. Once that fact has been established the discussion of particular delusional beliefs which are not generally accepted to be part of that faith can begin.[15]

Foggie thus begins in a different place. She urges chaplains to cross over into the experience of the patient and to listen carefully. Once chaplains are in such a position of innocent listening, they will begin to hear properly. Only when they hear properly can their task as spiritual guides begin. In this way, meaningful presence becomes a possibility. As Tim Fretheim has put it, chaplains come to learn "how to affirm authentic spirituality while recognizing some thoughts and experiences as psychotic fragments. A patient once said to me, 'God is not pleased with me. I heard the shutters rattling, and that means he is not happy with my behavior.' I replied, 'I don't doubt that God speaks to you and is concerned about your behavior. I think that the rattling shutters might be your schizophrenia talking, though.' He smiled and accepted my comment."[16] Such listening and responding is a subtle but necessary skill.

One might object to Foggie's suggestion that once we enter into the relationship and conversation in such a way, part of our task is to help people discern which beliefs are orthodox and which are heresy. Is this not exactly what she was complaining about in the first place? However, for the Christian chaplain who is dealing with Christians (as we have been throughout this book), that cannot be the case. All of us need spiritual direction, albeit sometimes retrospectively. All of us need guidance as we struggle to navigate the rainbow of beliefs within and without the church. Foggie's suggestion is a helpful way of conceptualizing and articulating the process of discipling and spiritual discernment in a situation that is complex, sometimes painful, but potentially deeply hopeful.

15. Foggie, "Orthodoxy or Heresy?," 25.

16. Tim Fretheim, "Many Will Come in My Name: Spiritual Care for Persons with a Delusion of Grandiosity with Religious Content," *Covenant Quarterly* 73, nos. 3–4 (August–November 2015): 24.

In the light of this, one might expect that Catherine could find solace, comfort, and empathic understanding in the company of Christian friends and those whom the church has set aside to help people living with enduring mental health challenges discern the nature and authenticity of their spiritual experiences. Unfortunately, it hasn't always worked out that way.

REPERCUSSIONS: THE SHADOW SIDE OF SPIRITUAL ELATION

At one level, Catherine's religious experience can be exciting and enticing, but it does have a shadow side. Intertwined with her deep sense of connection with God is a tendency toward dangerous behaviors, sometimes *because* of her powerful spiritual experiences:

> My delusions have repercussions. I mean, you just cannot exist like that in the world, in the real world, basically . . . you end up saying and doing things that are dangerous. I actually have thought I needed to kill myself so that I could be with God. I remember one time I was driving around [while talking] on the phone to my psychiatrist, saying I was going to be going to heaven and stuff. I remember reflecting on it after I got better and it was horrible. But even now I sometimes drive my car really fast and close my eyes and do things like that that are very dangerous, so afterwards it's, like, terrible.

Catherine's spiritual experiences are a strange and difficult combination of religious ecstasy, existential danger, and new spiritual possibilities that hold the potential for both growth and destruction. She needs people around her who see these dimensions clearly. She also needs professional help, albeit in a form that recognizes the significance of the spiritual experiences that occur in the midst of those experiences that are pathological. She is deeply moved by the intensity of her positive experiences with God, but at the same time, she remains aware that there can be a heavy price to pay if she does not manage her situation effectively:

> I do miss the high, and I do miss feeling really religious. That's what I miss the most. But I have children so . . . and also my husband has made it clear he'll stand by me through anything, but if I stop taking my medicine, he won't stand by me for that. And he's, like, I'll leave you if you do that, because it's destructive and we have children and you just can't do it. It would be a huge

cost, for an amazing experience. And if I was diagnosed with some other, terminal illness, then maybe I would do it. Like if the end of the world was coming. And also I'd lose my job, and that's really important to me.

Catherine works hard to remain within her therapeutic regime not because she wants to get rid of her religious feelings and experiences but because she realizes she has to make a choice, and she chooses to remain alive, to take medication, and to be with her family. But still she retains a longing for the intensity of the spiritual high.

Thinking about the Devil: Terrible beyond Terrible

The lows that Catherine encounters hold a good deal of danger, both physical and spiritual: "When I'm depressed, I can get very, like, confused. I start thinking about the devil. I think, sort of like, why I'm feeling bad, and why I want to kill myself—that might be the devil? When I think like that, I generally feel worse. I start asking people, but that can be bad as well." It is precisely here, when her thinking begins to drift into a darkly negative space, that she needs spiritual assistance. As her mood shifts her into dark places, so her interpretation of these dark places and the reasons for her being there begin to adopt a negative spiritual shape and form.

This is precisely the kind of complex interaction between spirituality and pathology that Foggie urges us to take seriously and treat with empathy and epistemic generosity. Catherine needs hopeful affirmation—a way of describing her situation that recognizes the significance of her diagnostic mental health description but also offers positive spiritual redescriptions that capture the subtleties and fullness of her experiences. Unfortunately, what she sometimes encounters is the *reinforcement* of her negative spiritual descriptions:

> I have a religious friend, and she is kind of, yeah, she tries to be nice about it. She's a very religious Christian, but she's been like, well, "Satan does exist," and I'm like, "What do you mean!" What does that mean? And she's like, "Well I'm just saying." So that's pretty horrible to think that you're possessed by the devil. . . . When she said that I just felt terrible. When you're depressed, you already feel so terrible. I always feel very guilty, like I've done something really horrible, and I'm terrible, beyond terrible. I don't even know what I've done but it's something that's really terrible. So then if somebody says that this is the devil's work, then it just adds to that.

Such negative spiritual explanations are not ascribed out of malice. Quite the opposite: the intention is concern and kindness. The outcome, however, is something quite different.

Demons Are Bad for Your Health!

It's interesting to reflect on Catherine's self-ascription of demonic activity and her friend's reinforcement of this in light of a relatively recent study in the *Journal for the Scientific Study of Religion,* which indicates that belief in demons and evil spirits is harmful to mental health.[17] The National Study of Youth and Religion, involving 3,290 Americans, found that belief in demons was a strong predictor of poorer mental health among youth and young adults. Importantly, poorer mental health did not lead to greater belief in demons. One of the authors of the report—Fanhao Nie of Purdue University—points out that

> there is a lack of sociological research on the dark side of religion to health. Most prior research tends to confirm the conventional wisdom that religion makes one better off in health. Even among the relatively fewer number of studies on the negative religious effects on health, researchers tend to ignore a very important element to most religions—the demons or evil spirits. However, beliefs in demons or evil spirits is not only integral to many major religions but also vividly experienced by most of us in our everyday life. During childhood, we were told that demons exist and they may tempt us to do things evil. To children and even many adults, we may fear that demons are watching us from behind and attack us off guard when left alone in a dark room. To people who are burdened or dismayed with life issues, the demons-cause-my-misfortune belief might be well accepted.[18]

The study showed that even after controlling for belief in the presence of a benevolent God, a strong belief in demons still leads to poorer mental health. In terms of mental health, this particular religious belief can be a double-

17. Fanhao Nie and Daniel V. A. Olson, "Demonic Influence: The Negative Mental Health Effects of Belief in Demons," *Journal for the Scientific Study of Religion* 55, no. 3 (January 2017): 498–515.

18. Eric W. Dolan, "Study Suggests Belief in Demons and Evil Spirits Is Harmful to Mental Health," PsyPost, February 23, 2017, https://www.psypost.org/2017/02/study-suggests -belief-demons-evil-spirits-harmful-mental-health-47783.

edged sword. The report suggests that parents and youth workers should be careful in the way they emphasize the demonic, as an overemphasis can be detrimental.

The Harm of Lazy Analysis

The observation that the ascription of the demonic can do harm has implications for Catherine's situation in at least two ways. First, it may well be that Catherine's friend was just doing the best she could to understand and help Catherine. But even if her motivation was positive, there are side effects to this kind of negative spiritual diagnosis. I am not suggesting that we dismiss the demonic out of hand in general terms, but if we use it as an explanatory framework, we must make sure our ascription is accurate. Otherwise, we inflict suffering rather than merely name its assumed source.

Second, the ascription of the demonic to Catherine's experiences moves her condition out of the realm of psychiatry and medicine (the description Catherine herself had decided was the most appropriate) and into the realm of "the spiritual." Now, Catherine does not have a "mental illness"; instead, she is possessed by a demon. Something from the outside has invaded her body and is controlling her experiences. She is not ill, she just needs the liberating power of Jesus! Her medical diagnoses gave her hope and positive opportunities for intervention and for the future. This new spiritual diagnosis simply made her feel worse and in principle tempted her to leave behind her medical description and stop using her medication, with all the consequences that would emerge from such a course of action. One has to wonder what it must feel like to be told by those who claim to care for you that your experiences are not in fact *your* experiences at all. Rather they are the manifestation of a malevolent force that has invaded your body. If Catherine had described her situation in this way—my body has been infiltrated by an alien being—she would have been assumed to be psychotic. For an "outsider" to do the same thing is apparently acceptable. Whose psychosis counts? might be a question worth reflecting on.

The Dangers of Ambiguity

Catherine's friend was not alone in describing her situation in negative spiritual terms. Within the realm of professional spiritual counselors, Catherine had encountered similar issues:

I've had some [other] really bad experiences. Once when I was in the emergency room I felt so depressed I was seriously thinking about killing myself. I asked for a chaplain, and I said to him, "Could I be . . . is it possible that I'm possessed by the devil?" And he was like, "I really don't know," which was like, kind of a horrible thing for him to say. I just thought maybe he should have been, like, no! But I don't know, I guess the answer *was* "maybe?" but that was pretty negative. Not the kind of truth I wanted to hear.

Responses such as those offered by Catherine's friend and the chaplain have serious consequences:

I've decided that if this happens again, and I'm sure it will, especially if I get psychotic, religious, and depressed—that I won't talk to anyone religious . . . because I guess you guys (I'm including you [John Swinton] as a religious person) feel the need to honestly answer questions. I don't know how people are trained to be chaplains with people in mental distress, but that experience of that person was just terrible. Even if he thought that, that was not the right thing to say. You just have to be really careful not to invalidate people's experiences. I mean if someone was suicidal and they think they're possessed by the devil, it might be best not to reinforce that even if you believe it! You could just say, "Don't worry about that, you're going to be fine."

This is an interesting situation. At one level, one might sympathize with the chaplain. If he believes in demons and is not sure whether Catherine's bipolar symptoms are the product of demonic activity, his ambiguous response is to an extent understandable. Likewise, if he thinks that as a Christian he has to tell the truth as he sees it, then again, we can understand his dilemma. However, if one asks *why* the chaplain thought it was possible that Catherine's experiences were demonic, and *why* he felt he had to tell her this in the way that he did, then the situation becomes much less clear. It is true that Christians are called to "speak the truth in love" (Eph. 4:15). However, perhaps we need to pay more attention to precisely what truth and love are, what they are intended to do, and why telling the truth in love might not be the most faithful thing to do in particularly tricky pastoral situations.

This is another example of *casual theodicy*: explaining the presence of perceived evil without thinking it through or exploring other plausible descriptions and explanations. Like theodicy proper, casual theodicy tries to explain an experience or phenomenon in a way that holds on to the goodness of God in the face of evil; except on this occasion it is not an intentional, considered intellectual endeavor but a passing comment that reflects a desire to too quickly find an explanation for an experience that someone finds disturbing and difficult to understand. Like casual racism (the unthinking use of negative stereotypes or prejudices made on the basis of race, color, or ethnicity), casual theodicy is not necessarily malign in intent. It is often hardly noticed by its perpetrators, but it can have deeply debilitating consequences. With so many medical, scientific, and indeed positively spiritual ways of describing Catherine's experience available, one has to ask why those who genuinely desired to be kind and helpful chose these particular descriptions in defining it.

Two Aspects of Suffering

Catherine's story informs us about the nature of suffering and some of the ways in which suffering emerges from the formal psychiatric description of bipolar disorder alongside other, more hidden areas. It is clear that there is an inbuilt mode of suffering that emerges from the biology of bipolar disorder and its attendant experiences. However, a spiritual dimension also rumbles on alongside the biological dimensions, and it can bring modes of suffering that are not always apparent. In what follows, we will focus on two aspects of spiritual suffering that are illuminating and challenging:

1   Suffering that comes from the ascription of demonic explanations

2   Suffering that comes from a certain understanding of the nature of truth telling

In reflecting on these two sources of suffering, we will begin to discover fresh possibilities for faithful responses that bring comfort and release.

The Suffering That Emerges from the Ascription of the Demonic

In the three mental health challenges we have looked at thus far, the demonic has emerged in different forms as a framework to explain unconventional mental health experiences. This has caused a good deal of distress.[19] The fact that something is distressing is not necessarily an argument for it not being true. The question is whether that description is accurate. We need to get this right. People deserve better than lazy, uninformed theodicies. Up to now we haven't addressed this issue in any detail. Here we will reflect on the question: *Are mental health challenges caused by demons?*

There are two dimensions to the issue. First, is there biblical evidence that what we currently describe as mental health challenges equate with what the Bible refers to as demons or the demonic? Second, should we be looking for the demonic within individuals living with enduring mental health challenges, or should we be looking elsewhere for the demonic?

The Old Testament View

The Old Testament has relatively little interest in the demonic. Within this worldview, the assumption was that both good and evil were the responsibility of Yahweh (1 Sam. 16:14–23). This perspective leads to some unusual and uncomfortable realizations; for example, think of Moses's calling in Exodus 4: "Moses said to the LORD, 'Pardon your servant, Lord. I have never been eloquent, neither in the past nor since you have spoken to your servant. I am slow of speech and tongue'" (4:10). God calls Moses to lead the people of Israel out of oppression and into the promised land. Moses responds by telling God (as if God didn't know) that he can't do it because he has a speech impediment. God responds not by healing Moses's disability but by telling him to do what he is told! But then, mysteriously, God says something rather odd: "The LORD said to him, 'Who gave human beings their mouths? Who makes them deaf or mute? Who gives them sight or makes them blind? Is it not I, the LORD? Now go; I will help you speak and will teach you what to say'" (4:11–12).

God is the author of all things. It is God who makes people blind, deaf, and unable to talk. If it is the case that God is good, and also that God is deeply implicated in disability, this indicates, at a minimum, that such experiences and ways of being are *not* the product of evil. God cannot do evil. Human beings may call some experiences evil, but if God truly is good and loving, then to do so, at least from this perspective, seems like a category mistake. In

---

19. It is worth noting the difference between the Islamic perspective on demons, which is somewhat benign, and the kinds of demons that Christians tend toward, which are much more malignant.

terms of Old Testament thinking, the casual ascription of evil and the demonic to human experiences of difference and suffering seems far too simplistic.

Demons in the New Testament

In the New Testament, the demonic came to be seen as the realm of Satan, who, it was assumed, *inter alia*, spoke to the world through demon-possessed people. Demons caused suffering (Mark 5:1–20; 2 Cor. 12:7); they became the objects of worship (1 Cor. 10:20–21). Demons were entities that had to be stood against (1 Pet. 5:8–9). Jesus cast evil spirits out of many people (Matt. 4:24; 8:16; Mark 1:32), and his ministry of exorcism was considered the first stage in defeating the demonic. Stories of the demonic are found mainly in the Synoptic Gospels. John has nothing at all to say about demons. Similarly, Paul doesn't talk about demons. He talks about sin in "demonized" ways, as a hostile, indwelling power that takes over the self (Rom. 7) but also operates through corporate, social entities. In the Gospels, six encounters with demons are given in any kind of detail:

- The demon-possessed Gerasene(s): Matthew 8:28–34, Mark 5:2–20, Luke 8:26–39
- A demon-possessed mute man: Matthew 9:32–34, Luke 11:14–26
- A demon-possessed blind and mute man: Matthew 12:22–28
- The Canaanite or Syro-Phoenecian woman's daughter: Matthew 15:22–28, Mark 7:25–30
- An epileptic boy: Matthew 17:15–21, Mark 9:14–29, Luke 9:38–43
- The man in the synagogue at Capernaum: Mark 1:21–28, Luke 4:33–36

The intercultural practical theologian Esther Acolatse suggests that "When we consider the bulk of the New Testament and its message versus the small percentage devoted to demons and spirits, we could say that there is a restraint on the part of the New Testament authors regarding demons and their activities."[20] The reason for this restraint is as follows: "The purpose of the early church was not to engage demonic forces in a power struggle, because they had learned through the death and resurrection of Jesus Christ that all the powers of darkness were subject not only to him but to all who belong to him.

20. Esther E. Acolatse, *For Freedom or Bondage? A Critique of African Pastoral Practices* (Grand Rapids: Eerdmans, 2014), 114.

Therefore the way to fight demonic powers was no longer to have a toe-to-toe engagement with them but to know and embody this truth."[21]

The church stands against the full force of the demonic. Yet that begs the question why the church (or individuals describing themselves as Christians) might choose to single out people with mental health challenges as particularly worthy of demonic recognition, particularly when one looks at the descriptions of what demonic manifestations actually look like in the Gospels.

What Does the Demonic Look Like?

There is no real, fixed pattern to the demonic narratives in the Gospels. They all reveal the demonic in quite different ways, notably with very little detail. So, for example, the Canaanite woman pleads with Jesus to free her daughter of a demon, but we get no details on how the demonic is manifesting itself in the girl. Scripture does not indicate that particular kinds of demons are responsible for specific sins: "No demon of lust was expelled from the adulterous woman (John 8), or from the woman of ill-repute mentioned by Luke (ch. 7), or from the incestuous people of Corinth (1 Cor. 5). No demon of avarice was expelled from Zacchaeus, no demon of incredulity from Peter after his triple betrayal. No demon of rivalry was expelled from the Corinthians whom Paul had to call to order."[22]

Also, as Marcia Webb points out, most of the demonic incidents seem to relate to *physical* rather than psychological conditions: "Thus we find that many incidents of demonic influence or possession in the New Testament are related in some way to physical ailments which today are understood in medical terms. It is significant that these narratives are generally not describing impairments of a psychological nature."[23] It would be unusual within contemporary church circles to ascribe blindness, for example, to the demonic, particularly in light of Jesus's response to the blind man in John 9, where he seems to make it quite clear that his blindness was not *the* product of sin. It is interesting to reflect on why some focus on psychological and not physical disorder as a primary locus of the demonic.

21. Acolatse, *For Freedom or Bondage?*, 115.

22. Léon Joseph Suenens, *Renewal and the Powers of Darkness* (London: Darton, Longman & Todd, 1983), 17.

23. Marcia Webb, *Toward a Theology of Psychological Disorder* (Eugene, OR: Cascade, 2017), 57–58.

"I Am Legion"

There are two stories that seem to describe demon possession in terms of psychological or social disorder. The first is the story of the demoniac who calls himself Legion, which is present in varying forms in all three Synoptic Gospels (Matt. 8:28–34; Mark 5:1–17; Luke 8:26–37). In all the stories, the demoniac is violent and self-abusive, roaming around naked in tombs and solitary places. The name Legion seems to indicate that the man believed he was inhabited by a legion of demons. Some have suggested some derivation of multiple personality disorder here. This is possible, although that is a highly contested diagnosis and bears no obvious similarity to the types of mental health challenges we have been looking at in this book.[24] Beyond that, we are given no real detail of this person's condition. This person may have been struggling with psychological issues, but we are not given enough information to make an informed judgment, never mind a clinical assessment.

The second incident is found in Acts 19:11–16, when some new disciples of Jesus are trying to exorcise a demon from a possessed man. They find themselves overpowered by the violence of the man. There is no indication here that the man has a mental health challenge, and there is strong evidence to suggest no direct connection between violence and mental health challenges.[25] Indeed, people with mental health challenges are much more likely to be the victims of violence than its perpetrators.[26] The fact that he was violent does not indicate the presence of mental health challenges. The connection between the man's demon possession and the presence of, or connection with, a mental health challenge is therefore somewhat tenuous.

Why, then, is the demonic ascribed to psychological issues like schizophrenia, depression, or bipolar disorder? This connection is certainly not based on the descriptions of the demonic we find in the Gospels. One can't help but wonder whether perceptions of the demonic are shaped more by Hollywood than by Jerusalem.

---

24. For an excellent exploration of the construction of multiple personality disorders, see Ian Hacking, *Rewriting the Soul: Multiple Personality and the Sciences of Memory* (Princeton: Princeton University Press, 1998).

25. Hind Khalifeh et al., "Recent Physical and Sexual Violence against Adults with Severe Mental Illness: A Systematic Review and Meta-Analysis, International," *Review of Psychiatry* 28, no. 5 (2016): 433–51.

26. H. Khalifeh et al., "Domestic and Sexual Violence against Patients with Severe Mental Illness," *Psychological Medicine* 45, no. 4 (2015): 875–86.

Mental Health Challenges Are Not Related to the Demonic

It is not my intention here to challenge the reality of the demonic. Readers are quite able to discern that for themselves. I am simply claiming that the ascription of the demonic to the types of mental health challenges we have looked at in this book is mistaken and not based on the descriptions in the biblical text. To ascribe the demonic to mental health challenges, one has to move beyond the text. When one moves beyond the text, discernment becomes much more complicated and much more human.

In his book *Strength for His People*,[27] Steven Waterhouse reflects autobiographically and theologically on his experience with his brother's schizophrenia. Toward the end of the book, he discusses the demonic. As an evangelical and Bible-believing Christian, he accepts the reality of demons. However, he sees no evidence that such a description is appropriate for people living with schizophrenia or any other mental health challenge. His argument is apropos to our current conversation. Waterhouse highlights six reasons why it is a mistake to think that mental health challenges are related to the demonic.

Attraction versus Aversion to Religion

In Jesus's conversations with the demons, they know who he is but are terrified! They have no desire whatsoever to relate to Jesus, because they know that Jesus has come to destroy them. Many people living with severe mental health challenges want very much to relate to Jesus. Indeed, one of the most painful experiences people can have is to feel that there is distance between themselves and Jesus. However, any such distance is not because of the presence of demons. Rather, it relates to the nature of their mental health challenges and echoes a commonly shared experience that has been present within Christian spirituality from the beginning. What we see in the demonic accounts recorded in the Gospels is not what we have discovered in this book.

Irrational Speech versus Rational Speech

The demons portrayed in the New Testament speak with a clarity and rationality that is simply not available for those in the acute stages of schizophrenia or in the wilder throes of hypermanic experiences. A possessed person is not

27. Steven Waterhouse, *Strength for His People: A Ministry for the Families of the Mentally Ill*, 2nd ed. (Amarillo, TX: Westcliffe, 2002).

unwell. He or she is perfectly well. The problem is the demon, which is why people instantly return to normal when Jesus exorcises them. For many people living with mental health challenges, such instantaneous cure is rare, if it happens at all. As we have seen, even when people recover, they often carry residual issues from their psychotic encounters.

Ordinary Knowledge versus Supernatural Knowledge

Demons in the New Testament often speak through people and offer knowledge that they could not otherwise have known were they not possessed. People with mental health challenges only know things they have come to know through ordinary means of learning. Koch and Lechler state, for example, "[that] clairvoyance itself is never a sign of mental illness, and a mental patient will never be able to speak in a voice or a language he has previously not learned."[28] Most people living with mental health challenges are just ordinary people trying to live well with difficult and unconventional experiences that may be extraordinary but are not supernatural. People may at times claim to have supernatural powers or extra special knowledge, but they don't.

Normal Phenomena versus Occult Phenomena

Waterhouse suggests that the presence of occult phenomena is necessary for something to be identified as demonic. It is not completely clear why he thinks this is the case, as there is nothing particularly occultic about the demonic narratives in the Gospels apart from perhaps the manifestation of abnormal strength and the "unnatural" knowledge of who Jesus is. Nevertheless, the distinction is interesting. The psychologist Craig Isaacs has done extensive research on the difference between mental health challenges and what he describes as possessive states disorder.[29] He concludes that while some aspects of mental health challenges could be interpreted as similar to demonic phenomena, the distinguishing features are the accompanying paranormal phenomena. The possessive states comprise seven common features:

28. Kurt Koch and Alfred Lechler, *Occult Bondage and Deliverance* (Grand Rapids: Kregel, 1970), 162.

29. T. C. Isaacs, "The Possessive States Disorder: The Diagnosis of Demonic Possession," *Pastoral Psychology* 35, no. 4 (Summer 1987): 263.

1 an experienced loss of self-control;

2 a sense of self that fluctuates between periods of emptiness and periods of inflation, or grandiosity;

3 the hearing of voices and seeing of visions;

4 the presence of other personalities within the person.

Also seen are phenomena seemingly unique to the possessive states:

5 behaviors that exhibit a person's extreme revulsion to religious items or matters, especially with regard to Christianity;

6 paranormal or parapsychological occurrences; and

7 phenomena that seem to affect persons in the vicinity of the patient.[30]

Helpful as this distinction may be in some senses, points 1, 2, and 3 seem to have no real basis within the demonic accounts that we find in the Gospels. Point 4 could be read into the story of Legion, but how representative this story is of all demon possession is debatable. Points 5 to 7 relate to the specific phenomenon of possession. None of these is present in people living with mental health challenges, and indeed, it is arguable whether they are present within the gospel accounts of demons. They are a different phenomenon.

The Claim to Be Possessed

Demons are secretive. They don't want their identity to be revealed. People who claim to be possessed most likely aren't. There is no instance in the Gospels in which people had any trouble recognizing the presence of the demonic. Speculation and debate on whether someone may be demon possessed indicate that the person is not.

---

30. Isaacs, "The Possessive States Disorder," 266.

The Effects of Therapy

Finally, Waterhouse points out that most people with mental health challenges respond to therapy or medication. Demons cannot be exorcised by antipsychotic medication, lithium, antidepressant drugs, or ECT (electroconvulsive therapy). Although I have been wary of the *DSM* criteria, the bottom line is that Scripture does not indicate that demons organize themselves into recognizable diagnoses and categories that can be treated by medication, or respond to it. On this occasion, the medical model is helpful in discrediting the spiritual stigma that accompanies the ascription of the demonic.

A Focus on the Demonic Distracts Us from the Demonic

It always struck me as rather odd that some people feel comfortable using the language of the demonic around some of the most vulnerable people in the world but tend not to use that kind of language when talking about corrupt politicians, bankers, and lawyers and oppressive social and legal systems—the places where significant demonic activity occurs. The close connection between culture and the experience of people living with mental health challenges has been mentioned frequently in this book. Johann Hari, in his critique of the biologization of depression, notes that human beings have basic needs that must be fulfilled, chief among them being the need to belong, the need for a sense of meaning and purpose. He argues that these basic needs are being eroded because of the kind of individualistic cultures that we have created in the West. Medication may be helpful for some, he argues, but it is not the ultimate answer. What we need is a different form of society that encourages different forms of relationship: "We need to be together. We need to deeply reconnect, with each other, with meaning, with purpose, with meaningful work. These are the paths out of the very deep depression and anxiety crisis. We need antidepressants. Most of the antidepressants we need are social, psychological, in the way we live."[31]

What is novel about Hari's proposition is his suggestion that we expand our understanding of what an antidepressant is. Rather than thinking about it in purely pharmacological terms, he suggests we view it in much broader and more social terms. Meaningful work, good housing, and basic income

---

31. Andy Goodman, "Johann Hari: To Treat Depression, Provide Meaningful Work, Housing & a Basic Income, Not Just Drugs," *Independent Global News*, February 2, 2018, https://www.democracynow.org/2018/2/2/part_2_johann_hari_on_uncovering.

are modes of antidepressants that relate to the type of society that we want to create, rather than the palliation of individual problems.

In our discussion of schizophrenia, we saw that a significant dimension of the suffering people experience relates to the pathological culture within which they experience their condition. The experiences that make up the diagnostic criterion of schizophrenia are exacerbated, sometimes grotesquely so, by societal structures and attitudes. Although issues of causality are not the focus of this book, many people who live with voices and have psychotic experiences have been exposed to some kind of trauma or abuse in their lives. One line of argument suggests that the voices a person hears are often the voices of abusers, abusive family members, or other authority figures who have traumatized the individual at some point.[32] In other words, the sinful behavior *of others* is manifested in the experiences of the person living with severe mental health challenges. Attributing the demonic to traumatized individuals and letting those forces that bring about the harm that people experience off the hook seems grossly unjust and wholly inappropriate. It's a bit like blaming someone for having cancer that is caused by secondhand smoke. We could then make an argument that a countercultural community that names and describes people differently—more kindly, compassionately, and faithfully—is an effective antipsychotic.

There is strong evidence that bipolar disorder is a biological condition that requires biological intervention. It is, nonetheless, highly stigmatized and still draws accusations of sinfulness and demon possession, even though the literature shows that this is an incorrect description. The problem seems to be that people do not explore the etiology of this condition. It is much easier to say that it is really the person's fault or that the person's openness to malignant external forces caused the ailment. In one sense, the latter is the case. Much suffering is caused by malignant external forces, but these forces are not demonic. They are very human.

Putting Ambiguity to One Side

There are thus strong grounds to suggest that Catherine's chaplain's ambiguity about the presence of the demonic was unnecessary. Likewise, neither her

32. E. M. Andrew, N. S. Gray, and R. J. Snowden, "The Relationship between Trauma and Beliefs about Hearing Voices: A Study of Psychiatric and Non-Psychiatric Voice Hearers," *Psychological Medicine* 38, no. 10 (2008): 1409–17; J. Read et al., "The Contribution of Early Traumatic Events to Schizophrenia in Some Patients: A Traumagenic Neurodevelopmental Model," *Psychiatry* 64, no. 4 (2001): 319–45; J. Read et al., "Childhood Trauma, Psychosis and Schizophrenia: A Literature Review with Theoretical and Clinical Implications," *Acta Psychiatrica Scandinavica* 112, no. 5 (2005): 330–50.

friend nor Catherine herself needed to be concerned about it. All three just need to spend a bit more time thinking through what the Bible *actually* says about the demonic. Catherine has a recognizable mental health challenge that manifests itself quite differently than does the phenomenon of demons (a phenomenon about which we know remarkably little and on which the Bible spends very little time). All three can find healing and release from that particular worry in the gospel narratives when they are brought into hospitable conversation with the details of Catherine's experiences and the expertise that comes to us from the professional mental health services.

The Suffering That Emerges from Truth Telling

The second aspect of suffering that emerges from our reflections on Catherine's experiences relates to truth telling. In response to her encounter with the chaplain's ambiguity about the presence of demons, Catherine commented: "That was not the kind of truth I wanted to hear." This is an interesting and slightly dissonant statement. What kind of truth did she want to hear? What kind of truth should she be told? Surely truth is truth. Both the chaplain and Catherine's friend felt compelled to "speak the truth in love," as Paul puts it in Ephesians 4:15. In itself this is a laudable intention, as long as we know what we mean by "truth," and are clear on what it means to speak the truth in love. We have seen the ambiguous nature of the so-called truth that was spoken into this situation. But there is another dimension to truth and truth telling that, in closing, we must draw attention to.

The question of what constitutes truth and truth telling is not straightforward. Stephen Plant, in his reflection on Dietrich Bonhoeffer's position on truth telling, points out that "telling the truth is not always a simple matter of accurately reporting facts; it demands that we discern the truth that lies beyond literal accuracy."[33] But what on earth might it mean to suggest there is a truth that lies beyond literal accuracy. Surely literal accuracy is what truth is all about, correct? Not quite, says Bonhoeffer.

Bonhoeffer and Truth Telling

For Bonhoeffer, telling the truth is not only a matter of moral character and literal accuracy: "It is also a matter of correct appreciation of real situations and

---

33. Stephen Plant, *Bonhoeffer*, Outstanding Christian Thinkers (London: A&C Black, 2004), 124.

of serious reflection upon them. The more complex the actual situations of a man's life, the more responsible and the more difficult will be his task of 'telling the truth.' . . . The ethical cannot be detached from reality, and consequently continual progress in learning to appreciate reality is a necessary ingredient in ethical action."[34] Truth telling is not simply a dislocated moral act; it has a context and an intention that are defined by that context. The context is God's ongoing work in the world, and that context shapes the nature of the intention of the truth that is told. In this view, truth telling includes but transcends straightforward adherence to moral rules.

Bonhoeffer is particularly concerned about the implications of principle- and rule-based approaches to truth such as Immanuel Kant's understanding of truth telling.[35] Kant argued that truth telling had to do with adhering to moral rules that determine the nature of what is and what is not true. In this view, to tell the truth is to correctly answer questions relating to what did or did not occur in any given situation. To tell a lie is to break with such a principle and, as such, is morally wrong. Kant offers an example: you open your door to a man with an axe looking for your friend. For Kant, the morally correct thing would be to tell the truth: "He is upstairs in the front bedroom!" Bonhoeffer begs to differ:

> From the principle of truthfulness Kant draws the grotesque conclusion that I must even return an honest "yes" to the enquiry of the murderer who breaks into my house and asks whether my friend whom he is pursuing has taken refuge there; in such a case self-righteousness of conscience has become outrageous presumption and blocks the path of responsible action. Responsibility is the total and realistic response of man to the claim of God and of our neighbour; but this example shows in its true light how the response of a conscience which is bound by principles is only a partial one.[36]

Telling the axe man where your friend is may be an appropriate framing of truth telling from the perspective of Kantian moral principles. It is certainly a certain kind of truth telling. However, in this situation, telling the truth serves to increase rather than decrease the possibility of evil. Principles have a part to play in the Christian life. It is good and proper that Christians should be known for being honest, straightforward, and trustworthy. However, there is a

34. Dietrich Bonhoeffer, *Ethics*, trans. Neville Horton Smith (New York: Simon & Schuster, 1995), 359–60.

35. Immanuel Kant, in Sissela Bok, *Lying: Moral Choice in Public and Private Life* (New York: Vintage Books, 1989), 282–86.

36. Bonhoeffer, *Ethics*, 359–60.

partiality about principle-based truth telling that requires a degree of freedom from decontextualized moral principles if what is good is to emerge. Truth telling, in Bonhoeffer's view, must be understood within a deeper moral context that cannot be authentically articulated in simplistic, moral a + b = c equations. Love is not an abstract principle. God—who *is* love—is a living being who is deeply involved with the world. Truth first and foremost reflects and images the intentions of this living and loving God. Within this perspective, truth is inevitably relational, always guided by the immediate love of neighbor rather than by unchanging principles that would drive one to endanger the life of one's friend for the sake of a moral principle. Christians do not simply have an obligation to tell the truth, they are also called to embody and live out that truth in a world that is complex and messy.

Let me give you an example. A few years ago a good friend of mine lost her brother to suicide. Both of her parents were in the later stages of dementia. When she told them about their son's demise, they were devastated. But a few hours later they had forgotten and were asking for him. She told them again. They were devastated. A few hours later they were asking how he was doing. My friend's truth telling was causing them to constantly be retraumatized. What was she to do? In the end she stopped telling them the truth and simply parked their questions about her brother when they came up. Did she lie to them? Yes, in principle she did. Was lying to them the most compassionate thing to do? Yes, it probably was. Was declining to tell them the truth the right thing to do? If Bonhoeffer is correct and truth is intended to participate in God's movement of neighborly love toward the world, then probably it was. I say "probably" because there is an inherent tension within this kind of truth telling that needs to be recognized rather than resolved. That tension is imbued with empathy and sensitivity to the power of words and the impact of truth.

In Bonhoeffer's perspective, truth is faithfulness to God, whose responsibility for the world shapes and forms our responsibility. God's command comes to us in a fresh and new form each day. God's will does not change, but situations, relationships, and perceptions do. Bonhoeffer is not talking here about situational ethics. His ethic is not intended to be ad hoc or occasional. He is suggesting that God is love (1 John 4:8), not that love is god. He wants us to see that Christians take responsibility for discerning the right thing to do, and also take responsibility for doing it. God takes ultimate responsibility for the world and manifests that responsibility on the cross. In a penultimate sense, Christians take responsibility for who they are, what they do, and the truths they tell. We tell the truth in order to demonstrate our "total and realistic response . . . to the claim of God and of our neighbour." Truth is for the "outcast, the suspects, the maltreated, the powerless, the oppressed, the reviled—in short . . . those who suffer."[37] Our moral responsibility is to learn how to see the world from the perspective of those who suffer and to respond accordingly. Truth telling is intended to increase our love for our neighbor.

Speaking the Truth in Love?

If Bonhoeffer is correct, then those around Catherine may have been wiser to consider not just the act of truth telling but also its impact. As has become clear, people cannot be certain that their description of her situation was correct. They "spoke the truth in love" but didn't really have the "truth" they claimed needed to be told. Ambiguity is not a truth statement; it's a sign of uncertainty. Responsible truth telling does not speculate or speak out in uncertainty or ambiguity. Telling the truth in love requires a much thicker account of the nature of truth than Catherine's helpers were working with.

SACRIFICE AND VOCATION

The final issue raised by Catherine's story relates to her *vocation*. We have seen that Catherine enjoys the highs but recognizes their dangers. The thing that holds her back from simply allowing herself to tumble into the high (stop taking her medication) is the love of her family and the love of her job. She is willing, as far as she has control over things, to sacrifice the excitement of her spiritual highs for the stability of her family. To sacrifice is to give up something valuable for the sake of something else that one regards as important or worthy. To achieve her vocation (to become a good doctor) and to maintain her heart's desire (to be a good mother and a good wife), Catherine has to sacrifice the spiritual high. That is not to say that she substitutes her family for God. She retained her belief in God (although without overt commitment to Christian religious structures) but decided to sacrifice something of her intimacy with God. While many aspects of spiritual care may apply to Catherine's situation, it strikes me that issues around *sacrifice* and *vocation* are rarely

37. Dietrich Bonhoeffer, *Letters and Papers from Prison*, ed. John W. de Gruchy, trans. Christian Gremmels (Minneapolis: Fortress, 2010), 52.

highlighted as central to the spiritual experiences of people living with mental health challenges. A disciple has a vocation and a calling from Jesus. Catherine's discipleship may be strange, but it is no less potent for that. What might it mean to try to untangle the complexities of her spiritual life in such a way that that which is of God might flourish and that which is not of God might be put to one side. In thinking through such a question, we must move on to the final section of this book and begin to reflect on the nature of healing and ecclesial participation for people living with severe mental health challenges.

Conclusion: Redescribing Healing

Theology That Drops Down into the Heart

> I'm here. I love you. I don't care if you need to stay up crying all
> night long, I will stay with you. If you need the medication again,
> go ahead and take it—I will love you through that, as well. If you
> don't need the medication, I will love you, too. There's nothing
> you can ever do to lose my love. I will protect you until you die,
> and after your death I will still protect you. I am stronger than
> Depression and I am braver than Loneliness and nothing will
> ever exhaust me.
>
> —Elizabeth Gilbert[1]

THUS FAR WE HAVE NOT DISCUSSED IN ANY DEPTH THE ISSUE OF HEALING.
In this conclusion, we will reflect, if only briefly, on the practices of healing as
they relate to the kinds of issues we have encountered in the previous pages.
To do this, we must clearly define what we mean by healing. The temptation
is to conflate healing with curing. When we do this, the quest becomes the
eradication of troublesome experiences with a view to initiating a return to
some kind of perceived psychological norm that, as we have seen, is often
determined by the expectations of culture rather than by the actual nature of
the experiences of individuals living with mental health challenges. However,
thinking about healing in terms of cure is only one way the issue can be addressed. Theologically, we might think of healing as much more than cure, if
in fact it includes cure at all.

Scripture has no equivalent term for biomedical understandings of health
that equate health with the absence of illness. The closest term is the Hebrew
term *shalom*, which has a core meaning of righteousness, holiness, right re-

---

1. Elizabeth Gilbert, *Eat Pray Love: One Woman's Search for Everything* (London:
Bloomsbury, 2017), 57.

lationship with God.[2] From this perspective, to be healthy is to be in right relationship with God regardless of one's physical or psychological state. One can be the world's fittest athlete, the world's richest, most hedonistic individual, or the most psychologically stable person on the planet and still be deeply unhealthy. Health in this perspective is not a medical or psychological concept but primarily a relational and theological concept. Health is not the *absence* of anything; it is the *presence* of God. In Judges 6:24 we discover that *Yahweh is shalom*: "Gideon built an altar to the LORD there and called it Yahweh-Shalom [which means 'the LORD is peace']." In Ephesians 2:14 Paul tells us that Jesus is shalom: "For [Christ] himself is our peace, who has made the two groups one and has destroyed the barrier, the dividing wall of hostility."

Health is therefore not an ideal, a concept, or a humanly achievable goal. Rather, it is a *person*. When Jesus says, "I have come that they may have life in all its fullness," it is this shalom life to which he is referring: life with Jesus in all times and in all places. Shalom is abundant life; it is what enables us to hold on to Jesus in the midst of the storms. Mental health, biblically speaking, is not defined by the presence or absence of "symptoms." Psychological distress is therefore *not* a sign of the absence of God. It is perfectly possible to be with Jesus even in the midst of deep distress. It is also the case that psychological disorder can bring about the experience of God's abandonment. However, as we have seen, this is not a sign that one's distress is caused by anything any individual may or may not have done. The absence of God is mysterious but not uncommon within the experiences of the people of God. It is distressing but not indicative of personal sin or transgression. God has promised never to leave us, but it doesn't always feel that way. That is so for all of us, even if it feels more acute during times of psychological distress. The pastoral task is to help people hold on to Jesus in these difficult times without unnecessary guilt or blame.

I remember giving a talk about this understanding of mental health at a conference in Edinburgh a few years ago. After it, a man came up to me and said: "You know, I have lived with schizophrenia for twenty-five years. I never realized that I was accepted just as I am without being cured. . . . *I just thought I was a bad Christian.*" How sad that the people of God had not been able to help him find the healing presence of Jesus without blaming him for his distress or demanding that he be cured of it. Shalom is liberation from false ideas about mental health and ill health, misguided expectations around curing, and

2. For a further development of this understanding of health, see David Wilkinson, *The Bible and Healing: A Medical and Theological Commentary* (Grand Rapids: Eerdmans, 1998).

unrealistic expectations concerning the nature of the good life we are called to live out with Jesus.

Within such a description of mental health, healing becomes something that may include cure but is not defined by it. Healing relates to those forms of practice in which the church engages, which can enable people to remain connected to Jesus at all times and in all places. In closing, let us consider seven dimensions of healing that have emerged from the narratives explored in this book and that can help us begin to respond to the issues in creative and thoughtful ways.

CULTURAL HEALING

Our discussions around schizophrenia and hearing voices revealed a pathogenic dimension to Western cultures that is deeply troubling. There is something about the way Westerners respond to this form of mental health challenge that causes an exacerbation of pathology and an abandonment of hope, which in turn results in deeply negative perceptions of and responses to schizophrenia by individuals and by culture as a whole. Cultural pathology requires cultural healing. Cultural healing requires exemplars that offer an alternative paradigm. Only as we come to *see* alternatives can we as a culture begin to see the possibility of alternatives and change.

The missiologist Lesslie Newbigin concludes his important book *The Gospel in a Pluralist Society* with a short essay titled "The Congregation as Hermeneutic of the Gospel." In it, he argued that the only way the world can understand the gospel is if Christian congregations live it out in the world. He didn't mean that we show who we are through our works. His point was that no one will believe the message of the church if what it says it is, is radically different from what it is actually seen to be doing in its day-to-day life in the world. Newbigin writes:

> I have come to feel that the primary reality of which we have to take account in seeking for a Christian impact on public life is the Christian congregation. How is it possible that the gospel should be credible, that people should come to believe that the power which has the last word in human affairs is represented by a man hanging on a cross? I am suggesting that the only answer, the only hermeneutic of the gospel, is a congregation of men and women who believe it and live by it. I am, of course, not denying the importance of the many activities by which we seek to challenge public life

with the gospel—evangelistic campaigns, distribution of Bibles and Christian literature, conferences, and even books such as this one. But I am saying that these are all secondary, and that they have power to accomplish their purpose only as they are rooted in and lead back to a believing community.[3]

The gospel is intended to reveal a new counterculture: the kingdom of God. This new culture is a place where people love one another, a place filled with people who live by the virtues of love, joy, peace, forbearance, kindness, goodness, faithfulness, gentleness, and self-control. Newbigin reminds us that when people look at the church, this is what they should see. The physical manifestations of the church are the interpretative principle by which the faithfulness of the world (understood as that aspect of creation that has not yet recognized Jesus) is discerned and assessed. When we look at the church, we should at a minimum see beautiful reflections of Jesus.

The tragedy revealed in the stories of people with mental health challenges is that such a noble aspiration is not always lived out. Loving-kindness is not always the church's first response toward them. Rather than functioning as an antipsychotic, many church communities tend to reflect the kind of pathogenic culture that is so destructive for people with schizophrenia, but ultimately is destructive for everyone. Nevertheless, Newbigin's plea for the church to reveal a counterculture has vital aspirational significance for the mental health ministry of the church. A pathogenic culture requires alternatives if it is to become shalomic (revealing of God's shalom) and healing. If the church is to become an antipathogen that understands and responds differently to mental health challenges, we need to be formed differently. Cultural healing requires liturgical healing.

LITURGICAL HEALING

Liturgy and the experience of worship are events of deep formation for the people of God. As we sing, pray, praise, sermonize, and form our bodies into the gestures of worship, we are shaped and formed into liturgical people who come to see that the shape of the liturgy is the shape of our lives. When we looked at depression, we discovered some of the issues that emerge from lopsided liturgical practices. If our liturgical practices do not take onboard the full breadth of human experiences, our formation will be incomplete. Liturgical

---

3. Lesslie Newbigin, *The Gospel in a Pluralist Society* (Grand Rapids: Eerdmans, 1989), 227.

healing relates to creating practices of liturgy and worship that bring about deep connections between human beings and God and names the silences for those who struggle to hold on to God in the midst of their mental health challenges. Such healing requires the creation of liturgical resources that people can use actively and passively. "If you are struggling to pray, find somebody else's words instead of your own." Holding one another in worship is a fundamentally healing practice.

Liturgical healing means holding one another in prayer and praying for *everyone*. As Jen put it: "People with mental illness aren't generally prayed for in the list of prayer concerns. You can sign up if you've had a heart attack or if your child's in the hospital, but rarely do we pray for people who are going through a depressive episode or who have had a psychotic break or any of those things. We don't name, we don't lift up mental illness in our litany of concerns, so people feel invisible." The suggestion that some people may become invisible in worship is deeply troubling. If worship is a place of formation, re-formation, fellowship, and holiness, and if some among us "disappear" because of the shape of our worship practices, then all of us are failing in our task to honor God and to love our neighbor. It is vital that we learn how to talk in public about mental health issues. When we learn how to talk, things change. Pat helps us see what that might look like: "My colleague developed an entire liturgy for people with depression. The church had never identified mental health directly, but because he named the fact that many people in the church lived with depression, he brought out the issue. He wrote a beautiful service using Scripture, candles, anointing with oil, prayers that he wrote specifically for people with depression. And I think things like that go a long way to making people with mental illness feel welcome in a congregation."

This is a beautiful practice. But what might it look like to do the same kind of gentle liturgy for people living with schizophrenia or bipolar disorder? What might that look like, feel like, be like? Worshiping in the fullness of the human experience—in lament, joy, confusion, elation—is a blessing for everyone. It helps the body of Jesus truly to be the body of Jesus.

BIBLICAL HEALING

When we think about biblical healing, we tend to focus on the miracles of Jesus and the eradication of particularly troublesome physical or psychological issues. Important as this dimension is, biblical healing is thicker than simply the desire for cure. Biblical healing involves developing an exegetical sensitivity to the purpose of the Bible and to its impact on those who hear its words and struggle to interpret it in ways that are healing and releasing. We have seen that the experience of mental health challenges can deeply impact the way Scripture is interpreted and acted out. The whole point of the Bible is to help us understand the things of God and come to love God, neighbor, and self more fully. If the ways in which we use the Bible contradict that goal, we need to contemplate a different hermeneutical approach. This might, as has been suggested, mean a person putting the Bible down for a season and allowing others to use it in faithful and creative ways to bring healing and relief to the person. This is a temporary move that requires a community that can hold an individual who is struggling under the weight of negative hermeneutics and desires to help get that person to a place where the Bible can once again bring blessing and positive connection.

Biblical healing has another dimension that relates to the practice of preaching. We might call this homiletical healing, that is, a deep pastoral sensitivity to the power of preaching and to the ways the preached word can bring both blessings and curses. The absence of preaching on mental health issues leads to a gap in the spiritual lives of a congregation in which the power of the gospel is not brought to bear on a fundamentally important issue in many people's lives. The word of God needs to be preached into all areas of human experience. Deep, thoughtful, and pastorally sensitive biblically infused sermons can be transformative forms of healing for individuals and communities. On the other hand, insensitive, ill-conceived, and uninformed biblical preaching can be deeply destructive. Careless preaching on healing, sin, demons, and the causes of mental health challenges brings unnecessary sadness and alienation and can be avoided if we just take a little time to think through the issues. Similarly, Bible study and preaching that do not take lamentation seriously deprive people of a powerful biblical resource—the psalms of lament—that has the potential to bring about the holy articulation of pain and sadness, which leads to a sense of shared experience belonging in the midst of brokenness.

I recently visited a church in Vancouver, Canada, where, before a preacher delivers a sermon, the preacher is required to run it past a committee that offers feedback and suggestions. Wouldn't it be interesting if such a group included people with mental health challenges? Imagine the richness of our preaching if we were able to capture the highs, the lows, the oddness, and the blessings of people's experience in ways that liberate all of us from stigma and open up the whole congregation to perspectives and understandings that could be transformative as together we strive to live faithfully and lovingly. Liturgical healing comes to the whole people of God when we begin to notice the liturgical significance of all of God's people. Developing a healing mental health hermeneutic at a pastoral, liturgical, and theological level may be the key beginning point for developing communities within which everyone has a sense of belonging. Such biblical and homiletical healing leads to theological healing.

THEOLOGICAL HEALING

Many of us in the church, and particularly those of us who engage with the academy, tend to focus on reason and intellect as fundamentally important for theological understanding. Clarity of thought, sharpness of reason, doctrinal awareness, and conformity of spiritual expressions and experiences seem to provide us with a sense of security that enables us to know, understand, and feel comfortable within the boundaries of life with Jesus.

However, as we have seen, Christians have all sorts of unusual experiences, all of which require serious consideration. I'm not saying we need to become unorthodox or unthinking. All I'm saying is that orthodoxy is more complex than we sometimes assume it to be. If all of us together are to minister faithfully with those living with mental health challenges, we need to develop a theological flexibility that recognizes the creedal parameters and boundaries of our faith but at the same time takes very seriously the ways in which these boundaries and parameters look different when different questions are asked of them. We need a theology that drops down into the heart.[4] By that I mean that we need to think clearly and carefully about the things of God while at the same time letting our thoughts about God, self, and others drop down into our hearts. Henri Nouwen describes the heart in this way:

> From the heart arise unknowable impulses as well as conscious feelings, mood, and wishes. The heart, too, has its reasons and is the center of perception and understanding. Finally, the heart is the seat of the will: it makes plans and comes to good decisions. Thus the heart is the central and unifying organ of our personal life. Our heart determines our personality, and is therefore not only the place where God dwells but also the place to which Satan directs his fiercest attacks. It is this heart that is the place of prayer.

4. I am grateful to my friend and colleague Bethany McKinney Fox for this lovely phrase.

The prayer of the heart is a prayer that directs itself to God from the center of the person and thus affects the whole of our humanness.[5]

A theology that drops down into the heart recognizes that all theological construction is intended to increase the presence of God's sovereign neighborly love. It realizes that the test of a good theology is not simply its intellectual coherence but the way it enables the people of God to see God more clearly and love God more dearly. Theological healing occurs when we learn to develop a type of theological flexibility that allows our theological understandings to move our hearts. If we find ourselves thinking that people hear voices because they are demon possessed rather than because they have been treated terribly in the past, we need to expand our intellectual and spiritual knowledge and become more aware of the significance of our hearts. Theological healing requires epistemic healing and epistemological generosity.

EPISTEMIC HEALING AND EPISTEMOLOGICAL GENEROSITY

Epistemic healing has to do with learning to understand and value the perspective of other people. It doesn't mean that we have to accept everything that people say. We need to enter into holy alliances with the mental health professions within which all of us together (including those bearing the mental health experience) can work through issues of meaning and significance. Epistemic healing does mean that we have to respect the things that people say and experience. Clearly, there is a tendency to downgrade or reject the opinions and perspectives of people with mental health challenges simply *because* they have mental health challenges. This is epistemic injustice, and it is the essence of stigma. If we do not take time to understand people's unconventional mental health experiences, we will never come to know them. If we never come to know them, we will never love them. If we never love them, then we have failed in our fundamental gospel task. There is, of course, a problem with that last sentence: Who are "we" and who are "them"? What we have learned in these pages is that there is no "we" and there is no "them." Even the most unusual experience that those who live with mental health challenges encounter is shared by many of us in different ways and to different extents. The call to love those with mental health challenges turns out to be a call to love everyone. What better way to describe the gospel? What more powerful

5. Henri J. M. Nouwen, *The Way of the Heart: The Spirituality of the Desert Fathers and Mothers* (San Francisco: HarperCollins, 1994), 77.

mode of healing could there be? Epistemic justice leads to epistemological generosity, which leads to the possibility of love. In turn, epistemological healing leads to testimonial healing.

TESTIMONIAL HEALING

One could frame this book as a book of testimonials in which people with difficult life experiences testify to a different way of describing their mental health experiences. Testimony is intended to inform, illuminate, entice, and bring about change. The intention of this book has been to try to do all these things. By listening to people's testimonies and trying to interpret, communicate, and theologize their experiences, I have tried to bring a degree of theological illumination that has the potential to make our mental health practices more faithful, potent, and healing.

Testimonial healing occurs when a person is freed to give his or her testimony in all its fullness without fear of judgment and retribution. John's Gospel is the gospel of testimony! The idea of testimony runs like a golden thread throughout that gospel. Those who know Jesus, those who have experienced his transforming presence, are called to testify to what they have seen. Testimony is a legal metaphor that originally related to standing up in court and telling the judge what you know and what you have seen. Testimonial healing comes about when you are able to stand before the people of God and honestly tell them what God has done *and what God has not done* in your life. We are used to the idea of testifying to all the wonderful things God has done in our lives. That is good, proper, and beautiful. But when was the last time we heard a public or private testimony that suggests that God is good but that God has not done the things we might want God to do? Being with God includes disappointment.

Testimonial healing requires that the fullness of people's testimonies is acknowledged and that together we both lament and celebrate the presence and perceived absence of God. Such honest testimony resonates closely with the psalms of lament and the psalms of joy and has the potential to open up spaces of healing and illumination, that is, assuming that we can overcome our uncomfortableness at the presence of dissonance in the lives of our brothers and sisters. Testimonial healing also means taking people's spiritual testimonies seriously. We have seen that it is very difficult for people to make sense of their spiritual experiences when they are in the thick of things. It's just too difficult and confusing to work out where God is and whether there are enduring spiritual things to be learned from these experiences when life feels chaotic and out of control. But as we have seen, after the fact, we can make sense of things and discover new and sometimes challenging things about God and God's presence. Testimonial healing requires that we develop the practice of *retrospective spiritual direction*. By this I mean finding ways to help people to work through what was and what was not of God in the more acute phases of their experiences. It's not enough to insist that all spiritual experience within the context of psychosis, bipolar, or major depression is inevitably invalidated by the fact that people were "ill." God was with them, and people need to understand what that might mean for the past, the present, and the future. Retrospective spiritual direction is a mode of spiritual discernment that allows people to see what God has done within contexts where at first glance it might appear that God has done nothing. Retrospective spiritual direction allows people to see where God was in the midst of the storms and to help them use that knowledge as an encouragement and source of hope now and for the future. Testimonial healing demands that we take people's spiritual testimonies seriously. Retrospective spiritual direction is one way in which we can move toward such a goal.

It is true that everyone in this book, apart from Allen, is anonymous. After his tragic death by suicide, his mother gave me permission to use his real name as a tribute to him. Andrew Solomon, in his work on depression, *The Noonday Demon: An Atlas of Depression*, states that the people in his study, for the most part, are not anonymous. He suggests that anonymizing people's experience is to reinforce stigmatizing attitudes that suggest that one should hide mental health challenges. I take his point, but I think he puts the cart before the horse. Before one can testify honestly, one needs to feel safe. For now, testifying to having a mental health challenge is not safe. As one of the participants in this study put it: "It think it's probably easier to come out as gay or LGBTQ than to come out as mentally ill. If I was to tell my employers that I had bipolar disorder, that would be the end of my career. When I told them I was gay, they thought that was great! So they think I'm a bit odd at times, but they will never know why." There is a time and a place for honest testimony. My hope is that this book helps move us a step closer to that time and that place. But for now, anonymity may be the best way to bring about love.

RELATIONAL HEALING

All these things lead to relational healing. Healing comes to us from God, but it also comes to us from other human beings. My kids often ask me what superpower I would like to have. I always tell them I'd like to have the power to be gentle and kind . . . at all times. They just laugh, and I can understand why. But I am serious. Such a superpower seems rather weak in the face of the ability to fly, to shoot spider webs from your wrists, to scale tall buildings, or to defeat the powers of darkness while talking to your beautiful girlfriend on your state-of-the-art mobile! But I think my superpower (even though it is more an aspiration than a reality) is more interesting. Imagine a world where people didn't judge one another, a world where gentleness, kindness, and tenderness were our priorities. Within such a world, being different or seeing the world differently would not be an occasion for rejection, humiliation, demonization, and loneliness. Rather, such experiences would be seen as an opportunity to practice kindness. It seems to me that is precisely the superpower that is given to us by the Holy Spirit and is manifested so beautifully and movingly in the life of Jesus: "Take my yoke upon you and learn from me, for *I am gentle* and humble in heart, and you will find rest for your souls" (Matt. 11:29). Jesus is gentle. Wow!

In Galatians 5:22–23, Paul informs us that "the fruit of the Spirit is love, joy, peace, forbearance, kindness, goodness, faithfulness, gentleness and self-control. Against such things there is no law." The process of understanding and responding faithfully to those living with unconventional mental health experiences is complex, but at heart it is not complicated. People living with mental health challenges, like all of us, just want to be understood, respected, and treated with love and kindness. What more can any of us desire? Such kindness is the essence of healing and the substance of Jesus's promise of life in all its fullness. As Margaret put it in relation to her experience of bipolar disorder: "Mental health ministry means finding a way to exhibit some ordinary human kindness. You don't have to be a special individual to do that; you're just a human being, and you're letting the God within you see the God within the other person. The church is meant to specialize in human kindness, isn't it?"

There is a tremendous power and beauty in the suggestion that the church is called to be a specialist in human kindness. Small acts of kindness, tenderness, and thoughtfulness bring healing. It's really not that complicated.

Appendix: Mental Health Resources

Sanctuary Ministries offers training, tools, and resources to equip the church to be a sanctuary for all people, at all stages of their mental wellness journeys. https://www.sanctuarymentalhealth.org.

The Mental Health Foundation is the UK's charity for everyone's mental health. With prevention at the heart of what they do, they aim to find and address the sources of mental health problems. https://www.mentalhealth.org.uk.

Mental Health First Aid is a skills-based training course that teaches participants about mental health and substance-use issues. https://www.mental healthfirstaid.org.

The Mind and Soul Foundation is a web-based organization that provides education on theology and mental health issues. Its goals are to educate by sharing the best of Christian theology and scientific advances; to equip by helping people meet with God and recover from emotional distress; and to encourage by engaging with the local church and mental health services. https://www .mindandsoulfoundation.org.

Pathways to Promise: Ministry and Mental Illness is a website hosted by the Missouri Institute of Mental Health "to promote a caring ministry with people with mental illness and their families." www.pathways2promise.org.

The National Institute of Mental Health is a US government site that provides information about mental health and specific mental disorders, mental health research, and links to more resources. https://www.nimh.nih.gov/index .shtml

National Alliance on Mental Illness (NAMI) is America's largest grassroots mental health organization dedicated to improving the lives of individuals and families affected by mental illness. NAMI provides information, advocacy, support groups, referrals, and more. https://www.nami.org.

Mental Health Ministries was founded by Susan Gregg-Schroeder, a United Methodist minister who has struggled with depression. This organization aims to destigmatize mental illness and help churches better care for those affected. www.mentalhealthministries.net.

Befriended Worldwide is a volunteer action group that provides emotional support to prevent suicide worldwide. https://www.befrienders.org.

Samaritans provides confidential, nonjudgmental support twenty-four hours per day for people experiencing feelings of distress or despair. www.samaritans.org.

Intervoice (International Hearing Voices Projects) is a charity, registered in the UK, that aims to support the International Hearing Voices Movement by connecting people, sharing ideas, distributing information, highlighting innovative initiatives, encouraging high-quality respectful research, and promoting its values across the world. http://www.intervoiceonline.org/about-intervoice/national-networks-2.

Depression and Bipolar Support Alliance offers in-person and online support groups for people living with a mood disorder as well as friends and family. https://www.dbsalliance.org.

The Royal College of Psychiatrists' spirituality and psychiatry special interest group (SPSIG) was founded to provide a forum for psychiatrists to explore the spiritual challenges presented by psychiatric illness and how best to respond to patients' spiritual concerns. https://www.rcpsych.ac.uk/members/special-interest-groups/spirituality.

Bibliography

Acolatse, Esther E. *For Freedom or Bondage? A Critique of African Pastoral Practices*. Grand Rapids: Eerdmans, 2014.

American Psychiatric Association. *Diagnostic and Statistical Manual of Mental Disorders*. 5th ed. (*DSM-5*). American Psychiatric Publishing, 2013.

Andreasen, Nancy C. *The Broken Brain: The Biological Revolution in Psychiatry*. New York: Harper & Row, 1984.

———. "DSM and the Death of Phenomenology in America: An Example of Unintended Consequences." *Schizophrenia Bulletin* 33, no. 1 (2007): 108–12.

Andrew, E. M., N. S. Gray, and R. J. Snowden. "The Relationship between Trauma and Beliefs about Hearing Voices: A Study of Psychiatric and Non-Psychiatric Voice Hearers." *Psychological Medicine* 38, no. 10 (2008): 1409–17.

Anscombe, G. E. M. *Intention*. 2nd ed. Oxford: Basil Blackwell, 1957.

Arrandale, Richard. "Madness, Language and Theology." *Theology* 102 (May 1, 1999): 195–202.

"Asperger Syndrome." National Autistic Society. Accessed October 28, 2018. https://www.autism.org.uk/about/what-is/asperger.aspx.

Augustine. Homilies on the Gospel of John (1–40). Edited by Boniface Ramsey. Translated by Edmund Hill. Vol. III/12 of The Works of Saint Augustine: A Translation for the 21st Century. New York: New City Press, 2009.

Barshinger, C. E., L. E. LaRowe, and A. Tapia. "The Gospel according to Prozac: *Can a Pill Do What the Holy Spirit Could Not?*" *Christianity Today*, August 14, 1995, 34–37.

Barth, Karl. *Church Dogmatics* II/2. *The Doctrine of God*. London: Bloomsbury, 1957.

Baughey-Gill, Sarah. "When Gay Was Not Okay with the APA: A Historical Overview of Homosexuality and Its Status as Mental Disorder." *Occam's Razor* 1, no. 2 (2002): 5–16.

Baxter, Richard. *Depression, Anxiety, and the Christian Life: Practical Wisdom from Richard Baxter*. Revised, updated, and annotated by Michael S. Lundy. Wheaton, IL: Crossway, 2018.

Beavan, Vanessa, John Read, and Claire Cartwright. "The Prevalence of Voice-Hearers in the General Population: A Literature Review." *Journal of Mental Health* 20, no. 3 (2011): 281–92.

Bennett, K., K. J. Shepherd, and A. Janca. "Personality Disorders and Spirituality." *Current Opinion in Psychiatry* 26, no. 1 (2013): 79–83.

Bentall, Richard P. *Madness Explained: Psychosis and Human Nature*. London: Penguin Books, 2004.

Blazer, D. B. *The Age of Melancholy: "Major Depression" and Its Social Origins*. New York: Routledge, 2005.

Boivin, Michael J. "Finding God in Prozac or Finding Prozac in God: Preserving a Christian View of the Person amidst a Biopsychological Revolution." *Christian Scholar's Review* 32, no. 2 (January 2002): 159–78.

———. "The Hebraic Model of the Person: Toward a Unified Psychological Science among Christian Helping Professions." *Journal of Psychology and Theology* 19, no. 2 (June 1, 1991).

Bok, Sissela. *Lying: Moral Choice in Public and Private Life*. New York: Vintage Books, 1989.

Bonhoeffer, Dietrich. *Ethics*. Translated by Neville Horton Smith. New York: Simon & Schuster, 1995.

———. *Letters and Papers from Prison*. Edited by John W. de Gruchy. Translated by Christian Gremmels. Minneapolis: Fortress, 2010.

Bortolotti, Lisa. "The Epistemic Innocence of Motivated Delusions." *Consciousness and Cognition* 33 (May 2015): 490–99.

Breggin, Peter. *Toxic Psychiatry*. New York: St. Martin's, 1991.

British Psychological Society. *Understanding Bipolar Disorder: Why Some People Experience Extreme Mood Status and What Can Help*. Leicester, UK: British Psychological Society, 2010.

Brueggemann, Walter. *Into Your Hand: Confronting Good Friday*. Eugene, OR: Cascade, 2014.

———. *The Practice of Homefulness*. Eugene, OR: Cascade, 2014.

———. *The Spirituality of the Psalms*. Minneapolis: Augsburg Fortress, 2002.

"Call for an End to 'Bashing' Psychiatrists." *Mental Health Today*, February 29, 2016. https://www.mentalhealthtoday.co.uk/call-for-an-end-to-bashing-psychiatrists.

Campbell-Reed, Eileen R., and Christian Scharen. "Ethnography on Holy Ground: How Qualitative Interviewing Is Practical Theological Work." *International Journal of Practical Theology* 17, no. 2 (2013): 232–59.

Changeux, Jean-Pierre. "Art and Neuroscience." *Leonardo* 27, no. 3 (1994): 189–201.

Clay, Sally. "The Wounded Prophet." Unpublished paper presented at the First National Forum on Recovery from Mental Illness, National Institute of Mental Health and Ohio Department of Mental Health, April 1994.

Coldiron, Katharine. "Fractured Origins in Esmé Weijun Wang's 'The Collected Schizophrenias.'" *Los Angeles Review of Books*, February 5, 2019. https://lareviewofbooks.org/article/fractured-origins-in-esme-weijun-wangs-the-collected-schizophrenias.

Coleman, Monica. *Bipolar Faith: A Black Woman's Journey with Depression and Faith*. Minneapolis: Fortress, 2016.

Colwell, John. *Why Have You Forsaken Me? A Personal Reflection on the Experience of Desolation*. Milton Keynes, UK: Paternoster, 2014.

Cook, C. H. *Hearing Voices, Demonic and Divine: Scientific and Theological Perspectives*. London: Routledge, 2018.

Cooper, D. G. Psychiatry and Antipsychiatry. London: Tavistock, 1967.

Cornah, Deborah. *The Impact of Spirituality on Mental Health: A Review of the Literature*. London: Mental Health Foundation, 2006.

Currier, J. M., J. M. Holland, and K. D. Drescher. "Spirituality Factors in the Prediction of Outcomes of PTSD Treatment for US Military Veterans." *Journal of Traumatic Stress* 28, no. 1 (2015): 57–64.

Davidson, Arnold. "Closing Up the Corpses." In *Meaning and Method*, edited by G. Boolos. Cambridge: Cambridge University Press, 2001.

Denzin, N. K. *Interpretive Interactionism*. Newbury Park, CA: Sage, 1989.

Dolan, Eric W. "Study Suggests Belief in Demons and Evil Spirits Is Harmful to Mental Health." PsyPost, February 23, 2017. https://www.psypost.org/2017/02/study-suggests-belief-demons-evil-spirits-harmful-mental-health-47783.

Dostal, Robert J., ed. *The Cambridge Companion to Gadamer*. Cambridge: Cambridge University Press, 2002.

Eiesland, Nancy. *The Disabled God: Toward a Liberatory Theology of Disability*. Nashville: Abingdon, 1994.

Federico-O'Murchu, Linda. "Farewell to Aspies: Some Families Reluctant to Let Go of Asperger's Diagnosis." Today, January 4, 2013. https://www.today.com/parents/farewell-aspies-some-families-reluctant-let-go-aspergers-diagnosis-1B7821891.

First, M. "Harmonisation of ICD-11 and DSM-V: Opportunities and Challenges." *British Journal of Psychiatry* 195, no. 5 (1999): 382–90.

Foggie, Janet. "Orthodoxy or Heresy? A New Way of Looking at Spiritual Care for People with Delusional Beliefs." *Scottish Journal of Healthcare Chaplaincy* 10, no. 1 (2007): 23–26.

Forde, Gerhard. *On Being a Theologian of the Cross*. Grand Rapids: Eerdmans, 1997.

Fretheim, Tim. "Many Will Come in My Name: Spiritual Care for Persons with a Delusion of Grandiosity with Religious Content." *Covenant Quarterly* 73, nos. 3–4 (August–November 2015): 14–29.

Fricker, Miranda. *Epistemic Injustice: Power and the Ethics of Knowing.* London: Oxford University Press, 2009.

Friedrich, M. "Depression Is the Leading Cause of Disability around the World." *Journal of the American Medical Association* 317, no. 15 (2017): 1517.

Gadamer, Hans-Georg. *Truth and Method.* London: Continuum, 1981.

Garfinkel, Alan. *Forms of Explanation: Rethinking the Questions in Social Theory.* New Haven: Yale University Press, 1981.

Geertz, Clifford. *The Interpretation of Cultures.* New York: Basic Books, 1973.

Gilbert, Elizabeth. *Eat Pray Love: One Woman's Search for Everything.* London: Bloomsbury, 2017.

Glover, Jonathan. Alien Landscapes? Interpreting Disordered Minds. Cambridge, MA: Harvard University Press, 2014.

Goffman, Erving. *Stigma: Notes on the Management of Spoiled Identity.* Englewood Cliffs, NJ: Prentice-Hall, 1963.

Goldacre, Ben. *Bad Pharma: How Medicine Is Broken, and How We Can Fix It.* New York: Farrar, Straus & Giroux, 2012.

Goodman, Andy. "Johann Hari: To Treat Depression, Provide Meaningful Work, Housing & a Basic Income, Not Just Drugs." *Independent Global News,* February 2, 2018. https://www.democracynow.org/2018/2/2/part_2_johann _hari_on_uncovering.

Gray, Benjamin. "Hidden Demons: A Personal Account of Hearing Voices and the Alternative of the Hearing Voices Movement." *Schizophrenia Bulletin* 34, no. 6 (2008): 1006–7.

Greenberg, Gary. "Does Psychiatry Need Science?" *New Yorker,* April 23, 2013. https://www.newyorker.com/tech/annals-of-technology/does-psychiatry -need-science#.

Greene-McCreight, Kathryn. *Darkness Is My Only Companion: A Christian Response to Mental Illness.* Expanded ed. Grand Rapids: Brazos, 2015.

Grover, S., T. Davuluri, and S. Chakrabarti. "Religion, Spirituality, and Schizophrenia: A Review." *Indian Journal of Psychological Medicine* 36, no. 2 (2014): 119–24.

Hacking, Ian. "Lost in the Forest." *London Review of Books* 35, no. 15 (August 8, 2013): 7–8. https://www.lrb.co.uk/v35/n15/ian-hacking/lost-in-the-forest.

———. "Making Up People." In *Reconstructing Individualism: Autonomy, Individuality, and the Self in Western Thought,* edited by T. Heller, 99–114. Stanford, CA: Stanford University Press, 1986.

————. *Rewriting the Soul: Multiple Personality and the Sciences of Memory.* Princeton: Princeton University Press, 1998.

————. *The Social Construction of What?* Cambridge, MA: Harvard University Press, 1999.

Haldeman, D. C. "Gay Rights, Patient Rights: The Implications of Sexual Orientation Conversion Therapy." *Professional Psychology: Research and Practice* 33, no. 3 (2002): 260–64.

Hari, Johann. *Lost Connections: Why You're Depressed and How to Find Hope.* London: Bloomsbury, 2019.

Harrington, Anne. *Mind Fixers: Psychiatry's Troubled Search for the Biology of Mental Illness.* New York: Norton, 2019.

Haslam, Nick O. "Natural Kinds, Human Kinds, and Essentialism." *Social Research* 65, no. 2 (Summer 1998): 291–314.

Hay, David, with Rebecca Nye. *The Spirit of the Child.* London: HarperCollins, 1998.

"Hearing Voices." Mental Health Foundation. Accessed October 28, 2019. https://www.mentalhealth.org.uk/a-to-z/h/hearing-voices.

Heller, Thomas C., Morton Sosna, and David E. Welbery, eds. *Reconstructing Individualism.* Stanford, CA: Stanford University Press, 1986.

Hellerstein, D. J., and J. W. Eipper. "Dysthymia and Chronic Depression." In *Clinical Handbook for the Management of Mood Disorders*, edited by J. J. Mann, P. J. McGrath, and S. P. Roose. New York: Cambridge University Press, 2013.

Herman, Peter. "Jesus Doesn't Want Me for a Sunbeam: Thoughts on Depression, Race and Theology." *Other Journal: An Intersection of Theology and Culture*, April 6, 2017. https://theotherjournal.com/2017/04/06/jesus-doesnt-want-sunbeam-thoughts-depression-race-theology.

Hurford, Irene. "Medicating a Prophet." *New York Times*, October 1, 2016. https://www.nytimes.com/2016/10/02/opinion/sunday/medicating-a-prophet.html.

Husserl, Edmund. *Cartesian Meditations.* The Hague: Martinus Nijhoff, 1973.

————. *The Crisis of European Sciences and Transcendental Phenomenology.* Translated by D. Carr. Evanston, IL: Northwestern University Press, 1970.

Insel, Thomas. "Transforming Diagnosis." National Institute of Mental Health, April 29, 2013. https://www.nimh.nih.gov/about/directors/thomas-insel/blog/2013/transforming-diagnosis.shtml.

Isaacs, T. C. "The Possessive States Disorder: The Diagnosis of Demonic Possession." *Pastoral Psychology* 35, no. 4 (Summer 1987): 263–73.

Jamison, Kay Redfield. *Night Falls Fast: Understanding Suicide.* New York: Vintage Books, 1999.

———. *Touched with Fire: Manic-Depressive Illness and the Artistic Temperament.* New York: Free Press, 1993.

———. *An Unquiet Mind.* New York: Vintage Books, 1995.

Jansson, Tove. *Finn Family Moomintroll.* Translated by Elizabeth Portch. London: Puffin Books, 1961.

Jaspers, Karl. *General Psychopathology.* Translated by J. Hoenig and M. W. Hamilton. 7th ed. Manchester: Manchester University Press, 1963.

Jay, Mike. *Mescaline: A Global History of the First Psychedelic.* New Haven: Yale University Press, 2019.

Jenkins, Janis H., and Marvin Karno. "The Meaning of Expressed Emotion: Theoretical Issues Raised by Cross-Cultural Research." *American Journal of Psychiatry* 149 (1992): 9–21.

Jennings, Willie James. "Joy That Gathers." An unpublished essay, presented as a work in progress to the Theology of Joy Project at the Yale Center for Faith & Culture consultation on "Religions of Joy?," August 21, 2014.

Kamens, Sarah. "Dr. Insel, or: How Psychiatry Learned to Stop Worrying and Love the Biomarker; A Response to RDoC." Unpublished conference paper, May 2013.

Kelly, Douglas F. "The Westminster Shorter Catechism." In *To Glorify and Enjoy God: A Commemoration of the 350th Anniversary of the Westminster Assembly,* edited by John L. Carlson and David W. Hall. Edinburgh: Banner of Truth Trust, 1994.

Khalifeh, H., P. R. Moran, K. Borschmann, C. Dean, H. Hart, and L. Howard. "Domestic and Sexual Violence against Patients with Severe Mental Illness." *Psychological Medicine* 45, no. 4 (2015): 875–86.

Khalifeh, Hind, Siân Oram, David Osborn, Louise M. Howard, and Sonia Johnson. "Recent Physical and Sexual Violence against Adults with Severe Mental Illness: A Systematic Review and Meta-Analysis." *International Review of Psychiatry* 28, no. 5 (2016): 433–51.

King, Martin Luther, Jr. *The Autobiography of Martin Luther King, Jr.* London: Abacus, 2000.

Kirsch, Irving. *The Emperor's New Drugs: Exploding the Antidepressant Myth.* New York: Basic Books, 2010.

Kitwood, Tom. *Dementia Reconsidered: The Person Comes First.* Buckingham, UK: Open University Press, 1997.

Koch, Kurt, and Alfred Lechler. *Occult Bondage and Deliverance.* Grand Rapids: Kregel, 1970.

Koenig, H. G., M. E. McCullough, and D. B. Larson, eds. *Handbook of Religion and Health.* New York: Oxford University Press, 2001.

Leede-Smith, S. de, and E. Barkus. "A Comprehensive Review of Auditory Verbal Hallucinations: Lifetime Prevalence, Correlates and Mechanisms in Healthy and Clinical Individuals." Frontiers in Human Neuroscience, July 16, 2013. http://journal.frontiersin.org/article/10.3389/fnhum.2013.00367/full.

Luhrmann, T. M. *When God Talks Back: Understanding the American Evangelical Relationship with God.* New York: Vintage Books, 2012.

Luhrmann, T. M., and Jocelyn Marrow, eds. *Our Most Troubling Madness: Case Studies in Schizophrenia across Cultures.* Berkeley: University of California Press, 2016.

Luhrmann, T. M., R. Padmavati, H. Tharoor, and A. Osei. "Differences in Voice-Hearing Experiences of People with Psychosis in the USA, India and Ghana: Interview-Based Study." *British Journal of Psychiatry* 206 (2015): 41–44.

Mahdanian, Artin. "Religion and Depression: A Review of the Literature." *Journal of Psychiatry and Behavioral Health Forecast* 1, no. 1 (February 23, 2018): 1–6.

Malla, A., R. Joober, and A. Garcia. "'Mental Illness Is like Any Other Medical Illness': A Critical Examination of the Statement and Its Impact on Patient Care and Society." *Journal of Psychiatry and Neuroscience* 40, no. 3 (2015): 147–50.

Mann, J. J., P. J. McGrath, and S. P. Roose, eds. *Clinical Handbook for the Management of Mood Disorders.* New York: Cambridge University Press, 2013.

Marsden, Patricia, Efthalia Karagianni, and John F. Morgan. "Spirituality and Clinical Care in Eating Disorders: A Qualitative Study." *International Journal of Eating Disorders* 1, no. 1 (2006): 7–12.

Martin, Emily. *Bipolar Expeditions: Mania and Depression in American Culture.* Princeton: Princeton University Press, 2007.

Matthews, Eric H. "Merleau-Ponty's Body-Subject and Psychiatry." *International Review of Psychiatry* 16, no. 3 (2004): 190–98.

McCarthy-Jones, Simon. "The Concept of Schizophrenia Is Coming to an End—Here's Why." *Independent*, September 4, 2017. https://www.independent.co.uk/life-style/health-and-families/healthy-living/concept-schizophrenia-coming-to-end-psychology-genetics-psychiatry-schizophrenia-a7925576.html.

McGruder, J. H. "Life Experience Is Not a Disease or Why Medicalizing Madness Is Counterproductive to Recovery." *Occupational Therapy in Mental Health* 17, nos. 3–4 (2002): 59–80.

———. "Madness in Zanzibar: An Exploration of Lived Experience." In *Schizophrenia, Culture, and Subjectivity: The Edge of Experience*, edited by R. J. Barrett, 255–81. Cambridge: Cambridge University Press, 2004.

Mitsumoto, Sato. "Renaming Schizophrenia: A Japanese Perspective." *World Psychiatry* 5, no. 1 (2006): 53–55.

Modrow, John. *How to Become a Schizophrenic: The Case against Biological Psychiatry*. Everett, WA: Apollyon, 1992.

Mohr, Sylvia, Laurence Borras, Carine Betrisey, Brandt Pierre-Yves, Christiane Gillieron, and Philippe Huegueler. "Delusions with Religious Content in Patients with Psychosis: How They Interact with Spiritual Coping." *Psychiatry* 73, no. 2 (2010): 158–72.

"Moral Treatment." Brought to Life. Accessed October 28, 2019. http://broughtto life.sciencemuseum.org.uk/broughttolife/techniques/moraltreatment.

Narvaez, Darcia. *Neurobiology and the Development of Human Morality: Evolution, Culture, and Wisdom*. New York: Norton, 2014.

Neelman, J., and M. B. King. "Psychiatrists' Religious Attitudes in Relation to Their Clinical Practice: A Survey of 231 Psychiatrists." *Acta Psychiatrica Scandinavica* 88 (1997): 420–24.

Newbigin, Lesslie. *The Gospel in a Pluralist Society*. Grand Rapids: Eerdmans, 1989.

NHS, Education for Scotland. *Spiritual Care Matters: An Introductory Resource for All NHS Scotland Staff*. Edinburgh: Scottish Government, 2009.

Nie, Fanhao, and Daniel V. A. Olson. "Demonic Influence: The Negative Mental Health Effects of Belief in Demons." *Journal for the Scientific Study of Religion* 55, no. 3 (September 2016): 498–515.

Nouwen, Henri J. M. *The Way of the Heart: The Spirituality of the Desert Fathers and Mothers*. San Francisco: HarperCollins, 1994.

Paris, Joel, and James Phillips, eds. *Making the DSM-5: Concepts and Controversies*. New York: Springer, 2013.

"Patsy Hague: Inspiration." Intervoice. Accessed October 28, 2019. http://www .intervoiceonline.org/about-intervoice/patsy-hague-inspiration.

Peerforck, S., G. Schomerus, and S. Pruess. "Different Biogenetic Causal Explanations and Attitudes towards Persons with Major Depression, Schizophrenia and Alcohol Dependence: Is the Concept of a Chemical Imbalance Beneficial?" *Journal of Affective Disorders* 168 (2014): 224–28.

Peters, E. "Are Delusions on a Continuum? The Case of Religious and Delusional Beliefs." In *Psychosis and Spirituality: Exploring the New Frontier*, edited by Isabel Clarke. London: Wiley-Blackwell, 2011.

Plant, Stephen. *Bonhoeffer*. Outstanding Christian Thinkers. London: A&C Black, 2004.

———. *Simone Weil*. London: Fount, 1996.

Puchalski, Christina. "Integrating Spirituality into Patient Care: An Essential Element of Person-Centered Care." *Polskie Archiwum Medycyny Wewnetrznej* 123 (2013): 491–97.

Rabinow, P., ed. "Psychiatric Power." In *Ethics, Subjectivity, and Truth*, by M. Foucault. New York: New Press, 1997.

Ratcliffe, Mathew. *Experiences of Depression*. Oxford: Oxford University Press, 2015.

———. *Real Hallucinations*. Cambridge, MA: MIT Press, 2017.

Read, J., N. Haslam, and N. L. Sayce. "Prejudice and Schizophrenia: A Review of the 'Mental Illness Is an Illness like Any Other' Approach." *Acta Psychiatrica Scandinavica* 114 (2006): 303–18.

Read, J., J. van Os, A. Morrison, and C. Ross. "Childhood Trauma, Psychosis and Schizophrenia: A Literature Review with Theoretical and Clinical Implications." *Acta Psychiatrica Scandinavica* 112, no. 5 (2005): 330–50.

Read, J., D. B. Perry, A. Moskowitz, and J. Connolly. "The Contribution of Early Traumatic Events to Schizophrenia in Some Patients: A Traumagenic Neurodevelopmental Model." *Psychiatry* 64, no. 4 (2001): 319–45.

Reed, Pamela. "An Emerging Paradigm for the Investigation of Spirituality in Nursing." *Research in Nursing and Health* 15 (1992): 349–57.

Repper, J., and R. Perkins. *Social Inclusion and Recovery: A Model for Mental Health Practice*. Edinburgh: Baillière Tindall, 2003.

Romme, M., and S. Escher, eds. *Understanding Voices: Coping with Auditory Hallucinations and Confusing Realities*. London: Handsell Publications, 1996.

Romme, M., S. Escher, J. Dillon, D. Corstens, and M. Morris, eds. *Living with Voices: 50 Stories of Recovery*. Ross-on-Wye, UK: PCCS Books, 2009.

Rüsch, N., A. R. Todd, and G. V. Bodenhausen. "Biogenetic Models of Psychopathology, Implicit Guilt, and Mental Illness Stigma." *Psychiatry Research* 179 (2010): 328–32.

Rutledge, Fleming. *Advent: The Once and Future Coming of Jesus Christ*. Grand Rapids: Eerdmans, 2018.

———. "Divine Absence and the Light Inaccessible." *Christian Century*, August 27, 2018. https://www.christiancentury.org/article/critical-essay/divine-absence-and-light-inaccessible.

Saks, Elyn R. *The Center Cannot Hold: My Journey through Madness*. New York: Hachette Books, 2008.

Schiller, Lori, and Amanda Bennett. *The Quiet Room: A Journey out of the Torment of Madness*. New York: Warner Books, 2011.

Sims, Andrew. "Is Faith Delusion?" Royal College of Psychiatrists. Accessed October 28, 2019. https://www.rcpsych.ac.uk/docs/default-source/members/sigs/spirituality-spsig/is-faith-delusion-andrew-sims-editedx.pdf?sfvrsn=59a019c0_2.

———. "Symptoms and Beliefs." *Journal of the Royal Society of Health* 112, no. 1 (1992): 42–46.

———. *Symptoms in the Mind: An Introduction to Descriptive Psychopathology*. 3rd ed. Edinburgh: Saunders, 2003.

Sommerfeld, Denise P. "The Origins of Mother Blaming: Historical Perspectives on Childhood and Motherhood." *Infant Mental Health Journal* 10, no. 1 (Spring 1989): 14–24.

Sousa, A. "Pragmatic Ethics, Sensible Care: Psychiatry and Schizophrenia in North India." PhD diss., University of Chicago, 2011.

Steiner, L. M., S. Zaske, S. Durand, M. Molloy, and R. Arteta. "Spiritual Factors Predict State and Trait Anxiety." *Journal of Religion and Health* 56, no. 6 (2017): 1937–55.

Strawson, P. F. *Scepticism and Naturalism: Some Varieties*. New York: Columbia University Press. 1985.

Suenens, Léon Joseph. *Renewal and the Powers of Darkness*. London: Darton, Longman & Todd, 1983.

Swinton, John. *Becoming Friends of Time: Disability, Timefullness, and Gentle Discipleship*. Waco, TX: Baylor University Press, 2017.

———. *Dementia: Living in the Memories of God*. Grand Rapids: Eerdmans, 2012.

———. "Medicating the Soul: Why Medication Needs Stories." *Christian Bioethics: Non-Ecumenical Studies in Medical Morality* 24, no. 3 (December 2018): 302–18.

———. *Raging with Compassion: Pastoral Responses to the Problem of Evil*. Grand Rapids: Eerdmans, 2007.

———. *Resurrecting the Person: Friendship and the Care of People with Mental Health Problems*. Nashville: Abingdon, 2000.

———. *Spirituality and Mental Health Care: Rediscovering a "Forgotten" Dimension*. London: Jessica Kingsley, 2001.

Swinton, John, and Harriet Mowat. *Practical Theology and Qualitative Research*. Rev. 2nd ed. London: SCM, 2017.

Swinton, John, and Stephen Pattison. "Moving beyond Clarity: Towards a Thin, Vague, and Useful Understanding of Spirituality in Nursing Care." *Nursing Philosophy* 11 (2010): 226–37.

Szasz, T. "The Myth of Mental Illness." *American Psychologist* 15 (1960): 113–18.

Tallis, Raymond. *Aping Mankind: Neuromania, Darwinitis, and the Misrepresentation of Humanity*. London: Routledge, 2011.

Taylor, Charles. "Gadamer on the Human Sciences." In *The Cambridge Companion* to *Gadamer*, edited by Robert J. Dostal. Cambridge: Cambridge University Press, 2002.

Thomas, W. I., and D. S. Thomas. *The Child in America: Behavior Problems and Programs*. New York: Knopf, 1928.

Torgalsbøen, Anne-Kari, Susie Fu, and Nikolai Czajkowski. "Resilience Trajectories to Full Recovery in First-Episode Schizophrenia." *European Psychiatry* 52 (2018): 54–60.

Torrey, E. Fuller. *Surviving Schizophrenia: A Family Manual*. 6th ed. San Francisco: Harper, 2013.

Vanier, Jean, and John Swinton. *Mental Health: The Inclusive Church Resource*. Kindle ed. London: Darton, Longman & Todd, 2014.

Vasegh, S., D. H. Rosmarin, H. G. Koenig, R. E. Dew, and R. M. Bonelli. "Religious and Spiritual Factors in Depression." *Depression Research and Treatment*, 2012.

Wang, Esmé Weijun. *The Collected Schizophrenias: Essays*. Minneapolis: Graywolf, 2019.

Waterhouse, S. *Strength for His People: A Ministry for the Families of the Mentally Ill*. 2nd ed. Amarillo, TX: Westcliffe, 2002.

Watters, Ethan. *Crazy like Us: The Globalization of the Western Mind*. New York: Little, Brown, 2011.

Webb, Marcia. *Toward a Theology of Psychological Disorder*. Eugene, OR: Cascade, 2017.

Webb, Stephen H. "God of the Depressed." *First Things*, February 19, 2016. https://www.firstthings.com/web-exclusives/2016/02/god-of-the-depressed.

Weil, Simone. *Awaiting God: New translation of* Attente de Dieu *and* Lettre a un Religieux. Translated by Bradley Jersak. 2nd ed. Scotts Valley, CA: CreateSpace, 2013.

Wilkinson, David. *The Bible and Healing: A Medical and Theological Commentary*. Grand Rapids: Eerdmans, 1998.

Woods, Angela. "The Voice Hearer." *Journal of Mental Health* 22, no. 3 (2013): 263–70.

World Health Organization. "The ICD-10 Classification of Mental and Behavioral Disorders: Clinical Descriptions and Diagnostic Guidelines." Accessed October 28, 2019. https://www.who.int/classifications/icd/en/bluebook.pdf?ua=1.

———. "The ICD-10 Classification of Mental and Behavioural Disorders: Diagnostic Criteria for Research." Geneva: World Health Organization, 1993. https://www.who.int/classifications/icd/en/GRNBOOK.pdf?ua=1.

———. "International Classification of Diseases (ICD) Information Sheet." Accessed October 28, 2019. https://www.who.int/classifications/icd/en.

Writer, H. "Recovering from Schizophrenia Not Rare." Healthy Place, last updated June 11, 2019. https://www.healthyplace.com/thought-disorders/schizophrenia-articles/beautiful-but-not-rare-recovery.

Yong, Amos. *Theology and Down Syndrome: Reimagining Disability in Late Modernity.* Waco, TX: Baylor University Press, 2007.

Zeki, S. "The Neurobiology of Love." *FEBSPRESS Letters* 581 (2007): 2575–79.

Index

affliction, 95–101, 102, 105, 107, 108
Andreasen, Nancy C., 39–41, 42
Anscombe, Elizabeth, 13
Arrandale, Richard, 4–5
Asperger's syndrome, 24–25
autism, 24–25

Barth, Karl, 80–81
Baxter, Richard, 99–101
bipolar disorder, 12; experiences of, 63–68,
  112; nature of, 165–69, 172, 190, 199; and
  responses to diagnosis of, 55–57, 62; and
  spiritual experiences, 171–74, 176–78,
  180–81, 185–87, 189, 214
Bonhoeffer, Dietrich, 200–203
Bortolotti, Lisa, 178
Brueggemann, Walter, 89–90, 91, 111–12

church/Christian responses to mental
  health challenges, 4–5, 46, 66–68, 132,
  151–52, 157, 184, 207–15; ascription of
  demonic to, 152–53, 189, 193; authentic
  worship and lament in, 86–88; and illumination (of Holy Spirit), 50–51; proper
  naming of, 160–61, 199
Coldiron, Kathleen, 119–20
Coleman, Monica, 63–68, 167
Colwell, John, 110, 112, 113

delusions: religious, and mental health
  care, 180–84; spiritual implications of,
  128–30, 171, 176, 177–78, 185–86; types of,
  125, 178–80

demons, demonic: and mental health, 67,
  131, 187–90; in Scripture, 161, 191–94;
  suffering from the ascription of mental
  health challenges to, 190–91, 195–200;
  and voice hearing, 127, 140–41, 151–54,
  156
depression, 209; and Christian joy, 74,
  79–83, 88; flattening of language about,
  75–79; nature of, 64–66, 68, 74–75, 83–85,
  96–97, 98, 198; spiritual experiences
  during, 91–95, 97, 99–105, 108–16, 214.
  See also bipolar disorder
diagnosis: and *Diagnostic and Statistical
  Manual of Mental Disorders*, 19–22, 25,
  27; and identity, 62–66; meaning and
  impact of, 12, 15–17, 55–56, 57, 59–62,
  119, 159–61, 167; medical vs. theological,
  66–68
*Diagnostic and Statistical Manual of
  Mental Disorders (DSM)*, 2, 25, 30–31;
  influence of, 19–22, 23–25; use of, 40–41,
  55, 198; validity of, 25–27

epistemic: injustice, 145–47, 176, 180–81;
  innocence and delusions, 178–80; justice,
  149–50, 183–85, 212–13; tension, 181–83

faith: and bipolar disorder, 65–66, 171–74,
  177–78, 180–84, 185–87, 189; and depression, 78–79, 94–95, 101–4, 109–10; and
  mental health challenges, 2, 6, 7; and
  schizophrenia, 125, 128–32; and voice
  hearing, 152–54